THE PEOPLE WORSHIP

THE PEOPLE
WORSHIP

A History of the
Liturgical Movement

Edited by Lancelot Sheppard

HAWTHORN BOOKS, INC. • PUBLISHERS
NEW YORK

First Edition, January, 1967

NIHIL OBSTAT

Joannes M. T. Barton, S.T.D., L.S.S.

Censor Deputatus

Mervyn A. Alexander

Censor Deputatus

IMPRIMATUR

✠ Georgius L. Craven

*Episcopus Sebastopolis,
Vicarius Generalis*

✠ Joseph E. Rudderham

Episcopus Cliftoniae

Westmonasterii
Die XVII MARTII MCMLXIV

Cliftoniae
Die II AUGUSTUS MCMLXV

The Nihil Obstat and Imprimatur are a declaration that a book or pamphlet is considered to be free from doctrinal or moral error. It is not implied that those who have granted the Nihil Obstat and Imprimatur agree with the contents, opinions, or statements expressed.

7241

CONTENTS

PART II: FUNDAMENTAL IDEAS OF THE
    LITURGICAL REVIVAL
*by the Sacerdotal Communities of
St. Séverin of Paris and St. Joseph of Nice*

PART III: THE PRINCIPAL ADVANCES MADE
    BY THE LITURGICAL RENEWAL

PART IV: FUNDAMENTAL DOCUMENTS
OF THE LITURGICAL RENEWAL

THE LITURGICAL RESTORATION: STAGE ONE

Surprise has been expressed in some quarters that the Second Vatican Council, after years of preparation, should have turned its attention first of all to what, it was alleged, is on the face of it only a matter of internal interest to the Church. At a period which has many of the marks of being apocalyptic, when great and urgent problems (the population explosion, the whole moral question of nuclear war, etc) face mankind the Council might have been better employed, it was considered, than in making rules about what goes on in church. Such a view betrays a total lack of comprehension of the nature of the Church and of what her worship is. Those who are in any doubt about what this worship means to the Church have only to read the first part of the Constitution on the liturgy to discover, indeed, that worship is, on a final analysis, what "the Church is about". It was also said, when some of the changes introduced by the Constitution came into force, that the whole reform had come so suddenly and that so many little changes of detail were being made one after the other, that it was really impossible to see any reason in any of it; the so-called reform was nothing else than the enthusiasm of liturgists run riot. It was not explained, however, in what way the liturgists had managed to persuade all but four of the bishops at the Council of the need for these reforms. In view of such misconceptions it may be worthwhile to take a glance back over the history of the liturgical movement for the past half century. We can then see how far it is true that the liturgical Constitution came suddenly.

The truth is, of course, that far from being a sudden reform produced by the Council it was in reality clearly adumbrated by events and movements in the Church long beforehand. Indeed, it might be said that the remote preparation for it went back beyond the half century mark to the work of Dom Guéranger, Edmund Bishop, Dom Lambert Beauduin, Pius X and others. Certainly the last half century has been a period of intense preparation and that the time was ripe for the Constitution can be gauged from the fact that, unlike other acts of the Council, the schema on worship was passed without the massive revision in detail that has been necessary for many of the subsequent Constitutions and decrees of the Council.

The liturgical renewal which had been going on for fifty years and more in the Church has thus come to fruition. On the face of it it seems odd that it should be necessary for there to be a special movement in the Church to lead men back to her liturgy, to the common worship of Christians, and it is some measure of the need for reform that such a movement, at work for upwards of half a century, should have been necessary. But before the Council assembled it had already become clear that the liturgical movement had gone as far vertically as it was possible for it to go—horizontally, of course, it still had far to go: there were millions in the Church entirely unaffected by it, who considered it, indeed, if they had ever heard of it, as something to do with rubrics—the rules, that is, for the external performance of worship—or else, regarded it as the province of monks and certain priests interested in such things. Yet the period of reform had begun as long ago as Pius X's decree on Church music (1903), telling the people to take an active part in the celebration of Mass, together with his decree on frequent communion. By these means he restored to congregations the two principal means of participation. Next he introduced, by his Bull *Divino afflatu* (1911) a reform of the Roman liturgy (it concerned the Breviary and Missal) so that the liturgy of the season was in some measure restored to its proper place in the Church's year. This was effected by the reduction in the number and importance of the feasts in the proper of saints. A new distribution of the psalms in the Roman Breviary enabled priests to recite the ferial Office or the Office of the season without being burdened by the great length of the former Offices (on Sundays particularly). The weekly recitation of the whole Psalter was assured at least for some weeks of the year; hitherto, in practice, certain psalms of the common of saints had been repeated almost daily. But it was the reform of the calendar that was the most important feature of this reform.

This was the first reform of the Roman rite since the publication of the Breviary (1568) and the Missal (1570) issued by Pius V as a result of the Council of Trent. But Pius X's reform made no real change in the structure of the Mass liturgy; in this the publication of the Easter Vigil (1951) was the first step, shortly followed by the reformed Holy Week services (1956). Both these provided some clue to the shape of things to come. Pius XII indeed in his Encyclical *Mediator Dei* (1947) had laid down certain principles and at the time this document was hailed as the charter of the liturgical movement; though it offered an authoritative definition of the liturgy, gave a certain encouragement and called for some positive measures, it was

perhaps too concerned to regulate certain practices and re-
strain the enthusiasm of certain sections of the movement
for it to give the necessary lead in the work of reform.

Still, it was under Pius XII that the reformed Holy Week
services were promulgated. It is worth noticing how this
reform, together with the simplification of the rubrics (1955)
and the new code of rubrics, although effected for pastoral
reasons were in fact a return to more primitive forms. By the
time that the first session of the Second Vatican Council
took place it was clear that a major reform of the Roman
liturgy had already been inaugurated. With the promulgation
of the liturgical Constitution it became even clearer that
this reform would be far more radical than that of Trent.
We are to have reformed liturgical books—the Constitution
calls for them—but reformed in a way that the Commission
resulting from Trent could never have imagined. The whole
emphasis is to be pastoral, for the people. While it is true,
of course, that any liturgical reform must of necessity have
a pastoral content, it remains true to say also that the reforms of Trent were directed towards the clergy and were
aimed at the suppression of certain abuses which had crept
in. The present reform is far wider in scope and far more
radical in nature.

It must be borne in mind that the Council's liturgical Constitution is not the end of reform, but merely the beginning
of the first stage. This is evident from the Constitution itself
and from the documents that have subsequently appeared.
On January 25th, 1964, came the *motu proprio* of Paul VI
(*Sacram liturgiam*). The details can be seen in the document
itself (see pages 228–233);what is of particular importance
is that it fully confirms the interpretation given to the Constitution on the liturgy and itself can be regarded as the real
preface to the first stage of the reform. It explains why the
Church has considered it necessary to proceed by a series of
successive and partial changes instead of awaiting the time

when the whole reform was ready and could be promulgated all at once. Some have been grievously disappointed by the comparison between the very great promise inherent in the provisions of the Constitution and the comparatively small amount that has been achieved. Others are irritated by the many small changes and constant need to alter, in some detail or other, the manner of celebration. *Sacram liturgiam* shows the two factors involved in the decision to proceed with the reform in this way. In the first place, the whole work of liturgical restoration is an enormous undertaking, involving not only a radical reform of all the liturgical books, but also a considerable change in the outlook of many Catholics, clerical and lay, all over the world. Patience is necessary for the fundamental ideas inherent or expressed in the Constitution to be grasped by all. On the other hand the pastoral need is so great and the liturgical restoration is so urgent and full of so many benefits for an adult Christian life, that it is really impossible to await the full reform which requires a considerable amount of preparatory work.

The rightness of this decision has been shown by the general welcome given to the introduction of the vernacular into the Mass.[1] Of course, there have been some who were genuinely distressed by this upset of their long-established habits; many of these have subsequently found, and acknowledged, that with the use of English they obtained not only a new insight into the meaning of the texts, but also a new conception of what Christian public worship is really meant to be. There is, it must be admitted, a vocal minority which has declared opposition not only to the introduction of the vernacular, but to the whole concept of reform. This is not the place to examine the genesis, development and roots of this movement, interesting psychological and sociological study that it

---

[1] And the Breviary. It is extraordinary how many of the clergy who were opposed to English in the Mass were willing, and indeed demanded, to have it in the Office.

would be; it must suffice to say that it exists in the United States, in Great Britain, in France and elsewhere. On the continent of Europe, particularly, it seems bound up with a form of extreme right wing politics that in the past has already done more than a little harm to the Church.

The advantage of introducing the reforms by stages was shown by the simplification of the formula for giving Communion. If it had been introduced in the context of a major reform of the whole rite of Mass it would probably have passed almost unnoticed; by itself it furnished a useful opportunity for preparing people's minds for what is to come. This rite forms an excellent example of the whole spirit of the reform and demonstrates how words and liturgical actions can be the symbol of the mystery that is accomplished. Previously there was a formula, muttered by the priest, which accompanied the action (namely the giving of the host). It hardly seemed to matter whether the communicant heard the words or not, however, because they did not form an integral part of the rite. But now we have a formula which is a constituent part of the rite.

> The proclamation of the mystery becomes an occasion for the communicant to proclaim his faith. The rite is now a complex action in which both priests and faithful collaborate, and in which the formula has the meaning of an authentic liturgical action. It reflects in miniature the whole movement for the revival of the liturgy; understood in this way it is quite beside the point to compare the old formula said by the priest with the new one to find if one is better than the other. There was no question of introducing a more "beautiful" formula or of changing it for the sake of change, or even of returning to a practice, however venerable, of the primitive Church, but of creating a rite which should be the expression of a new liturgical teaching method.[2]

A further stage in the reform is represented by the publication of the instruction *Inter oecumenici* by the council for

[2] T. Léonard, S.J., in *Etudes*, March 1965.

the carrying out of the Constitution on the liturgy (September 26th, 1964). This important document (it is reproduced on pp. 234–264) recalls the fundamental principles of the reform, the general rules for the liturgical training of the clergy, religious and laity; it treats of the divine Office, the arrangement of churches and altars in order to facilitate the active participation of the faithful. Here, then, we have the spirit of the reform embodied in practical prescriptions which affect the entire rite of liturgical celebration, from the religious culture of all, priests and faithful, down to the arrangement of churches. The changes in the Mass, of course, are the most striking feature of the document (they are contained in articles 48-60); and it is to be noticed that they are now obligatory and have a place in the rubrics.

These changes have been incorporated in the new *Ordo Missae*. In it, too, the final touches have been put to the first part of the Mass; it can now take place at the ambo or at the celebrant's seat at the side; but even if the priest remains at the altar the various parts are all said at the middle—the expressions "Epistle" and "Gospel side" no longer have any place in the liturgical vocabulary.

If all the changes in the liturgy, as they are enumerated in the various documents mentioned, are considered in detail the general impression obtained may be of complexity and not a little confusion. Yet in reality the actual purpose is a greater simplicity, not for its own sake, but because, in the words of the Constitution, "both texts and rites should be drawn up so that they express more clearly the holy things which they signify; the Christian people, so far as possible, should be enabled to understand them with ease and to take part in them fully, actively and as befits a community". To what extent this has been achieved appears clearly enough if we examine the Mass rite as it has so far been reformed.

The three rites which together make up the liturgy of the Mass are the entrance rite, the liturgy of the word and the

Eucharist proper. Before the latest reforms it could be said that the two first mentioned hardly fulfilled their function and appeared almost as vestigial elements which had to be gone through before the Eucharist began: the celebrant on arrival at the altar said the preparatory prayers and then recited the introit which should have been sung as he approached the altar; the lessons meant for the people's instruction were said by the celebrant or at a high Mass sung by the appropriate minister in Latin and not facing the congregation. Now, if the introit is sung at the entrance the celebrant has not to recite it and the lessons are read to the congregation in their own language. The latter change is, in fact, a useful pointer to the radical reasons for the reform. If the lessons were to perform their function they had to be in the vernacular so the reform was introduced as a matter of functional necessity, a point often missed in much of the controversy about the vernacular.

It has been argued in some quarters that the reform has not gone far enough, that it needs to be much more radical if it is to achieve an enduring result. But it is really beside the point to argue in this way. We are at the beginning, not the end, of a very radical reform of the Roman liturgy, and the only way that this can be successfully achieved is by first laying down the principles to be followed. When these have been established and generally accepted the necessary reforms will follow almost of themselves—it will be plain to all how necessary they are. This period of transition will in all probability be far too short for the work of education that needs to be done. But we are in transition to what amounts to a new liturgical world where there will be no longer rites that are performed for their own sake, passages of Scripture that have to be recited, but not necessarily understood, ritual gestures that are devoid of meaning. We are in transition to a liturgy of authentic acts, the real gestures of a community worshipping in "spirit and in truth".

Lancelot Sheppard

PART I

SHORT HISTORY OF THE
LITURGICAL MOVEMENT

The liturgical movement came into being because it was necessary. Under the influence of modern individualism and rationalism, the worship of the Church with its magnificent forms, lofty considerations and concentration on the totality of revealed realities, had been increasingly relegated to the background. Spiritual life had assumed very largely a subjective and private character. It therefore became necessary that from within the Church should arise the desire to regain what had been thus set aside. Scientific and historical research was then carried out in an endeavour to revive the liturgy in its purity and to restore to it the place belonging to it in religious life. But there soon arose a further tendency to attribute to it an importance that it does not possess. . . .

*(Letter from Romano Guardini to the bishop
of Mainz, 1940)*[1]

A remark that holds good for the whole of this short book requires to be emphasized in regard to this first part. In a concern for clarity the subject has been divided up into sections—their artificial nature will strike the reader at once—dealing with monastic influences, research institutes and parochial and youth movements. This distinction, which is based on the very rough historical succession of events in the liturgical renewal, should not cause us to forget the interpenetration that has fortunately taken place between the various elements in this renewal. And it must not be lost sight of that

[1] *La Maison-Dieu* 3, pp. 7–24. (*La Maison-Dieu* is hereafter quoted as *MD*, followed by volume and page numbers.)

the movement which began in the monasteries, together with the institutes and centres specializing in pastoral liturgy, still continues to make its contribution to the generality of parochial and other communities in a kind of continual "circumincession". It is only for reasons of method that the three following chapters have here been separated, and this separation, as will be seen, is very relative.

The Sacerdotal Communities
of St. Séverin of Paris
and St. Joseph of Nice

CHAPTER I

MONASTIC SCHOOLS

At the very beginning of his Encyclical *Mediator Dei et hominum*[1] Pius XII pointed out the essential part played by monks in the liturgical renewal. This official acknowledgement has led us to begin this history of the liturgical movement with its monastic origins and, at the end of this chapter, in order to present an unbiased account, to point out its limitations as well as its beneficial results. In company with Fr Bouyer, Dom Olivier Rousseau and a large number of recent monographs about the liturgical movement, we go back to Dom Guéranger, although the history of the liturgical movement in the proper sense of the term might be seen to begin with Pius X and Dom Lambert Beauduin.

DOM GUÉRANGER AND SOLESMES

At Solesmes is to be found what at the birth of the liturgical movement can be called its original sin. But it must at once be added that it was a *felix culpa*. At Solesmes, in fact, began the general movement which has led to a renewal of divine worship, even though at present this movement is contriving to correct and, in some sense, to deny its origins.

After ordination to the priesthood for the secular clergy Dom Guéranger (1805–75) restored the abbey of Solesmes in the Sarthe *département* in France and sought to re-establish in this peaceful corner of the country an outpost of Roman Catholicism by a fervent return to the Middle Ages as to the golden age and the ideal period of Christendom. Thus his

---

[1] Hereafter quoted as *Mediator*.

action was influenced by the philosophical traditionalism of the period and neo-Gothic romanticism. It was also inspired by fierce opposition to the neo-Gallicanism of the times and, generally speaking, by systematic disparagement of everything that was not strictly "Roman". These extreme positions profoundly influenced the liturgical outlook of the first abbot of Solesmes and were blemishes on the two great works that he bequeathed us—his *Institutions liturgiques* and especially his *Année liturgique* (recently republished). Dom Guéranger's work belonged to the category of what has come to be termed "archeologism", since this tendency was stigmatized expressly by the Encyclical *Mediator*. It lays itself open to the reproach, also, that the apparently spiritual and theological tendency of this reform can be seen to be at the same time the expression of a certain policy dubbed reactionary by its opponents and still supported by a certain section of the Catholics in France and elsewhere.

Apart from these controversial aspects of the movement which originated at Solesmes its more authentic and positive implications should be acknowledged. In the eyes of the historian of the Church Dom Guéranger must be given the great credit for having caused the liturgy to be known again and loved; for having restored it to a worthy, sober and really religious style; for having put forward the Roman liturgy as a model, for him the only model, and an especially privileged one and worthy of imitation; for having laid the foundations for the restoration of liturgical chant and its re-introduction into worship; finally, by his return to certain forms of worship in the Roman Church which, though in a special category, bear the stamp of universality, for being the promoter, despite himself, it is true, of ecumenism. Indeed, it requires to be said that he had no idea at all of the legitimate liturgical and disciplinary diversity in the Church; the Eastern Churches, even those in union with Rome, he regarded in their rites and customs as merely tolerated by the Roman Church.[2]

[2] Cf. H. Chirat's review of Dom Rousseau's *Histoire du mouvement liturgique* (Paris, 1945; English translation, *Progress of the Liturgy*,

BEURON AND THE WOLTER BROTHERS

The liturgical movement which grew up in Germany with the new Benedictine Congregation of Beuron was in the beginning modelled on that of Solesmes. Nevertheless, it received additional and probably more authentic inspiration from the work of Möhler (1796–1838), the theologian, who was the promoter of the patristic revival at the theological faculty of the university of Tübingen. This revival Möhler successfully combined with a strong love of the Church and with tradition as a whole; as a result, without himself being directly interested in the liturgy, he endowed the movement, which drew inspiration from him in this matter, with a more solid foundation than that formed by Solesmes's attachment to medieval forms.

All the same it is true that the two Wolter brothers, priests of Cologne who became Benedictines as Dom Maur and Dom Placid respectively, achieved a satisfactory combination of the heritage received from Dom Guéranger, in whose abbey they made their novitiate, with—in reaction to the *Aufklärung*—a

Westminster, Md, 1951) in *MD* 7, 137–47: "Dom Guéranger states that the Holy See has taken the oriental rites under its protection (he refers to acts of Pius IX and Gregory XVI).... These measures appear to him to be inspired principally by pure condescendence and by reasons of expediency. They are aimed at not embittering or wounding the peoples who practise these liturgies and it is 'to make this invitation more pressing', to 'avoid every pretext which could postpone the longed for day of reunion' that 'Rome... does not cease to evince her motherly regard for these liturgies... enshrined in languages very different from her own'. The apostolic see, he does not hesitate to write, 'has been excessively tactful... in the face of the susceptibilities of these unfortunate peoples, by taking under her protection the Eastern liturgies'. The Eastern liturgies appear to him as 'barriers' which make 'more difficult' the duty of 'remaining united to the centre of Catholic communion' although 'this fidelity is always possible with the help of divine grace'. In spite of their venerable antiquity they are 'make-shift', compromises, even 'a misfortune for those Churches which do not share in the Roman liturgy'. He feels himself authorized to 'think that a time will come when the language of Rome, like her faith, will be for the East, as for the West, the only means of unity and regeneration'." (References in the review quoted above.)

concern for the revival of patristic tradition. The elder brother compiled what amounts to an anthology of the Fathers in his *Praecipua ordinis monastici elementa*; there should also be mentioned his commentary on the psalms in five volumes (*Psallite sapienter*); this, too, is full of quotations from the Fathers.

MAREDSOUS AND SAINT-ANDRÉ

Dom Placid, Dom Maur's younger brother, became the first abbot of the Belgian abbey of Maredsous which was founded from Beuron. To this monastery belongs the merit of having published the first complete translation of the Missal for the use of the laity, a work which emerged victorious from the controversies on the legitimacy of translating the sacred text of the liturgy and especially that of the canon of the Mass.[3]

It is clear, then, how to the concern for liturgical restoration, referring back to a particular point in tradition, was joined the supplementary concern, acknowledged as fundamental, to bring the liturgy within the reach of the ordinary laity. The archeological tendency was eliminated and Maredsous began the struggle, still going on, to bring the liturgy out from the antiquated framework within which it had been confined and in God's light to set it out before his people.

Thus, a year after the publication of the Missal, during the liturgical congress held at Liège in 1883, Dom Gérard van Caloen read a paper, which attracted some attention and a certain amount of controversy, on the subject of communion during Mass. Subsequently, he founded the first liturgical review, *Le Messager des fidèles*, which afterwards under Dom Germain Morin, a follower of Dom Wolf's and through him of Scheeben's, became *La Revue bénédictine*, a critical and learned organ.

Meanwhile, Maredsous made a foundation at Louvain (Mont-César), which we shall encounter again with Dom

---

[3] It is perhaps worth pointing out that an English translation of the Missal by Dr Husenbeth (1796–1872) antedated the French one by at least half a century. (*Trans.*)

Lambert Beauduin, and Dom Gérard van Caloen established a house at Saint-André, Lophem, near Bruges, which was to achieve considerable development in the liturgical and missionary fields. Here it was that the tradition begun by Dom Gérard was to be perpetuated and reach its full stature; its first phase was the work of Dom Gaspar Lefebvre whose Missal, in many editions and various languages, has sold hundreds of thousands of copies; the second phase came with the review *Paroisse et liturgie* which at the end of the last war developed from the *Bulletin liturgique et paroissial* and at the present moment, with its editorial team under Dom Thierry Maertens, represents the most clearly defined pastoral trend among liturgical reviews in French.

At this point we can conclude this first sketch of the liturgical renewal which issued from monastic sources, leaving mention of the Rhineland abbey of Maria Laach, which has a more direct connection with the achievements of liturgical research, and of Dom Lambert Beauduin, to the starting-point of what in the strict sense of the term is called the "liturgical movement"—that is, as it is based on pastoral work in parishes and the various movements.

Indeed we have already reached this point with Maredsous and Saint-André so that we can conclude this chapter with mention not only of the benefits of the monastic liturgical renewal but also of its limitations.

MERITS AND LIMITATIONS OF THE MONASTIC LITURGICAL MOVEMENT

The great merit of the monastic liturgical movement is that it made a start. In addition, right from the beginning, it brought with it a guarantee of religious authenticity that many of the so called pastoral improvisations are far from possessing. Thus the monasteries preserved and renewed the liturgy at a period when other institutions in the Church did not understand it and would probably have made matters even worse if they had attempted anything in this field.

On the other hand, monasticism shows certain limitations and sometimes the following disadvantages in the matter of liturgy. In the first place, there is the tendency to archeologism, a danger pointed out by Guardini to the bishop of Mainz and by Pius XII in *Mediator*. This danger is to be discerned to some extent with Dom Casel (as we shall see) as well as with the two Wolter brothers or Dom Guéranger. It is to be supposed that the "preservation of ancient monuments" mentality, which is contemporary with the first liturgical restoration, finally spread to this field also. The title of the great dictionary edited by Dom Cabrol and Dom Leclercq (*Dictionnaire d'archéologie chrétienne et de liturgie*) is not without significance in this respect.

Then, there is the tendency to aestheticism of which a famous example is to hand in Huysmans' conception of liturgy which he derived from its presentation in monasteries, or again, Claudel's idea of it, though he is far less monastic, as it is to be seen in *La Messe là-bas*. This tendency is to be clearly seen in the fact which is still usual that the monks celebrate and officiate while the faithful are onlookers. It is even general for it to be forbidden for the laity to sing during a monastic office. And this is not abnormal since the "congregation" in the monastic order of things is formed by the choir of monks alone. But in this case the danger is considerable when this liturgy is put forward as an example to be imitated in parochial liturgies. To cite but one disadvantage, there can be a tendency to make the solemnity of the liturgy consist in its external splendour and its performance by the officiants alone. Now the solemnity of the liturgy resides, as Dom Thierry Maertens has pointed out, in the presence of the people of God taking their own part in the common prayer.

Another limitation of the monastic liturgical renewal comes from the value itself of monastic life. The monk, accustomed to reading the Bible, easily penetrating the full meaning of the prayer, feels no need for the teaching function of the liturgy, the living language and more expressive forms. He is less inclined to recognize the needs of initiation among the faithful, needs that of course are constituent parts of the liturgy which is itself a catechetical initiation, as we shall see below.

For all these reasons the monastic liturgical movement has in the past suffered from the danger of keeping the liturgy as the special preserve of a humanly and religiously cultured caste; this is one of the most serious choices that can be made, quite legitimately of course, by this or that monastic community in which the liturgy is deliberately made to fall into line with forms of life, civilization and culture regarded as classical and ideal but which cannot be considered as invariably applicable to every kind of human group within the Church.

To sum up: the advantages and limitations of the monastic liturgical effort enable us to discern two apparently strongly contrasting laws. The first is that the liturgy is fundamental on the same score as Christianity itself (it is not a workshop open to all), hence the providential rôle of the monasteries as "conservatories" of liturgy. But at the same time the limitations of a monastic presentation of liturgy at the pastoral level are a verification of Fr Jungmann's remark: "Liturgical reform cannot come only from above."

CHAPTER II

LITURGICAL CENTRES, INSTITUTES AND CONFERENCES

In dealing here with the various centres of liturgical research and propaganda we hardly leave the monastic setting with which we have so far been occupied, for this chapter deals principally with certain institutions which have been established in different countries with the help of monks and sometimes also under their direction. But in continuing to follow the pastoral trend of the liturgical movement, which it began to take at Maredsous and Saint-André, we could hardly give here, even in abridged form, the history of the various branches of ecclesiastical science which have contributed to this movement. To do so would have meant following the history and providing a list of all the archeological and literary documents, both in Scripture and patristics, discovered and interpreted by scholars and researchers of the calibre of Duchesne, Andrieu or Bishop.

RESEARCH INSTITUTES

Germany: the school of Maria Laach

The German liturgical movement, as we have already noticed, has its roots in a rediscovery of the Fathers and of ecclesiology, the two great artisans of this work being the theologians Scheeben and Möhler. But beyond all question to the abbey of Maria Laach belongs the honour of having laid the foundations of the modern liturgical movement on a firm doctrinal basis and of having put a varied selection of its practical applications to the proof. Three names stand out in this connection—Dom Ildephonsus Herwegen, Dom Odo Casel and Fr Johannes Pinsk, respectively, abbot, monk and friend of Maria Laach, have made this monastery the centre of liturgical life in the German-speaking countries. (Klosterneuburg in Austria, mentioned below, owes much to Maria Laach and its work is closely connected with it.)

The various movements and institutions depending on Maria Laach can be clearly seen as belonging to two categories; there are those which are concerned principally with the Mystery in liturgy and those which give more attention to anthropology and sociology. Maria Laach forms their inspiration and their principal source at the levels both of doctrine and research; it is for this reason that it has been included in the present chapter.

The principal achievements of the three men mentioned above should be briefly mentioned. Dom Ildephonsus Herwegen (†1948) gave a number of conferences which he afterwards collected together in volume form. He founded a yearbook of liturgy (*Jahrbuch für Liturgiewissenschaft*) and a periodical (*Ecclesia Orans*) together with an academy of patristic studies and a centre for sacred art. But his principal achievement was to get away from the romantic, medieval notion of liturgy that had been current since the work of Dom Guéranger. Dom Herwegen was able to show, to the surprise of many, that the Middle Ages were not, in liturgy at any rate, the Christian era *par excellence*, and that during this period the worship of the Church became overlaid with all sorts of fanciful interpretations, developments foreign to its nature, thus paving the way "for the abandonment of the liturgy by Protestantism and its final disgrace and neglect in so much of post-Tridentine Catholicism".[1]

The *Jahrbuch* founded by Dom Herwegen was carried on

[1] L. Bouyer, *Liturgical Piety*, p. 15.

by Dom Odo Casel (†1948), the most original thinker of the group. He was the author of *Das Christliche Kultmysterium* (1932; English translation referred to in the Select Bibliography), a work which caused some controversy on its first appearance and indeed still continues to do so, though it has also been hailed as the most outstanding theological work of the century. Dom Casel also produced other works on the mystery of feasts and the mystery of the Mass. His teaching is examined below in chapter VI.

Fr Johannes Pinsk was profoundly impressed by the liturgical realism of Maria Laach. After a post as chaplain to students in Berlin he was one of the principal leaders of the *Akadermikerverband* and then parish priest of Lankwitz, Berlin. As editor of a liturgical review, and the author of two books on certain aspects of worship, he exerted a certain influence on the liturgical movement in Germany. His two series of articles, one on the liturgical year and the other on the sociological, anthropological and pastoral conditioning of the liturgy, have been regarded as classics of the liturgical revival.

France: the Centre de Pastorale liturgique

The Centre de Pastorale liturgique (usually referred to as CPL) in France has been compared to the German centre at Maria Laach. It might be objected that this comparison is based on a mistaken classification of the work of the CPL which is thereby effectively denied its pastoral quality and relegated to the category of a research institute. But this classification has been maintained for two reasons: the first is the undeniable high quality of the studies undertaken by the CPL and their extraordinary proliferation; the second is the access that these studies give to the results of scientific research in the field of liturgy—to those matters, in fact, which, as was mentioned at the beginning of this chapter, cannot be dealt with here. Indeed the CPL deserves high praise for the fact that by calling on specialists in all branches of ecclesiastical learning it has been instrumental, both in France and outside it, in preventing the liturgical movement from turning into a series of merely practical prescriptions for liturgical propaganda—a danger, always present, which has not been avoided in some countries, when work of this nature is not based on real research and theological thought. There can hardly be cause for complaint that at the present moment the CPL, despite its numerous public manifestations and the services of a pastoral nature that it renders, appears rather as an academy for liturgical research and thought. This is particularly true since the foundation of the *Institut supérieur de liturgie* at the Institut Catholique in Paris, under the joint direction of the CPL and the abbey of Mont-César, for training seminary professors in this branch.

The present stage of evolution of the CPL was obvious from the beginning, for it started immediately after the war, being founded by two Dominicans, Frs Duployé and Roguet, with Canon Martimort, and sought to group men of learning, theologians and pastors. On the other hand, its legitimate concern to guard against the insubordination of certain unenlightened elements in France, as in Germany, and to give complete assurance to the hierarchy, certainly helped it to maintain itself in the loftier and calmer sphere of ideas and principles. Perhaps it was led thereby, sometimes unconsciously, to discourage other teams which, if less well equipped, were possibly more actively engaged in the pastoral field, by condemning them, practically speaking, to silence.

In any case, as early as 1946 the *Osservatore Romano* bore undeniable witness to the approval that the CPL had obtained at the highest level of ecclesiastical authority and to its general policy. In a laudatory note published on January 17th, 1946, the semi-official journal of the Roman curia emphasized the various indications that led it to believe that the liturgical movement had reached a decisive turning-point of its history and would take the right road; it praised the CPL as being "the consoling and flowering springtime of a Christian spirituality coming from and fed by the pure springs of the *lex orandi*".

Further testimony, if needed, is to be found just ten years

later in the success of the Assisi congress. Although this was not the exclusive work of the CPL it came to the fore as the leader and king-pin of the movement.

Usually the CPL seeks to exert an influence at the parochial level by its public meetings and liturgical weeks and among the Christian public in general through its popular illustrated periodical *Fêtes et Saisons* which has a high circulation. Its permanent activities find their expression in the quarterly review, *La Maison-Dieu*, and the basic works published in the series *Lex Orandi*. With the CPL and the Institut Superieur, already referred to, the Church in France was very well placed for an early implementation of the liturgical constitution.

THE LITURGICAL MOVEMENT IN ENGLISH-SPEAKING COUNTRIES

Great Britain and Ireland

Just as it would be wrong to say that there are no signs of a liturgical movement in Great Britain, so it would be to assert that up to the end of the last war this movement had taken a firm hold on the Church in these countries. Certain ideas had penetrated from abroad, but in general they remained at the notional level or were adopted by some as ready-made practical solutions of the liturgical problem, and this occurred in both instances because the necessary preliminary theological thinking and liturgical research had been done by others and was not the product of native effort. An authentic movement requires some at least of the preliminary spadework to be done on the spot and not to be left to the scholars and liturgists of other countries.

Nevertheless, as appears later in this section, there are signs of much improvement. Of course, there were several reasons for the tardy start of the liturgical movement in Great Britain, reasons which go back to the nineteenth century and beyond to the time of persecution.

The historical position emerges plainly from such a book as

Dom Rousseau's *Progress of the Liturgy* where of the twenty short pages devoted to England (the restriction to the one country is Dom Rousseau's) all but three of them are concerned with Anglicans. There can be no quarrel with this for it represents accurately enough the real position: a little over a hundred years ago Anglicans—or at least that portion of them actively concerned with the Oxford movement—were occupied in those tasks of *ressourcement* which we nowadays realize to be of capital importance, while the Catholics, emerging from a period of persecution, with very different problems on their hands (for example, the influx of poor Irish due to the famine, the difficulties inherent in the re-establishment of the hierarchy in 1850, lack of financial resources, etc.) though benefiting in some degree from the research done by Anglicans were largely preoccupied with other matters.

It has also to be borne in mind that though the Catholics were doctrinally the heirs to the pre-Reformation Church in England, professing the same faith and using the same liturgy as their forefathers, what can only be called the ethos of the pre-Reformation Church seemed to have lingered on among certain sections of Anglicanism. For this reason many converts to Catholicism, endeavouring to make a clean break with their immediate religious past, identified themselves with an expression of Catholicism as it was to be found in some parts of Italy in the nineteenth century, and adopted various devotional practices which, while no doubt picturesque among the Italian peasants where they evolved, were out of place in England and out of tune with the English religious mind. Fr Faber was an obvious example of such a reaction.

The influences at work in Germany and France were not without their impact in England. Dom Rousseau points out that there is a certain affinity between Newman and Möhler and he quotes Fr de Grandmaison's remark that "if in the iron age of theology constituted by the first three-quarters of the nineteenth century a name of destiny and enduring renown is sought, the first to appear is Möhler's, standing almost alone with Newman's". Newman frequently quotes Möhler and liked to regard him as his precursor. Neither of them was directly concerned with liturgy but the connection between them for what concerns us here is to be found in their love of Christian antiquity and the Fathers and in their appeal to them in their efforts to rechristianize their own period.

Dom Guéranger, too, was not without influence since his *Liturgical Year* appeared in translation soon after its original publication; this was the work of Dom Laurence Shepherd. But the same forces were at work in England as in France; as a rule any attempt at liturgical restoration went hand in hand with the "Gothic revival" in architecture and was conceived in terms of a return to the Middle Ages; most of the work done among Catholics was merely rubrical or else strictly historical. Dr Husenbeth, as has already been mentioned, translated the Missal; Dr Daniel Rock (1799–1871), a priest esteemed by his contemporaries for his learning, produced a treatise on the liturgy of the Mass that went through several editions: *Hierugia, or the Holy Sacrifice of the Mass* (London, 1833). He also produced a three-volume work on the Sarum rite and its ordinary, attributed in those days to St Osmund. But all this was largely archeology rather than what we are concerned with here.

Nevertheless, Dr Rock's work, like Dr Husenbeth's Missal, is symptomatic of a frame of mind and an approach to the liturgy of the Church that differed considerably from the type of worship that was introduced by, for example, the Oratorians in London in the middle of the nineteenth century. Husenbeth and Rock both belonged to the old English Catholic tradition which is also exemplified by Bishop Challoner's *Garden of the Soul*. This popular prayerbook, which has run through so many editions that it is probably impossible now to enumerate them all, has, unfortunately, been almost edited out of recognition. In its original form it contained a wealth of material from the worship of the Church, psalms and hymns and the like, that is now no longer included. The same tradition is revealed by the earlier volumes of the *Catholic Directory*, or the later volumes of the *Laity's Catholic Directory*; therein it may be discovered that High Mass and Vespers of a Sunday were the usual church services provided for Catholics in London in, say, 1829, and that the number of churches with Sunday Vespers then was far greater than it is today. Moreover, there were books in print which provided the laity with the text of this Office in their own language as well as in Latin.

But practically speaking the romantic medieval attitude towards liturgy, or else the rubrical approach, prevailed in Great Britain until well on into the twentieth century and it was only after the First World War that the real implications of the liturgical revival at the parochial level gained gradual recognition. Even so this realization was confined to a small number of clergy and laity. With the publication of *Mediator* (1947) and subsequent decrees, the reform of the Holy Week services, the directives about dialogue Mass, gradually a different mentality has begun to emerge among the younger clergy, but in the absence of clear leadership and encouragement from the bishops progress has necessarily been slow. That was the position prior to the Liturgical Constitution of the Second Vatican Council; this has given an entirely new perspective to the whole liturgical question in the British Isles.

Yet it is not true to say that, generally speaking, there has been little progress. Judged by the standard of even twenty years ago progress has been enormous. Before the Council dialogue Mass was widespread and real efforts were being made in some places to make the worship of the Church a living reality. Then the publication of books like Fr Charles Davis's *Liturgy and Doctrine*, which is fundamental, is just one symptom of the kind of work being done; in this book the theological revival and the liturgical revival are all linked together, showing the fundamental nature of the latter. It is a good example of the kind of theological preparation needed for an authentic liturgical movement. Of course, there have been many translations from the French and German, and it is good for English-speaking people thus to be in touch with thought in Europe, but translations rarely have the impact of a book which has been thought out in the language in which it is presented to readers, and which confronts a concrete situation in the experience of authors and readers alike.

The Society of St Gregory, founded between the wars with a predominant interest in plainchant, after the Second World War enlarged its scope to promote the liturgical revival in accordance with the principles laid down in *Mediator*. Its periodical *Liturgy* (formerly *Music and Liturgy*), ably edited by Fr J. D. Crichton, now publishes informative and valuable material and contrives to keep readers in touch with developments elsewhere; by means of its summer and other "schools" the Society of St Gregory has done much useful work. The Vernacular Society exists for the purpose indicated by its name; it is not widely supported but it has possibly exerted an influence in excess of its membership. Certainly, the symposium that it sponsored (*English in the Liturgy*, edited by C. R. A. Cunliffe, London, 1956) aroused considerable comment. Now that its principal purpose has been achieved it could usefully devote its energies to other work in the liturgical field.

In Ireland a beginning has been made in post-war years with the annual conferences for clergy held at Glenstal Abbey. Much has been done in recent years to promote a more realistic attitude towards the liturgical movement by the monthly review *The Furrow*; edited from Maynooth, a fact not without importance, since here a great number of the clergy who are to work in Ireland are trained, it has wisely not confined itself to liturgy, but has been concerned with the whole problem of the presentation of Christianity to the modern world. Certainly all the signs are that if the liturgical movement has begun to exert an influence in Ireland at a late stage in its development it has at least started on the right lines and with an entirely pastoral outlook, thus avoiding the mistakes made elsewhere.

Evidence for this is to be found in the *Collectio Rituum* published in 1960. This bilingual ritual for use in all the dioceses of Ireland is not just a reprint of the Roman Ritual with a translation of certain of its rites; the opportunity has been taken to revise some of the rites in order to make them better suited to conditions prevailing in Ireland at the present time. In this respect the Irish bilingual Ritual compares very favourably with the *Excerpta e Rituali* published at about the same time for use in England and Wales; in this no attempt has been made at adaptation and the book contains a straightforward translation of certain portions of the Roman Ritual.

Since 1954 an annual liturgical congress has been held in Ireland at Glenstal Abbey the papers of which have been published in two volumes (*Studies in Pastoral Liturgy*, I and II); these reveal very clearly that those taking part are very much alive to the problems of Christian worship in modern times and to the danger of taking over ready made the solutions arrived at elsewhere. The Editor of the latest volume of *Studies in Pastoral Liturgy* puts this very clearly:

> Obviously we have much to learn in Ireland from countries where the liturgical movement can be traced back to the beginning of this century; it would be, nonetheless, an unwise policy simply to transpose to this country practices in vogue on the continent and to impose them on our people—a policy of eclecticism which would be assured of no lasting results. We must work out our own solutions in the light of the Church's teaching, liturgical tradition and pastoral experience.[2]

All the signs are, then, that the liturgical movement in Ireland made a start which though late was healthy.

The United States

In the United States the liturgical revival owes its origins and much of its later development to the Benedictine monks of St John's Abbey, Collegeville, Minnesota. Indeed, more than anywhere else, the introduction of the revival to the U.S.A. was the work of one man, Dom Virgil Michel. His efforts

> had effects on the life of the Church throughout the whole of the United States and in varying degrees throughout the English-

[2] *Studies in Pastoral Liturgy*, II, p. viii.

speaking world. For in the mid-1920's an organized movement was brought from Europe and launched at St John's by Michel with the support of his abbot which Theodore Maynard in his *Story of American Catholicism* has termed the most significant aspect of contemporary religious life. It is called the liturgical movement, or more correctly the liturgical revival.[3]

The actual birth of the movement may be said to have taken place with the publication of the first number of *Orate Fratres* under Dom Virgil Michel's editorship in Advent, 1925. It is significant that Dom Virgil combined liturgical knowledge with an active social concern; his inauguration of the movement therefore avoided many of the pitfalls encountered elsewhere. *Orate Fratres* (which changed its name to the more appropriate *Worship* after the Second World War) has continued to make progress. From the Liturgical Day, held at St John's Abbey in 1929, to the first national Liturgical Week, under Benedictine sponsorship, in 1940, progress has not been slow. Certain names stand out: Fr Godfrey Diekmann, O.S.B., successor to Fr Virgil Michel as editor of *Orate Fratres* (*Worship*), in 1963 completed twenty-five years service in that position. During this period Fr Godfrey Diekmann has unquestionably been one of the most prominent and influential figures in the American liturgical movement. He is now vice-president of the Liturgical Conference and is acting as *peritus* on the liturgy commission of the Second Vatican Council. Fr Gerard Ellard was another pioneer. From the time that he began writing in 1923 until his sudden death in 1963, Fr Ellard contributed steadily to the liturgical apostolate through his numerous books and articles, both popular and scholarly, through his numerous lectures throughout the country and through his many years as a teacher. Fr Michael Mathis, C.S.C., was another significant figure in the American movement. Perhaps his best known contribution is the founding of the Summer School of Liturgy at the University of Notre Dame.

In recent years the most influential figure has been Fr

---

[3] Colman J. Barry, O.S.B., *Worship and Work* (Collegeville, Minn., 1956), p. 264.

Frederick R. McManus, J.C.D., a professor of canon law at the Catholic University at Washington, a *peritus* on the liturgy commission of the Second Vatican Council. His books, his monthly column in *Worship*, his numerous lectures and his work as President of the Liturgical Conference have established him as an international authority on liturgy. Other outstanding names are Mgr Hellriegel and the late Fr Laukemper with their work for the promotion of liturgical life as the normal manifestation of the parish and Fr Rheinhold with his lively and well-informed articles and books.

A recent survey has indicated that something like sixty per cent of the 140 dioceses in the United States have set up liturgical commissions, and although it is impossible to provide an accurate figure on the number of parishes in which the congregation participates actively in the Mass, it is certainly safe to say that there is some degree of active participation in more than half the parishes of the country.

Thus there are signs that the fundamental ideas of the liturgical movement have made considerable progress among the Catholics of the U.S.A. In addition the publication and authorization of the bilingual Ritual in 1954, five years before the jejune compilation authorized for England and Wales, showed that the Church authorities were alive to the problems of the day. This book, containing revisions of some of the rites, was probably the best of the bilingual Rituals in the English-speaking world, and closely rivalled its German counterpart in excellence. Unfortunately, the second edition, published in 1961, authorized far less English than the previous edition.

The first national Liturgical Week was held in 1940 under the sponsorship of the Benedictine Liturgical Conference and the Week has been held annually ever since. At the twenty-fourth Week, held in August 1963, there were fourteen thousand registrants who filled the Convention Hall in Philadelphia —significant progress since the first meeting held in the basement of the cathedral in Chicago. In 1943 it was decided that the Benedictine Liturgical Conference should be dissolved in favour of a more representative organization; in 1944 it was reconstituted and incorporated as The Liturgical Conference.

The liturgical revival in the United States was indeed fortunate in its founder. After Dom Virgil's early death in 1938, Fr H. A. Rheinhold wrote:

> It is almost beyond human comprehension to grasp the completeness with which he absorbed everything that Austria, Belgium and Germany had to offer. But greater yet was what he did with it. Instead of dragging his find across the border as an exotic museum piece, he made it American as only an American mind can make it. He had seen the high sweep of German ecclesiology and sacramentalism; he had admired the Belgians for their clear grasp of a new spirituality and their critical awareness of all that stood in the way of liturgical ecclesiastical piety from traditional carry-overs; he had learned in Austria what the common people could gather from the Church's treasures without fright, but he did not come back to force these foreign and incoherent moulds on the American Church. Besides, his clear realism and his burning apostle's heart had one urge none of the great masters in Europe seemed to see; the connection of social justice with a new social spirituality. For Virgil Michel the labour encyclicals of Leo XIII and the liturgical reforms of Pius X did not just by accident happen within one generation, but were responses to cries of the masses for Christ, who had power and gave the good tidings. They belonged together.[4]

EUROPEAN COUNTRIES OTHER THAN FRANCE AND GERMANY

It can hardly be said that the liturgical movement has made great strides in Spain, Italy and Portugal. In Spain the liturgical renewal is promoted principally by the Benedictine abbey of Montserrat in Catalonia, which is a well-known centre·not only of pilgrimage but also of liturgical worship and of the publication of books popularizing the fundamental ideas of the liturgical movement. There should also be mentioned the abbey of San Domingo de Los Silos in the province of Burgos

[4] *National Liturgical Week Proceedings* (1947), p. 11.

which publishes a review *Liturgia*. Since 1954 annual congresses of pastoral liturgy have been organized and less intermittent activity has been pursued in the seminaries. In 1955 a central committee for the liturgical apostolate was set up in Toledo.

In Italy, to the extent that liturgical progress can be distinguished from directions given by Rome, there may be mentioned the existence of the *Centro di Azione liturgica* which publishes a *Rivista liturgica*; once again this is a Benedictine work since it is published by the Abbey of Finalpia in the province of Savona; here too is organized an annual liturgical congress. It is worth pointing out, also, the connection between the work of Cardinal Schuster, a Benedictine monk who became archbishop of Milan, and that at the present day of Cardinal Lercaro, archbishop of Bologna. The works of both are certainly typical of their respective generations. Thus it is interesting to observe how the period of research as represented by Cardinal Schuster's work has led to that of a pastoral approach, intelligently open to the data of sociology. The particular significance of Cardinal Schuster's work in connection with the Italian liturgical movement since its origins is emphasized below.

CONCLUSION

At the end of this chapter, devoted to the various centres of research and propaganda in the sphere of pastoral liturgy, an attempt may be made to classify the various branches of the ecclesiastical sciences employed by workers in the field, whether scholars or pastors, who have combined in the liturgical movement learning and piety. There is nothing original about this since right at the beginning of the century a monk of Solesmes, Dom Aubourg, portrayed in the *Revue Grégorienne* his conception of the ideal liturgist. The following extracts are offered for the entertainment as well as for the edification of the reader:

The scientific equipment of the ideal liturgist should comprise at least the following: a good general education, a solid theological foundation, five or six ancient languages, and the same number of modern ones.... And those are only the preliminary and Latin—will be familiar to him. He should possess a thorough knowledge of the political history of the Middle Ages and an equally thorough knowledge of the history of the Church, of her dogmas and her discipline.... Set your mind at rest, we are only at the beginning. The liturgist's own particular task begins with the study of the liturgical texts, the texts of all the liturgies, which he must submit to painstaking analysis and continual comparison. From the data that he thus extracts from them he will be able to construct a doctrine of the liturgy or to retrace its history.... But this is only the stage of accumulating materials. The final work consists in the fusion of doctrine and history in a synthesis which should make clear to men's minds the gradual development of the first seeds of the Christian mysteries in the infinite frondescence of liturgical rites.

This passage, which is not without its exaggerations, can be summarized in a less colourful manner. The principal branches of learning, which in actual fact have been utilized in liturgy, are the following:

In the first place, history and archeology, particularly in connection with the Bible and the patristic and medieval periods, and even to such an extent that Pius XII was obliged to utter a warning against an excessive and unhealthy preoccupation with things of the past, declaring that it would be "neither wise nor praiseworthy to reduce everything to antiquity by every possible device" (*Mediator*). On the other hand, these branches of learning are especially allied with liturgy, which is essentially conservative, by its unchanging character expressing in some sort a sign of transcendence and instinctively resistant to any kind of fanciful innovation as well as to any unjustified modification.

Secondly comes ecclesiastical law, in its various aspects, but specifically as liturgical law, on a final analysis degenerating into knowledge of rubrics: just as with "archeologism", it is almost superfluous to protest against such a debased and narrow view of the subject.

Then, there is theology, and especially ecclesiology. Indeed, it seems almost commonplace now to point out a genetic development occurring between ecclesiology, derived from its biblical and patristic sources, and the liturgical movement.

Finally there is a branch of knowledge, which while being an art and not a science in the proper sense of the word, appears to be most important of all: this is the pastoral aspect. The title of Fr Jungmann's paper at the Assisi congress in 1956 was significant in this respect: "Pastoral care, the key to the history of the liturgy." It can be said that it was pastoral needs which brought the liturgical forms into being in the primitive Church: and so it is this which enables us to discover the reason for the liturgical forms of the past and which can devise forms adapted to the present needs of the faithful. The truth of this emerges clearly from the whole effort of liturgical catechesis and it can be seen, too, in the fact that in Pius XII's liturgical reforms the principal motivation was to be found generally in pastoral reasons.

But all this brings us into the perspective of other sciences which until a few years ago were still wholly unknown to the pastoral clergy. These are the auxiliary sciences, mostly of a clearly secular character, which nevertheless prove as necessary as the so-called ecclesiastical sciences. In passing, we can mention, for example, ethnology and the history of religions, sociology and individual and crowd psychology. This short list is indicative that pastoral liturgy, if it is not to be merely imitative of the past, even of a golden age for the Church, or, with greater reason, merely a matter of innovation, must enlarge its views to embrace the whole religious world in order to obtain a certain number of fundamental ideas and especially the laws and, so to say, the constants of the individual and collective religious mind. For it is these that it is important to promote in the present conditions of societies and their respective civilizations.

CHAPTER III

PAROCHIAL
DEVELOPMENTS

The views touched on at the end of the last chapter in connection with the social and cultural evolution of the contemporary world, together with its religious diversity, scarcely suspected, it seems, by Christians, should not discourage us from returning to consideration of more modest matters. In these, indeed, can be discerned the authentic effects of the liturgical movement at the present time.

As an introduction to this chapter we can consider a further piece of history which might well have found a place at the beginning of either of the preceding chapters or serve as a summary of the whole volume. This is the outstanding work of Dom Lambert Beauduin.

DOM LAMBERT BEAUDUIN

It is fitting and right that just a few years after his death a short account of Dom Lambert Beauduin's work should appear at the head of these few remarks on the parochial development of the liturgical movement. The liturgy is rightfully the worship of the Christian people: but in fact it is due to Dom Lambert Beauduin that its pastoral dimensions have been discovered in the present renewal. Many others after him, and some even before him, worked on the same lines. But beyond all question to him belongs the credit for the primary intuition, even to the extent that it is possible to date the liturgical movement in the proper sense of the term from the first expression that he gave to this intuition in 1909. It has been said indeed that "Dom Beauduin's intuitions form, no doubt, the principal characteristic of his genius".

But if that is true it is important to consider his thought on the pastoral implications of the liturgy in conjunction with two other intuitions of his without which it would lose much of its value. Yet it is on account of these further intuitions that Dom Beauduin is indeed the patriarch and patron of all workers in this field, whatever their special interest in it.

Dom Lambert Beauduin's view on the pastoral implications of the liturgy (he was a former parish priest and workers' chaplain), through which he gave fresh impetus to the liturgical movement, must be taken in conjunction with his attitude to the Eastern Church in general and Eastern liturgies in particular. In this field he became the leader of a school, and his work was continued, in the face of great difficulties, it must be acknowledged, in particular by the Benedictines of Amay-sur-Meuse, subsequently established at Chevetogne.

The same pastoral approach to the liturgy must be acknowledged as the basis of the scientific and learned work through which Dom Beauduin was effectively aided at Mont-César by the review *Questions liturgiques et paroissiales* and especially by Dom Capelle and Dom Botte.

Having thus delineated Dom Beauduin's fundamental attitudes we can recall some of the facts of the story and its subsequent developments. The origin of the liturgical movement, then, is to be found in 1909 at the Catholic Congress at Malines, in a paper by Dom Lambert Beauduin which earned the support of Cardinal Mercier. On July 7th, 1910 a report was sent by Mont-César to the abbot of Beuron suggesting the setting up of a school of liturgy at Louvain. This report was based on the following premises: liturgical renewal is necessary, it can be directed by the Benedictines and Mont-César seems indicated as the appropriate centre.

At that time, indeed, Dom Beauduin had in mind the holding of liturgical "weeks" (these were later held at the rate of two a year), the establishment of a liturgical review (this was achieved with the founding of *Questions liturgiques et paroissiales*) and finally the founding of a liturgical institute; this unfortunately proved impossible at that time.

In this way the principal characteristics of the liturgical movement of the abbey of Mont-César were that it was brought up to date and adapted to social requirements in all its bearings; as a consequence, its influence was felt far and wide and it found imitators in all countries.

So far as Belgium was concerned Dom Beauduin's liturgical work can be summed up in the threefold aspect which it assumed, corresponding at all points with the trend of the work at Saint-André (referred to above, p. 14). In the first place liturgy is for the service of the parishes, as they are; then, the liturgical renewal is the centre and also the starting-point of a complete parochial renewal; lastly, an attempt must be made to use what we already have; in the light of this experience reform can be effected; there must be neither rigid conservatism nor irresponsible innovation; the primary need is that an attempt should be made.

It was on account of this threefold aspect that this section on Dom Beauduin was placed at the head of the subject which is now to be treated—the liturgical renewal coming out from the monasteries and specialized centres to influence the parishes and popular movements. Germany, where the movement developed especially between the two wars, is here given special mention, followed by France, where the principal expansion took place after World War II. But to begin with some information is offered about the movement at Klosterneuburg in Austria because of its extensive influence and the sympathetic character of the work which was undertaken modestly but methodically in the simple setting of a parish church.

AUSTRIA: THE MOVEMENT AT KLOSTERNEUBURG

The school of Maria Laach, somewhat aristocratic and erudite, had evolved a theology of the liturgy in the tradition of the Fathers and through it influenced an intellectual élite among the faithful. Pius Parsch and his closest collaborator, Joseph Casper, a priest of the Byzantine rite, basing themselves on the principles of Maria Laach, were concerned particularly by what they called *Volksliturgie*, a tautological term perhaps, but one which clearly expresses the fact that liturgy is the people's work, the people's affair.

Yet what is striking at first in the Klosterneuburg movement, a parochial undertaking, is the solid nature of the organization. The basis of it is a publishing company (*Volksliturgische Apostolat*) which forms the financial and administrative side. This company is responsible for a review, *Bibel und Liturgie*, and a remarkable series of the liturgical propers for each week ("Life with the Church"), manuals of all sorts, editions of texts and pictures.

The purpose of one organization was the apostolate among the faithful through the liturgy. Now there are two ways of being concerned with the liturgy. It can be considered in itself, its origins and its symbolism studied, an attempt can be made to arrive at absolute purity of text and rite and to establish the authentic rubrics. That is the purpose of the various specialized institutes. Or the faithful can be brought back to an understanding of the liturgy to enable them thus to understand the ceremonies and to return to the ultimate source of authentic prayer. The Klosterneuburg movement was concerned with this latter way of regarding the liturgy.

In the first place it envisaged the restoration of the Mass to its true place and its true meaning—a sacrifice offered by the community and a sacrificial meal. For this purpose was developed a form of preaching directly inspired by the liturgy and evening services were restored to a place of esteem. By evening services were meant the singing of psalms, Compline, Bible reading, ceremonies during which the whole parochial family really takes part in the liturgy. But an important though modest preliminary is to have a proper care for the dignity of the sanctuary; everything in it should contribute to make the altar stand out for it is the place of sacrifice and the centre of liturgical unity.

The chief inspiration of this movement was certainly Dom Pius Parsch, a canon regular of Klosterneuburg. He was ill at ease in the great abbey church (a romanesque church which underwent restoration at the Baroque period) but he managed to restore as the parish church a magnificent little romanesque church dedicated to St Gertrude and situated a few hundred yards from the monastery. It was this church which was referred to in the remark: "The movement became a powerful ferment with enormous influence on parishes and religious communities."

THE MOVEMENT IN GERMANY

The history of the German liturgical movement can be divided conveniently into three stages—the first between 1918 and 1933, the second corresponding to the period of National Socialism and the Second World War, and the third stage after the war.

The first stage which drew its inspiration equally from Klosterneuburg and Maria Laach, and corresponds therefore with the development of frequent communion (under the form of monthly communion), is characterized principally by the return of youth to Christian sources hitherto ignored. Here Guardini's rôle was preponderant: "It was perhaps the first time for centuries that an author who was theologian, philosopher, artist and man of letters, embodying the whole living culture of his times, could be so cordially received." In addition to Guardini there should be mentioned several youth movements and also Mgr Volker who was the first to introduce dialogue Mass.

When the Nazis came to power the Church was deprived of all means of external action and was obliged to fall back on her own internal life. This was almost providential for the altar became the centre of Christians' lives and they began to feel that they were back in the period of the primitive Church. At this time the Oratorians at Leipzig and afterwards at Munich undertook their well-known work in the liturgical field. In addition, the important work done by military chaplains should be emphasized.

On obtaining her freedom again the Church was faced with the problem of the direction her activities should take; was she to base everything on the parish? Would she rediscover her former organizations? In point of fact these latter reappeared, together with others like the Young Christian Workers. But there seemed to be a certain paralysis of the liturgical movement. It was to continue at the scientific level under the direction of Maria Laach, but the movement continued to make its way with varying fortunes and at the mercy of more or less serious incidents under the leadership of the episcopate and the impetus given by two congresses.

In 1920 the bishop of Passau proposed at Fulda that an episcopal commission should be set up with a sub-committee of specialists (Jungmann, Kahlefeld, etc.). The commission was established and an Institute of Liturgy was founded at Trier.

Since 1943 four categories of eucharistic celebration are to be found in Germany. These are *Gemeinschaftmesse* (dialogue Mass), *Bet-undsangmesse* (Mass accompanied with prayers and hymns), *Hochmesse* (high Mass in plainchant, somewhat unusual in Germany) and *Deutschehochmesse* (German high Mass in which the ordinary is sung in German). This German high Mass was authorized by Rome in 1950 for all German-speaking-countries.

Two congresses took place, at Frankfurt (1950) and at Munich (1955). The first concluded with a resolution calling for the continuance of evening Mass on weekdays, mitigation of the eucharistic fast, and the reading of the lessons at Mass to be in German. The second congress, at which two thousand people took part, was concerned with the important problem of liturgy and personal piety. Two resolutions were passed, the first asking for the reform of all the Holy Week services, the second for the direct reading of the lessons at Mass by the priest in German.

A further step was taken officially. This was the publication of a new catechism bearing a very pronounced liturgical and scriptural stamp and the issue of a new collection of hymns and chants better adapted to the requirements of the liturgy. Lastly, in 1955, came the German ritual. By this time dialogue Masses were in use everywhere. Guardini's translation of the psalms was recommended by the bishops. The new Easter liturgy encountered considerable success and, it is important to note, new churches were built in accordance with the requirements of the liturgical renewal.

Yet clear-sighted priests were seriously concerned. They could observe that, generally speaking, from the liturgical point of view there was a kind of paralysis. For most people, liturgy meant something for show, it did not affect daily life. Does the language of the psalms, they asked, have any meaning for modern man? Sociological conditions at the present day make the liturgical assembly of the faithful difficult. In the provinces there are great numbers of those who are on the threshold of the faith, but the liturgy ought to be the gathering together of the *plebs sancta*. These preoccupations formed the inspiration of the following propositions, about which it can be said general unanimity was achieved.

There can be no question of "archeologism". The liturgy, therefore, must be authentic. Sacred Scripture must have its full and proper place in liturgy. The relationship of liturgy and personal piety must be made clear (allowance must be made for times of silence). The relationship between liturgy and life are equally in need of emphasis; liturgy must be an expression of life. In connection with the liturgical language Kahlefeld proposed that a trial should be made of Gregorian chant to German words for the proper of the Mass; this was not allowed by Rome at the time. It remains to be seen how, after the Second Vatican Council, the liturgical reform which it promulgated will take effect in Germany.

THE MOVEMENT IN FRANCE

"The new phenomenon is that with St Pius X the liturgical movement was freed from the restricted circles of the previous

generation and returned to its own field which is the parish."
Fr Doncoeur, the author of these lines, was himself one of the
intrepid workers in achieving this successful return. We can
see now how at his instigation it was primarily in the youth
movements and the specialized groups that this return
occurred.

Another promoter of the French liturgical renewal, Fr
Bouyer, the occasional acidity of whose criticism is compen-
sated for by his humour, offers us the following account:

> How did our liturgical movement begin? It is difficult to say
> exactly, but it seems that the beginning can be found in the
> youth movements connected in some sort with Catholic Action.
> The Scout movement in the first place was influential here both
> by the kind of liturgical life that it required and by the re-
> actions that it provoked in those that it had trained. . . . At the
> material level it seems difficult to imagine how all the accessories
> for benediction of the Blessed Sacrament could be packed up in
> a haversack. Thus for many the Roman Mass began to re-
> appear in all its stark simplicity and vigour. Around an altar,
> which in the nature of things was without gradines, reredos,
> vases or those long sham candles, and in the absence of all
> those "devotional" objects which, though washable in warm
> water cannot, thank God, be carried about, these young men
> rediscovered that the celebration of Mass was a eucharistic
> sacrificial meal.[1]

This amusing account may afford us the occasion to express
if not reproaches at least a certain regret. For if the liturgical
movement rapidly had effect among certain youth movements
and, through them, the parishes, its backwardness, or even its
non-existence, is to be deplored in a great number of institutes
and colleges under the direction of religious, clerics or nuns.
In any case, there are far too many of these places where the
religious exercises could not be better calculated to disgust
(the word is not too strong) the students for the rest of their
lives with every manifestation of religion. Timetables and cere-

---

[1] L. Bouyer, "Réflexions sur le mouvement liturgique", in *Dieu
Vivant* 19, 85.

monies, usually obligatory, combine together to make the children's practice of religion a sort of nightmare. It is a very great pity that, despite the liturgical renewal, some of the things that we can remember from our schooldays are still to be found today.

Now this is deplorable in two ways. For not only should religious institutions be in a position to celebrate a "living liturgy" more easily than elsewhere but also with the help of well-trained teams they ought to help less-favoured centres. This is what has been done by one Belgian institution in which, instead of sending the children home during Holy Week, or keeping them within the four walls of the school, sent properly trained teams to help neighbouring parishes with the cere- monies of the Easter triduum. If this festival falls at a date inconvenient to scholastic requirements there are nevertheless many similar occasions during the year.

What has been suggested in regard to schools might well be applicable and fruitful *a fortiori* with elder groups, particularly university and other students. It is certainly excellent and attractive to encourage numbers of them to set off on pilgrimage, and it is easy enough to do. On the other hand, how many groups assume adult responsibility in respect of the liturgical renewal by endeavouring to achieve a real insertion of the student element into adult communities?

At the parochial level, after 1920, side by side with the youth movements a few sporadic attempts were made in certain parishes. Canon Rémilleux, parish priest of Saint-Alban in Lyons, was the forerunner of them all. He went to Germany to study and lived for a time in Austria. He regarded Pius Parsch as his great master. Rémilleux's fundamental conception was to establish his parish as a praying community. Four points in this programme need emphasizing: an extraordinary sense of Christian charity; the one centre of the parish is the altar; the sacraments are the occasion of bringing to the liturgy those who only occasionally come to church; there is no authentic liturgy without a very thorough biblical formation.

Following Canon Rémilleux's example various parishes took

steps to place the liturgical renewal in the forefront of their pastoral preoccupations. To take two examples from among many, Mgr Chevrot at Saint-François-Xavier in Paris was well known, and in the dechristianized Parisian suburbs the Benedictine parish of Hay-les-Roses makes the liturgy the centre of its pastoral activity.

After Mgr Chevrot (†1958) a different style appears. In this case it is not a question of liturgy and still less of preaching. Liturgical pastoral methods are entirely integrated into a more comprehensive conception of the specifically missionary character of a Christian community, which ought to have no other reason for its existence. The classical formulation of this truth, which ought to be self-evident after the revelation of *France Pagan?*, was given in Abbé Michonneau's *The Missionary Spirit in Parish Life* (1952).

The situation has so far evolved that one can no longer speak of pastoral liturgy. The expression has become too narrow. Pastoral liturgy is only one element in missionary pastoral methods or, better still, in catechumenal pastoral methods. For if the first stage of the parochial liturgical movement consists in transforming the parish, by means of the liturgical renewal in particular, beginning with an administrative organization (civil parish, district, etc.) into a living community (first stage), and within this community of prayer and charity there grows up an awareness of missionary needs (second stage), the third and last stage still awaiting the renewed parish is a complete reconstruction bringing it back to its primary purpose which is the incorporation of new adult members by means of the catechumenate. The stages are, then, from administration to living community, from living community to missionary community, and from the latter to catechumenal community.

This is what a group of parishes in Paris and the provinces have endeavoured to achieve and to formulate in the review *Paroisse et Mission* with its counterpart in the series *Mission et Sociologie*. The purpose, among others, of these publications is to prevent the feeling of self-satisfaction when some small advance has been made liturgically, and to integrate liturgical endeavour in the general work of the apostolate without depriving worship in normally constituted communities of its place as the starting-point and as the end of the apostolate. Of course there is no question of confusing everything together, nor of sacrificing anything, but rather of distinguishing clearly the various functions in the Christian community and of subordinating them hierarchically in the conscience and in the practice of pastors and the laity concerned. Now a part of the present generation has perhaps been too exclusively concerned with the liturgical renewal (though the greater part of this generation has not yet awakened to the fact of the liturgical renewal, when, that is, it does not despise or oppose those who are alive to it). At present it is a matter of so acting that the liturgical movement as a whole assumes a missionary aspect (if it does not it will wither away) and that the missionary movement brings about a return to an authentically renewed liturgy, a "catechumenal" liturgy, as it really was in the springtime of the Church. It was already a great step forward when the liturgical movement passed from the monasteries into the parishes, but it still remains a talent buried in the ground if its place in the whole scheme of the Christian witness of the ecclesiastical community is not given proper emphasis. And this community will, or will not, be catechumenal.

At this point we come directly to the points raised by Mgr van Bekkum, Bishop of Ruteng (Flores, Indonesia), at the Assisi congress. He was speaking, of course, of pagan peoples in missionary countries in the proper sense of the term.

Having shown that with the emerging Afro-Asiatic nations a solely western liturgy would rightly or wrongly revive hostility to foreign influences and that pagan devotional worship should be considered as a preparation for Christian worship (complete abolition of all pagan forms of worship and the substitution of skimped and incomprehensible low Masses results in a devitalization of converts' piety) the missionary bishop went on to show that, of its very nature, the liturgy, although it includes, of course, the proclamation of the Word in the Christian community, in the face of the pagan world is missionary by right. That may be a banal observation for many pastors for whom authentic rites and ceremonies, well carried out, form a privileged means of reaching unbelievers at a genuinely religious level. And so it would be wrong to put "liturgy" on one side and "mission" on the other.

To return to the present state of French Catholicism which, unlike that of other countries, particularly England and Ireland, comprises a minority of practising Catholics among a mass of those who call themselves believers and do not practise (and who probably have never had the faith preached to them): in these circumstances pastoral liturgy and missionary work should in many cases be closely entwined—the liturgy of the dead, baptism, first communion, instructions to engaged couples, marriage (at the present time this sacrament corresponds to baptism administered to adults in the primitive Church), the teaching given at the great Christian festivals to the practising Catholics, and to the others also because these recurrent occasions of the year have passed into popular folklore, all these offer innumerable opportunities for pastoral initiative of the first importance. It is on these frequent occasions that Canon Martimort's words find complete verification: "It seems quite clear nowadays that liturgy and evangelization far from being contradictory are two complementary functions which must both be accomplished without the right of choosing between them or of opposing one to the other."

Liturgy, therefore, is missionary in so far as it is initiation, but there are certain limitations in fact and in law where evangelization is concerned. For liturgy is only really authentic for those who are initiated, for those, that is, who have been awakened to the whole faith by the Word of God and by catechumenal contact with the Christian community. It encounters the same limitations as the parish which under the present territorial organization does not always reach people where they are.

For these reasons, in addition to the urgency of the reconstruction of the parochial system, we have emphasized also the reconversion of the liturgical movement which, if it is true that it fulfils its aim in the parishes, with them runs the danger, nevertheless, of becoming ineffective. At the end of this short historical sketch of the liturgical renewal it was important to show in this way that the story has not yet come to an end; indeed it has only just begun.

THE RÔLE OF THE BISHOPS

In many cases the liturgical renewal at the parochial level has been given a certain impulsion by the bishop at the diocesan level—diocesan liturgical sessions and congresses, episcopal regulations and pastoral letters have revealed the increasing interest of the bishops in the liturgical renewal.

It is principally by the issuing of directories for pastoral liturgical practice that the authority and zeal of the bishops for the liturgy has been proved. In Italy, there is Cardinal Lercaro's directory for the Mass and the pastoral letter by Cardinal Montini (now Pope Paul VI) on liturgical education (Lent, 1958). In Belgium can be mentioned the directory issued by the bishop of Tournai and those issued by other Belgian bishops. Finally, in France, after the directory authorized by the bishop of Nancy, came that issued on the authority of all the bishops of France. The directory for the Mass (1955) followed that for the sacraments (1951).

The directory for the Mass which appeared to some as a check on their activities proved for the majority of the parochial clergy a decided stimulus; it is a clear manifestation of the rôle of the bishops of France in the liturgical movement, and especially of the national commission, under the chairmanship of the archbishop of Rouen in the name of the Assembly of cardinals and archbishops.

This Assembly, on the other hand, has shown its effective interest in the liturgy by publishing a note on liturgical efforts which unfortunately has not been sufficiently appreciated or utilized.

In any case, it seems quite obvious that the liturgical renewal can only make real progress at the diocesan level. Nothing worthwhile or enduring can be done if the leader of the diocese is not effectively behind it. On the other hand, there is room for considerable hope if the bishop gives sympathetic encouragement to his parish priests. For the bishops are the guardians of the liturgical laws; they have now considerable powers in the matter of liturgical customs and adaptation under the Constitution on worship of the Second Vatican Council.

In these circumstances, the fact that the Second Vatican Council will regulate the position and prerogatives of the bishop in the Church—questions which unfortunately were not reached by the First Vatican Council in 1870—by delineating clearly the active rôle of the bishops in the Church and the steps that they can legitimately take. It may well be thought that this question could with advantage be considered in regard both to the bishops in dechristianized lands and those in missionary territories in the light of the powers recognized by tradition as belonging to the apostolic patriarchs of the East.

Meanwhile, the following example of the action of a liturgical and missionary-minded bishop, working within the Italian liturgical movement, is of interest: we refer to the reforms instituted by Cardinal Lercaro, archbishop of Bologna.

Mgr Moglia was a pioneer of the Italian liturgical renewal; in 1922 he founded at Genoa the *Collegium Tarsicii et Caeciliae* for the liturgical training of the laity; he also founded at Genoa a form of liturgical apostolate with the purpose of joining priests and the younger laity in one and the same liturgical effort. In Mgr Moglia's school were trained the two leaders of the Italian liturgical movement, Cardinal Siri, future archbishop of Genoa, and Cardinal Lercaro, future archbishop of Bologna.

Cardinal Lercaro's liturgical reforms can be grouped together under three heads, each expressive of pastoral concern:

1. *The active participation of the Christian people in the Eucharistic Mystery* which is given concrete form in his directory for the Mass, a practical and complete handbook to enable

the faithful to rediscover the Mass. It encountered great success in Italy and numerous translations were made.

2. *The Paschal Mystery, the centre of all liturgical life.* The importance of the Paschal Mystery has been emphasized by the establishment of Lenten "stations", by the children's procession on Palm Sunday and finally by the Mass on Maundy Thursday which gathers round their bishop all the deans of the diocese, taking their part on this day as priests, deacons and subdeacons and expressing, thus, by this *communicatio in sacris*, the fundamental unity of the liturgical assembly with its twofold hierarchical and community nature. At the end of this Mass the deans take the holy oils to their deaneries for distribution to the parish priests. (For the ritual for the reception of the holy oils in the parishes, see Cardinal Lercaro's *Guida del Commentatore dei Riti della Settimana Santa*, Bologna, 1959.)

3. *Liturgical training of the faithful* is ensured by a diocesan centre of liturgical action of which Cardinal Lercaro is president. There are three sections; scientific studies, sacred music and missionary work are the subjects of conferences given to the priests of the diocese, thus training a new generation of clergy who in their turn will ensure the spread of this renewal of pastoral liturgy in the parishes. In each deanery a priest, after following a complete course of studies at the centre lasting two years, is put in charge of liturgical activities. A centre for church architecture, also founded by Cardinal Lercaro, in 1955 organized a first congress of architecture and sacred art; it also publishes a quarterly review, *Chiesa e Quartiere*.

PART II

FUNDAMENTAL IDEAS OF THE LITURGICAL REVIVAL

*by the Sacerdotal Communities
of St. Séverin of Paris
and St. Joseph of Nice*

CHAPTER IV

BIBLE AND LITURGY

LITURGY AND ECUMENISM

The impact of the liturgical revival is not nowadays confined to the Catholic Church. Similar preoccupations are to be found elsewhere as well. This corresponds with a general need of man in our times, and also with new possibilities, arising from a better knowledge of history and therefore of the original meaning of rites and attitudes. It is probably necessary to take this further still; in the psychological context of the world today it is easier than in preceding centuries to rediscover the real significance of community and communion.

This state of mind, which forms the foundation of the ecumenical movement, leads us to emphasize here the ecumenical significance of the liturgical renewal.

The liturgical activity that is going on within the Protestant Churches[1], and which is well represented by the reformed community at Taizé (Saône-et-Loire), is especially significant in this respect. The places of worship in certain Protestant Churches had finally come to look more like lecture halls than places of worship. The pulpit took the place of the altar, and the neglect of communion, which formed such a disastrous feature in the evolution of religious practice among Catholics in the Jan-

[1] The problem of the liturgical renewal does not occur in quite the same way in the Eastern Churches—see Chapter X, p. 121, for what is said about the Catholic portions of these Churches. The distinction raised here concerning the Protestant Churches explains why we have referred to ecumenism at the beginning of this chapter on the Bible; in the Churches issuing from the Reformation Scripture is given a privileged and on occasion an exclusive place.

senist centuries, was even more prevalent in the current practice of Protestantism. The publication, in 1955, by the French Reformed Church, of an "official order of worship" can be regarded as a turning-point in this history. From the outset, in the introductory note, care was taken to point out that "this liturgy takes into account the movement that in our Churches increases the frequentation and the frequency of the Lord's Supper. By dissociating it from Sunday worship our Church was separating itself from the primitive Church." We have there on one particular point, though it is one of fundamental importance, evidence of a new spirit which is to be found on every page of this liturgy which is characterized by the Preface as follows: "The liturgy, work in common, making its own Christian prayer of all times and places, is the living and unanimous prayer of the Church."

This effort is tending to diminish to some extent the divergence to be found in the past between Protestant worship and the liturgies of the Latin and the Oriental Churches. This ecumenical spirit finds expression throughout the Sunday worship, particularly in the very centre of the celebration of the Lord's Supper where, after the words of institution, is to be found the prayer from the Didache: "As the ears of wheat, once scattered over the mountains, and as the grapes, once scattered over the hills, are now made one in this bread and this wine on this table, so Lord, may your Church be gathered together from the ends of the earth in your kingdom." The Sunday worship of the new liturgy of the Reformed Church of France includes also a special mention of the Roman Church: "We pray you for the Roman Church. Fulfil your work in her. In our difficult dialogue with her grant us always to profess the truth in charity."

The example of the Reformed Church of France is of particular significance. Other Churches which sprang from the Reformation had preserved greater fidelity to traditional Western liturgical forms. In England the Oxford Movement resulted among Anglicans in a certain pastoral and liturgical renewal; the ritualist movement is one expression of these preoccupations. Its influence was to make itself felt on the Continent and particularly in the Church of Sweden where a certain satisfaction began to be felt that the Reformation and adherence to the doctrines of Luther had not totally abolished the traditional liturgy; people usually speak not of a service in a meeting place but indeed of Mass (*mässa*) in a church and the minister of worship is called indifferently "pastor" or "priest" (*präst*). The order of ceremonies in the language of the country follows the order of the Latin liturgy. The liturgical movement, in England as in Sweden, has made a considerable contribution in the preparation of men's minds in both countries for the rôle of capital importance that they have played in the origins of the ecumenical movement. In the same spiritual context a "High Church" movement has also emerged among German Lutherans, as well as among those of Scandinavia.

Simultaneously with this evolution among Protestants, Catholics under the influence of the liturgical renewal were returning to the Bible. Of course, even if there had been no Reformation, the invention of printing would have resulted, sooner or later, in provoking a revival of interest in the Scriptures. Even in those centuries when the masses were illiterate, all the great movements of spiritual renewal in the Church have always included a rediscovery of the Bible. It will be sufficient to recall here St Jerome and the evangelism of St Francis of Assisi.

The division in Western Christendom in the sixteenth century provoked among Catholics reactions of defence and opposition which had held back a movement capable nowadays of reaching maturity more easily, as a result precisely of the need to rediscover, instead of a purely literal fidelity to rites that are somewhat fossilized, the primary inspiration which gave them birth: the whole purpose of the reform instituted by the Second Vatican Council is the return to this primary inspiration.

Catholics and Protestants are able nowadays to appear far less irrevocably opposed to each other than in past centuries. It may well be thought that the day will come when Catholics will no longer consider that they can "fulfil their obligation" by arriving at Mass for the offertory, with little or no interest in the "liturgy of the Word" while Protestants are becoming increasingly aware of the importance of the eucharistic liturgy. The need has been clearly seen for a more complete use of the biblical texts in the liturgy and the reformed Roman Missal, called for by the Second Vatican Council, will contain a more complete course of Scripture readings in place of the previous annual and somewhat arbitrary choice of the same recurring pericopes.

The same need has caused the Church of Sweden to carry out a liturgical reform which, while retaining the lessons of the Roman Missal in the course of a year, regarded as a basic year, proposes other lessons for a second and third year in a way that restores, perhaps not exactly the *lectio continua* of the Fathers, but at least a far more comprehensive meditation of the Scriptures. In the same spirit, there remains to be restored, it would appear, the lessons of the Old Testament which are still almost systematically neglected. In any case, even with the resolution of these questions, it requires to be observed that the hopes raised by the ecumenical movement cannot be better served than by the quest for authenticity and truth in the liturgy.

BIBLE AND LITURGY: THE PRINCIPLES

Whatever the importance of the services rendered by the progress of historical research to the liturgical movement, the liturgical renewal will be neither a return to the Middle Ages, as Dom Guéranger seems to have hoped at the time of the Romantic movement, nor even a return to the age of the Fathers, as Dom Casel seemed to propose; principally it is a return to sources, to the Bible which remains the sacred foundation of all Christian liturgy.

There is a very close connection between the renewal of biblical piety and the liturgical renewal. At the Assisi Congress Cardinal Bea pointed out that "the congregation of the faithful which gathers together for the celebration of the eucharistic sacrifice is the most auspicious place for the reading and fruit-

ful explanation of the Word of God". Indeed it is only in the
context of the liturgy that the Bible is within the comprehension of the great majority of the faithful. Thus it is very necessary for the liturgy to be made apt for this rôle which has too
often been lost sight of in the last centuries.

Just as there is continuity between the Old and the New
Testaments in the unity of the same sacred book, which is the
Bible, so is there continuity between the worship of the Old
Covenant and that of the New, as the Epistle to the Hebrews
puts it. The rite of the paschal lamb prefigures Christ's sacrifice and through it the eucharistic rite of the Christian liturgies.
The synagogal meetings are continued in the Christian liturgy
of the Word: it is significant that the word "synagogue" and the
word "church" are the Greek translation of the same Hebrew
term. The Mass is nothing else than the juxtaposition of these
two liturgies, namely, the liturgy of the word and the eucharistic liturgy.[2]

To speak merely of juxtaposition is an understatement. It is
not only for reasons of convenience that the two liturgies follow
one another immediately. In the fervent Christian communities
at an early date the need was felt for a second meeting for
prayer on Sunday evenings; and this was the origin of the
widespread custom of Vespers. Thus the liturgy of the Word,
it would seem, might well have been separated in this way from
the eucharistic liturgy. Yet since Christian antiquity there is no
trace of such a practice. Right from the time that the first
Christians, excluded from Judaism, no longer frequented the
synagogue, it seems that their worship was immediately
organized in accordance with the fundamental pattern to be
found in all liturgies; a Mass beginning with the liturgy of the
Word and continuing immediately with the eucharistic liturgy,
this latter being placed, so to say, in the prolongation of the
former, since eucharistic communion was preceded by a com-

---

[2] The fundamental difference between worship in the Old and the
New Testaments is mentioned below; in fact, the change in structure
occurred in the "sacrifice", but the "synagogal" setting for prayer remained the same in Christian worship.

munion of minds in faith in the Word of God, liturgically proclaimed.

Even at the end of the Middle Ages this close connection of the two liturgies of the Mass had not been forgotten. *The Imitation of Christ* includes a chapter in which the Bible and the Eucharist are considered together: there are two "tables" at which the Christian is to be fed—*Una mensa est sacri altaris, habens panem sanctum, id est Corpus Christi pretiosum, altera est divinae legis, continens doctrinam sanctam* (Book IV, 11)—"There is one table of the holy altar with the sacred Bread, that is, the precious Body of Christ, the other is the table of divine law, with the sacred teaching."

If, nowadays, the Bible has regained a place of honour, a greater place perhaps than ever before, in the life of the Christian, if he feels the need to find his true nourishment in it, particularly in a world where he is tempted by all sorts of profane reading, in the ordinary course of events he will be led to pay particular attention to the liturgy of the Word. And he will do so because fundamentally it is intended to place him in communion with the Bible and to proclaim it in the congregation of the faithful in fellowship among themselves in their awareness of being the Church of God. Obviously this is something quite different from a mere reading carried out in isolation, a form of study that can turn into idle curiosity. In the liturgy the Word of God resounds in the holy place which is constituted by the gathering together of the members of the Body of Christ, in the unanimity of a same prayer offered to the Father in the name of Christ. The proclamation of the Word is a sacred action, a "sacrament", and it is with the utmost reverence, in a spirit of adoration, that it is to be received.

In these conditions, preaching no longer appears as an interlude or something extra. It forms an integral part of the liturgical action. There can be no question of giving a lesson, or a conference, of making a show of oratory or wit; rather must the preacher, in the name of the bishop, the successor of the apostles, open the minds of his hearers to the understanding of the Word of God. For the sermon is a part of the liturgical celebration: the celebrant officiates, *locum tenens*, taking the place of Christ himself, both when he preaches and when he pronounces the words of consecration. All that the congregation hears, whether it is the sacred readings or the homily, although of course in different degrees and varying intensity, is received by it as a living Word, always a reality because it is a message of an eternal nature, addressed to it by Christ himself, present in its midst.

BIBLE AND LITURGY: THE FACTS

It must be admitted that the foregoing ideas have been quite lost from view during the past few centuries. It has even been said that if the Protestant is a Christian for whom after the sermon is over the rest is of little account, the Catholic is one who does not mind arriving at Mass for the offertory and makes a point of missing the sermon. There is a germ of truth in this caricature. The popularization of a certain form of casuistry led to the belief that the liturgy of the Word was unimportant and to some extent optional; arrival at Mass before the end of the *Credo* "fulfilled the obligation". Thus the Word is proclaimed before the congregation has gathered together, in a half-empty church, amid the noise of people arriving.

This is an entire reversal of the whole aspect of the congregation gathered for the liturgy in comparison with what it was formerly. In earlier days it was the liturgy of the Word which was the most crowded since the catechumens and penitents left at the beginning of the eucharistic liturgy in which they did not take part. At the present time, many of those present at the eucharistic liturgy come to it to fulfil a precept of the Church whose real meaning they do not even seek to understand. And there have even been occasions in the past when there has been refusal to give communion during Mass, just as it was sometimes urged that it was better to communicate before Mass in order to be able to make a proper thanksgiving, if there was no time for it after Mass. This shows clearly that the whole meaning of eucharistic liturgy had been lost sight of, for Eucharist, as the term shows (but it is a Greek word), is nothing else than a thanksgiving.

It is, of course, easy to discover a certain number of factors that contributed to this lack of understanding of the Mass. The meaning of the Bible, which is quite naturally made clear where proclamation of the Word does not take place, paradoxically, in a language that has become incomprehensible to the congregation, had become foreign to the faithful. And this despite the care taken to read the translation of the Gospel before the sermon. Moreover, the latter has not always been preached on the texts of the day's liturgy. The almost complete freedom left to the preacher, in sharp contrast with the inflexibility of the rubrics, enabled him to consider other passages with no concern for those just read, and thus to compensate in some measure for the disadvantages arising from the fact that year by year the same passages from the Bible were read on the same days, while the remainder of the sacred text was never officially proclaimed to the people.

What is astonishing in all this is not the uneasiness increasingly felt in the face of such a situation, but that it could have come about and endured for so long without anything being done about it until the end of 1963 with the promulgation of the decree of the Second Vatican Council. It would be outside the scope of this book to discuss the historical reasons for such a state of affairs in order to understand a point of view that is undoubtedly outmoded nowadays. It will be sufficient to note the fact of a returning awareness of traditional values that were lost to view for too long.

CONCLUSION

"Word of God and word of man, all proclaim the Mystery and thus, in the liturgical structure of the Mass, we pass naturally from the proclamation of the Word of God to the sacramental celebration: there is no word without sacrament, no sacrament without liturgy of the Word. We have access to the Mystery only through the theology of the Word of God, which is Christ, the intervention of God in history, the recapitulation, the new beginning and the definitive condition of history." As was thus well said at the Strasbourg congress in 1957, without understanding of the Bible the liturgy remains only an illegible sign. That is why the catechumens, in ancient times, before having access to the eucharistic Mystery had for long been made familiar with the Bible through the liturgy of the Word in which they took part from the time of their admission to the catechumenate.

APPENDIX: THE PROBLEM OF THE MISSAL

As was pointed out above, the honour of first popularizing the translation of the Missal with explanatory notes for the use of the faithful in modern times must be attributed to Dom Gérard van Caloen and Dom Gaspar Lefebvre. Nowadays, Missals for the use of the laity exist in so many editions and formats that it is difficult even to offer a list of them. It will be useful however to mention here certain matters of more general interest in this connection.

Properly speaking the Missal is no affair of the congregation's. The lessons are read aloud in order to be heard and not to be read by each one in private. The anthems (introit, offertory, communion) are the refrains of processional chants meant to be sung and not read rapidly.

In fact, in the present state of affairs, and even with the people's part of the Mass in the vernacular, the Missal has a part to play in the liturgy, and it has certainly made a contribution to the liturgical revival. Dom Lefebvre's Missal, for example, has done much to educate the more fervent among the faithful. It can also be said that the Missal is and will always remain a valid means of personal liturgical study. In particular, the Missal helps the faithful to grasp the fundamental connection between the Bible and the liturgy. Everything, or almost everything in the Missal, is either taken directly from the Bible or at least directly inspired by biblical texts. It might even be said that the Missal is the Bible re-composed by the Church for the purpose of the liturgical year. Moreover, good editions of the Missal always give the scriptural references. Thus the principal events of the history of salvation are re-lived through the liturgical cycle and the Missal thereby becomes a very living and spiritual introduction to the Bible.

These advantages of a Missal, however, must not cause us to lose sight of the fact that in the first place liturgical celebration is *hierarchical*. There should be no question of everyone reading silently whatever the celebrant, reader or choir read or sing. Each individual should play his proper part in the celebration. Then, the Mass is a *community affair*; it is not a silent gathering of individuals with their noses in their books. The church on Sunday is not a reading room or, to quote a comparison made by Cardinal Lercaro, a restaurant where each person appears to be taking his meal in isolation. The emphasis placed by the Second Vatican Council on the congregation's participation should go far to make such an individualist approach impossible.

CHAPTER V

LITURGY AND CATECHESIS

"Catechesis" is a fashionable word at the present time. Its facile use in reviews and conferences may well deprive it in a short time of any precise meaning. It can be recalled simply that the term "catechesis" implies the presentation of the Christian message in a fairly developed and elaborated form. Thus catechesis is to be distinguished from kerygmatic proclamation which simply announces the message of Christ, who died and rose again for us, with no attempt to elaborate its implications.

But the patristic flavour of the word catechesis immediately conjures up the biblical, liturgical and spiritual context, together with implications of conversion and initiation which the less high-sounding term of "religious instruction" seems to exclude. Nevertheless, religious instruction, if it is true to its name, implies everything included in catechesis, and it must be admitted, if for the moment we forget the fleeting magic of words, that at the present time religious instruction and catechesis are synonyms.

And so there will be several forms of catechesis—of children at the age of reason, of adolescents, of catechumens, of adults. In some cases the emphasis will be on initiation, in others more importance will be given to bringing out the religious understanding of the message and its coherence. But in all cases it is the same duty of education of faith that is being discharged.

So far as the subject of the present chapter is concerned it must be pointed out that a considerable effort is required in pastoral liturgy to make clear the need for liturgical life by means of teaching. This liturgical catechesis, following the example of the Roman Catechism of the Council of Trent and of the Ritual, is principally conceived as preaching on the sacraments based on the rites themselves in accordance with the method used by the Fathers of the Church.

LITURGY AN ILLEGIBLE SIGN WITHOUT CATECHESIS

It is an absolute necessity for those in a human world, in a world of signs, and not only of things, that they should be initiated into the meaning of these signs. Without this knowledge they will be lost, just as they would be in a foreign country of whose language and customs they were ignorant. Those who "know" have to impart knowledge of these signs, gestures and customs of the community to those who come from outside and "do not know". Especially must initiates reveal to those who are not the ends pursued by the community and how the signs, gestures and customs used serve the ideal which gathers the community together.

Therefore catechesis is needed for the uninitiated, for the catechumens and for those whose position is tantamount to being a catechumen. But catechesis is necessary also for the initiates, even for the most fervent, so that continually they can revitalize their liturgical observance by thorough study and by ceaselessly returning to fundamentals; otherwise, it is more than likely that they will fall into formalism and entire lack of understanding.

Both for initiates, and for others as well, the mental effort required for understanding of the liturgy is no small one. The liturgical Constitution of the Second Vatican Council has indeed laid down that the rites "should be distinguished by a noble simplicity" and that they should be "short, clear and unencumbered by any useless repetitions"; they are to be "within the people's powers of comprehension" and not require normally very much explanation. Yet it still remains true that the whole universe of worship is difficult for modern man, the product of a civilization very different from that in which the Church's worship grew up; even with a reformed liturgy catechesis will be necessary, though possibly to a smaller degree than hitherto. Its purpose, therefore, is to decipher for us the whole universe which has grown up outside us, and to communicate to us the minimum that is indispensable to enable us to be at ease in our own fatherland.

THIS CATECHESIS WILL BE BIBLICAL

Thus, just like the biblical renewal, the liturgical renewal implies a certain cultural concern. And there is nothing astonishing in the fact that the concern for liturgical culture is to be found in those countries where the general cultural movement is most active. It is the duty of the clergy to watch over and satisfy this need of culture among Christian people. Good intentions and pastoral zeal are insufficient to bring this culture into play. Both pastors and people must be willing to make the effort to enter a foreign land and receive the biblical texts used in the liturgy. In some sort, it means entering a land that is doubly foreign, for liturgical tradition has transplanted biblical texts into a very different cultural context from that in which they first saw light of day. Pastors, if they wish to educate their people, must be in a position to obtain some grasp of the relativism of the different cultures that biblical and liturgical tradition has passed through during the centuries. In the endeavour to acquire this liturgical culture some idea of historical relativity must be shown, a quality which only too often is lacking and yet is one which enables what is essential, enduring and of present importance to be sifted out from the various cultural forms that the Bible and the liturgy have assumed. The danger nowadays is one of superficiality, of pastors being satisfied with "timeless" commentaries through lack of knowledge of the vital situations in which the liturgical forms arose, developed or, on the contrary, became fossilized.

But the other danger is to remain at the stage of mere

historical explanation without spiritual implications for the faithful; lack of theology is the cause of this. A certain type of liturgical exegesis, inadequate in all speculative thought, which does not seek to reach what is permanent, and therefore of real interest, is impoverishing for pastor and faithful alike for it takes no count of the essential, personal and community needs of our religious life.

What we need is an authentic understanding of the rites without our getting bogged down in the necessary but inadequate archeological investigation. It requires to be repeated that, for the lack of speculative effort, of an all-embracing and unifying viewpoint, the liturgical movement is in danger of seeing its pastoral influence diminish. But this effort of thought must always be exerted on the basis of the rites themselves. Thought about the liturgy is no initiation to the liturgy, it is the liturgy which initiates to the liturgy—on condition that its catechesis is enlightened, properly elaborated and communicated. For the liturgy itself is a catechesis and it is this which we have now to examine.

THE LITURGY IS ITSELF CATECHESIS

The liturgy is itself catechesis. It is intended to "guide the faithful to a conscious Christianity". The liturgy is catechesis by reason of the Word of God which it transmits. This immediately raises the problem of the hearing and understanding of the Word of God by the people. The subject is treated below in connection with the subject of liturgical language.

As the vehicle of the Word of God the liturgy forms the normal introduction to the Bible and it is by means of the passages proclaimed in the liturgical assembly that people are normally to be led to a taste for and an understanding of the Scriptures. But the matter must be regarded in realist fashion and it must be recognized that this introduction to the Bible by means of the liturgy is effected only very partially by reason of the present form of the liturgy. A selection of short passages, often arbitrarily chosen, can hardly constitute a genuine introduction to the Bible. What is required is a restoration of the *lectio continua*, that is, the consecutive, well ordered systematic presentation of the principal biblical passages suitably adapted to a given community. The present system of lessons, represented by the Sunday Epistles and Gospels, is only haphazard and therefore unable to provide a catechesis worthy of the name, that is, of communicating a spirit and a form of thought. A better selection of passages of Scripture is promised in the reformed Roman Missal to be issued in due course.

What is the place of the sermon is this catechetical dimension of the liturgy? It has to be recognized that considerable progress has been made in the course of half a century. In 1913 the French Jesuit review *Études* began a controversy—one that is nowadays quite an affair of the past—by publishing an article by Fr Navatel, S.J., on "The Liturgical Apostolate and Personal Piety". In it the liturgy was defined as the perceptible ceremonial and ornamental part of Catholic worship, contrasting with it, among other things, preaching.

It is generally recognized nowadays that the sermon is a liturgical act. And this has been made quite clear by the Constitution on Liturgy passed by the Second Vatican Council. Preaching does not form a sort of parenthesis in the Mass. It must be regarded in such a way that it can be integrated into the liturgy. The sermon has its starting point in the celebration and leads to a more enlightened and united celebration. That is its nature. The Sunday sermon is not in the same category as a Lenten course which is intended to give systematic and exhaustive teaching on a particular subject, or a mission sermon which should cause its audience to discover afresh the heavy and exacting requirements of Christian life. That is why it is more normal for the celebrant himself, and not some priest in a surplice who happens to be on duty that day, to give the Sunday sermon.

Again, liturgy is catechesis through its rites, and through the gestures and attitudes that it requires of the community.

These rites, gestures and attitudes convey a spirit, they direct the development of the religious mentality in individuals and communities. They are the primary form, anterior to words, of the total Christian mentality. Thus the liturgy is a catechesis which embraces the whole being. Through liturgical observance doctrinal values are in some sort verified because they are apprehended in an experience. The liturgy is the royal road maintaining a close link between doctrine and life.

It must even be said that the liturgy leads to a moral commitment. It places us in an attitude of listening, offering and obedience in relation to God, of fellowship in relation to our brothers. It disposes us to act in a Christian way, and this without moralism. But that does not mean that the liturgy is in a position automatically to educate Christian behaviour in all its practical decisions. Ivan the Terrible seemed to take part in the liturgy of his times with his whole soul while giving evidence in his behaviour of a state of mind at utter variance with Christianity. At the other end of the scale, there is an approach to morality, as for example in the post-Tridentine school of casuistry, which is entirely unconnected with liturgy.

The Christian education effected by the liturgy is something at a far deeper level than any particular approach to the subject. The liturgy imbues us with the fundamental themes of the faith by making us live in that relationship which it establishes between God and us. In the liturgy, indeed, we do not pray in a sentimental fashion or in a state of spiritual independence, but by relying on the truths of faith. The eucharistic prefaces are rich in doctrinal themes: they are the creeds—the symbols of the faith—in action. And in its festive aspect the liturgy sets before us doctrinal truths in the most suitable way to motivate Christian joy (Jungmann, *MD* 47–8, pp. 55–6).

Year by year the liturgy educates us to a further deepening of our understanding of the fundamental Christian truths and values, to thanksgiving and to our approach to God through Christ (*per Christum Dominum nostrum*). Every year it causes us to celebrate the redemptive mysteries (events) of our Lord. "When thus week by week, year by year, our Lord and his work appear to the spiritual gaze of the faithful, they must come to understand very well what it means to be a Christian."

That is why Christianity has been able to continue to exist at periods when there was no preaching, when there was no reading. That is why it continues still to exist in vast regions like Russia where the liturgical celebrations are the only means of religious activity. There is no Christian truth that is not expressed in one way or another by the liturgy. In Pius XI's phrase, "the liturgy is the principal organ of the ordinary magisterium of the Church".

Liturgical education, following the example of the catechumenate in patristic times, must form part of the first introduction to the faith. A great step forward was taken when it was rediscovered that already in adherence and awakening to the faith the part to be played by the rites of the Church was of capital importance. In practice in many places converts (that is, catechumens) are interviewed individually in an office or room attached to the church for the purpose of receiving a series of instructions from a priest or a nun. And it is to these individual interviews that the catechumen's contact with the Church is confined until the day of his baptism. But since 1962 there has been the possibility for the catechumen while following the course of instruction for baptism to take part in community rites by means of which the faith that he comes to ask of the Church is not only explained but made active. It was in 1962, in fact, that the Congregation of Rites gave permission for the rite for the baptism of adults to be performed in seven distinct steps, spaced out in accordance with the progress made in catechetical instruction. This permission has been confirmed and enlarged in the Constitution on liturgy of the Second Vatican Council. It lays down that the catechumenate for adults is to be restored and to comprise several distinct stages. "In this way, the time of the catechumenate, which is intended to be a period of suitable instruction, may be sanctified by sacred rites" which are to be celebrated at definite intervals during the period of preparation for baptism.

THE PROBLEM OF LITURGICAL LANGUAGE

It would be wrong to think that the liturgical Constitution of the Second Vatican Council has finally abolished Latin as the liturgical language of the Roman rite. On the contrary it states quite clearly that the "use of the Latin language is to be preserved in the Latin rites". On the other hand, it has made wide concessions for the use of the mother tongue in the public worship of the Church, in the Mass, the administration of the sacraments and other parts of the liturgy, so that *in practice*, with the permission of the local hierarchies, what amounts to the people's part of the liturgy may be in the vernacular, together with much else besides.

The debate that has gone on ever since Trent over the use of the mother tongue in the worship of the Roman rite is in its own way another manifestation of the left-right or conservative-progressive conflict. And the controversy over liturgical language has also been in part a cultural conflict. This cultural aspect of the problem of Latin and its historical origins has been analysed by Cyril Korolevsky:

> In the sixteenth century the doctrinal errors of Protestants led to a strong reaction at the Council of Trent. But the Council nevertheless did not formally condemn the principle of the use of living languages in public worship, considered in itself; what it did was to forbid such use on the ground that it was inopportune at that time, and because of the very great prestige which Latin still enjoyed. However, the circumstances of this prohibition were not properly understood, and it brought about a state of mind in which an opportune measure of suitability was interpreted as a formal condemnation; and this mentality governed all that was done during the succeeding centuries.
>
> Today, the increasing desire of many clergy and people for "more vernacular", the development of the liturgical movement, pastoral requirements and the need to make public worship more intelligible if Christianity is to continue to hold people in contemporary conditions, have led to experiments some of which are not happy; and this increases the desire and need for a reform. . . .

Quite involuntarily, the community of faithful is split between two categories: those, generally the economically better off, who have some classical culture and can understand and appreciate the Roman liturgy, and those who do not understand it properly and have no means of doing so. The Church is the society of all the faithful; but if there be, to use the modern jargon, a sort of bourgeois aristocracy among them, then the exclusive use of Latin at public worship tends not to unify but to divide.[1]

Fr A. M. Roguet wrote as follows:

The whole of Mass proclaims the Word of God. If the Word is not understood, it is not a word. And if it is understood only by means of a Missal and individual effort it is no longer the Word of God in public worship which is understood by me. I receive the Word of God, of course, but through the intermediary of an instrument lacking authority and in the solitude and uncertainty of my own personal study.... And so it is to be hoped that one day the Holy See will put into effect the resolution that it has itself approved (at the Lugano Congress): that the celebrant may one day proclaim the Word of God directly in the language of the faithful.[2]

The people must understand the liturgy and the liturgy must increase the understanding of the faith by the people. For this to come about the liturgical language must be within the grasp of the faithful. And indeed such was the practice of the Church. The primitive Church, as she made her way into the Greek world, at once adopted the Greek language instead of clinging to Aramaic. When she spread from the Greek communities to take root among the peoples of the West she adopted Latin to make herself understood.

We should not be surprised that the expression "Latin, the language of the Church" is entirely incomprehensible and indeed unthinkable with reference to a Christian of the East, even a Catholic, if it denotes a certain exclusivism. Latin is *a* language of the Church, it is even the language for a

[1] Cyril Korolevsky, *Living Languages in Catholic Worship* (London and Westminster, Md, 1957), pp. 113–14, 164.

[2] *Parole de Dieu et liturgie*, IV, p. 140.

privileged period of a Church which is the Mother of all the Churches of the West and moderator of all the others, and to this extent Latin belongs to the universal Church, as a common possession, but no more.

Moreover, it must be recognized, as Canon Martimort has pointed out, "that the discipline of the Western Church on the subject of liturgical language is far from being as severe as it appears at first sight; it is even capable of evolving according to circumstances and might well, one day, from missionary necessity come to match the practice of the Greek and Egyptian missionaries."[3]

The three authors quoted above were writing, of course, before the Second Vatican Council, but in dealing with the history and development of the liturgical movement it was necessary to show how the climate of opinion has changed in the course of the last quarter of a century. Twenty-five years ago, although the possibility of an extensive use of the vernacular was being canvassed in some quarters, generally speaking it was held that such a change of practice would be against the "mind of the Church", though the exact meaning of this last expression was never very clearly defined. Then came the Second World War. That and its aftermath brought home very sharply to many working among prisoners of war, with the armed forces or in the great industrial centres, the need for a living liturgy and the impossibility of any serious progress so long as worship, that is, the *public* worship of the Church, was conducted in a dead language. This is the explanation of the change, a change that appears to many as a complete revolution, that has been enacted by the Second Vatican Council.

In the Constitution on liturgy there are references to an extended use of the vernacular in the rites of the Church. Although Latin remains the language of the Roman rite it is conceded that the "use of the mother tongue is frequently of great advantage to the people in the Mass, the administration of the sacraments and in other parts of the liturgy". This con-

[3] *MD* 11, 84, 130.

cession is to apply in the first place to the lessons (Epistle and Gospels, etc.) at Mass and to those prayers and chants which are the congregation's part in the rite. In addition the whole of the rites for the administration of the sacraments may be in the mother tongue and this includes even the essential forms. At the same time the Council has called for a large measure of revision in the Roman Ritual because, as it pointed out in the Constitution, with the passage of time "there have crept into the rites of the sacraments and sacramentals certain features which have rendered their nature and purpose far from clear to the people of today so that changes are necessary to adapt them to the needs of our times".

Thus it is clear that what is here implied is a far larger question than the understanding of a language. It must not be imagined that when the Word of God and the liturgical texts have been translated they will automatically become intelligible. Think, for example, of the difficulty encountered by an average congregation in taking part in the Easter vigil, even when preparation has been made for it by instruction on the various symbols of fire, water, light and so on. What is needed is a whole education of the congregation in their entire approach to the Easter mystery; this cannot be reduced to a question of Latin or English. Continuous effort over the whole field is required to raise the faithful to the level of liturgical understanding. In this way, by providing Christian people with suitable instruction, will be laid the foundations of a liturgy more adapted to its purpose, for then both people and hierarchy will realize the appropriate conditions for a living liturgy.

Lastly, it may be well to return to a point of view mentioned above. The position adopted by the Church with respect to the special problem of liturgical language or languages will depend on the way in which she is able to solve the more general problem of culture in the modern world. Between the nationalist movements, which she must take into account, and her universal vocation, a fundamental attitude is still easy enough to determine. It is more difficult to conceive and create a culture for humanity which without doubt is seeking unity and, on the basis of this culture, liturgical forms in relation with it. This cultural aspect of the problem is brought out clearly by the following quotation from Möhler, the great German theologian, which will serve as a conclusion to this part of the book:

> In all circumstances of life every people makes use of the language which God has given it; why then do we not make the finest use possible of this divine gift, namely in the communication of religious sentiments during the most solemn action of the whole of our worship? Am I not therefore to put before God a prayer of thanksgiving in the language which he has given me? And if the language of the liturgy must itself be changed, with an essential perfection of the national language, is not that in the nature of things? Would we thereby accuse God of not having given each people its perfect language at the outset? Language is always the most perfect image of the cultural state of a people; thus its language, whatever it is, is always the best for it.

The Second Vatican Council, by leaving to the local hierarchies the application of the provisions for the introduction of the vernacular in worship, has recognized the existence of the cultural problem alluded to above and, by implication, the truth of Möhler's remarks in the foregoing quotation.

CHAPTER VI

LITURGY AND CHRISTIAN LIFE

The starting point and the principal features of the fundamental ideas of the liturgical movement emphasized here are to
be found almost completely in the work of Dom Odo Casel,
monk of Maria Laach. In Chapter VII of his book *Liturgical
Piety* [1] Fr Bouyer has given a well-balanced and critical
explanation of this work and of the doctrine elaborated in it.
We cannot do better than quote Fr Bouyer's explanation of
Dom Casel's teaching on the Christian mystery.

But what, then, is the Christian mystery? If we mean to ask
what it is in its deepest reality, it is nothing less than the *tran-
situs*, the passage from death to life, by faith, through the cross
to the resurrection, which was once for all accomplished in
Christ. The Mystery, therefore, is an action; and it is an action
which took place in the past and can never be repeated, because
it is perfect. The Mystery is the cross of Jesus, the cross seen
primarily as an accomplishment ... the cross seen also in the
fullness of its wonderful fecundity, that is, as including the resurrection of Christ, his ascension into glory, and, through the
Christ who has now himself become *Pneuma*, life-giving Spirit,
the radiance of all the wonderful gifts which he has given to
man. This action is as it were the inner essence of the Mystery.
But the Mystery is permanently embodied in the liturgy—more
especially in the Mass, but also in all the sacraments and even
in the sacramentals, in the Divine Office, in the feasts of the

[1] English edn, *Life and Liturgy*. See Select Bibliography.

liturgical year, and in the whole Christian life, since this life is nothing less than the expansion of what is given in the sacramental order. In all this, of course, the mystery is hidden. Nothing is present of the historical circumstances by which the divine action was set in its place in time and space. But the substance of the action is present, in a mysterious way, entirely real to faith; and it is through this substance that the Christ-*Pneuma* encounters the lives of all men and diffuses in them his own life.

The grace of Christ cannot be separated from his Person; his life *in* us is not a different thing from his life lived *among* us and for us ... in and through the liturgy, the all-saving act of Christ, giving life through his death, is truly and really present in its fullness as in its unity.[2]

In this explanation of Christian worship Dom Casel took as his starting-point the "mysteries", a term used as a common name for the Eastern religions which were being introduced into the Roman Empire at about the same time as Christianity. Each of them was a *dromenon*, that is, a kind of religious drama, the liturgical representation of the death and resurrection of a god. By being associated, in the actual performance of this representation, with the saving act of the deity, the initiates or "mystes" were to be saved. They were to be thought of as born again to a new and divine life, the life of the god himself triumphing over death.

For Dom Casel, these mysteries were a sort of providential preparation in human nature for what God was to do for it in Christ. The pagan mysteries did not, properly speaking, influence the beginnings of Christianity, but they provided a frame for Christianity to fill with its divine grace, the pattern which would make that grace appealing to human nature, as showing how grace brought with it precisely what human nature most desires and had been attempting to attain for itself. Christianity had really given in the liturgical mysteries what paganism had only contrived to adumbrate or desire in its "mysteries".

[2] Bouyer, *op. cit.*, pp. 87–8.

There is no difficulty in seeing the importance of this point of view, not only for the history of Christianity but also, and especially, for the spiritual life of the Christian. For this spiritual life can no longer be considered as a quest, and still less as an individual adventure, under the guidance of personal imagination, sentiment, intelligence and will. But all these faculties joined together will find in perfect assimilation to the person of Christ the effective realization of the destiny of the human person, and this assimilation is effected ordinarily by means of the liturgy. The liturgy gives to all those who come to it the mystery of Christ, as a personal destiny which is offered as an integration, a personalization of the destiny of man both as individual and as community.

This economy of the mystery of salvation must indeed form a protection for the destiny of thousands of human beings who do not normally or visibly come into contact with it. Here we have the whole problem of the salvation of the unbeliever. But having raised this important distinction, we do not feel it an exaggeration to state that Dom Casel's theory offers the most realist and most rewarding view of the Christian life.

In fact, it is a doctrine rather than a theory and it has been handed down to us by the Fathers of the Church and liturgical tradition. It has certainly been keenly debated and it must be admitted, with Fr Bouyer especially, that its historical foundation based on the parallel between Christian mystery and pagan mystery does not stand up. But even if these and other corrections are admitted, it may still well be thought that this doctrine of the mystery, far from being contrary to the ordinary teaching of the Church, is in agreement with it on many of its fundamental and catechetical aspects. For a better understanding of the mystery of Christian worship, and for a clear comparison of the teaching of the Encyclical *Mediator* with Dom Casel's ideas, which at one time some chose to see in opposition with each other, we reproduce here a part of the comparison made by Dom Hild between Pius XII's teaching and Dom Casel's thought:

The liturgy is living and transcendent, it is worship, the whole priestly life of Christ and his Church. . . . The eucharistic mystery is the mystery of worship par excellence, it is the liturgy. . . . Holy Mass is shown as being truly a mystery of worship and not as being purely and simply a commemoration of the passion and death of Christ. Sacramentally, Christ is present and does again what he once did for us. . . . The whole Christ . . . in all the states of his existence is present in the liturgical mystery. . . . The liturgical presence of the whole Christ is expressed as the mystery of the Christian feast (Dom Casel's expression, *Festenmysterium*). The liturgical year, in so far as it is something sacred, in so far as it is mystery, must guide and nourish Christian piety.[3]

The Encyclical again tells us clearly that living the liturgical year consists not only in meditation on the mysteries of salvation, but especially in contact with Christ himself. For "the liturgical year . . . is not a cold and lifeless representation of the events of the past, or a simple and bare record of a former age. It is rather Christ himself who is ever living in his Church. Here he continues that journey of immense mercy which he lovingly began in his mortal life . . . with the design of bringing men to know his mysteries and in a way to live by them."

In a very special way these mysteries of Christ are the sacraments. But the Encyclical *Mediator* says more than once that "Christ is present not only in the Mass and the sacraments, but in every liturgical action, and even in the Divine Office in which the Church prays in common with her Lord and Bridegroom. Every liturgical act is an act of Christ himself, every liturgical rite constitutes a *sacramentum*, it contains and effects what it signifies."

It is obvious that this way of putting things necessarily takes us back beyond the scholastic formulas to the Fathers' ampler presentation. Now that is the teaching of the mystery of Christian worship. That does not mean to say, however, that at present it has been completely formulated. Dom Casel's scholarly elaboration of it—somewhat encumbered perhaps by

[3] From an article in *Les Questions liturgiques et paroissiales* 48, 186–203.

its historical setting—still stands in need of a formulation that is, so to say, kerygmatic, and can be incorporated in the people's catechesis and faith, just as the narrower formulation of scholastic theology has been.

Now it is this that the Encyclical *Mediator* means to teach us by asserting so clearly the presence of Christ in every liturgical act. This sacramental realism, in harmony with the mystery of the Church as a whole, is strictly speaking the mystery of worship. And by this mystery our Lord genuinely perpetuates his redemption in the Church, leading us all in his train in an ever increasing eschatological perspective to the Parousia, *donec veniat*.

Dom Casel found in this point of view a perfect expression of his own views, but it remains to be seen whether all the details of his particular teaching on the Christian mystery will stand the test of time. The Second Vatican Council does not refer to the subject like *Mediator*, though in its definition of the liturgy and its remarks on the Christian year it reflects the climate of opinion provoked by Casel's work. Thus it can be seen that it is from the liturgy that in reality Christian life is to be derived, since it is in the liturgy that, through Jesus Christ, we can come to an encounter with the living God. "Under the species of an evocation of the past, the liturgy brings to us in the present Christ in person."

There follows from this—it is a subsidiary point but of great importance—the hope of a Christian revival as a result of the whole liturgical reform initiated under Pius XII with the revision of the Holy week rites and continued by the Second Vatican Council in more radical fashion. The Paschal Mystery, the fundamental mystery of our worship, has been restored to the centre of Christian life. It is not merely a rubrical change, but Christian life which has been restored to its true sources.

In concluding this account of Dom Casel's teaching, and of its confirmation by the magisterium of the Church, it is worth while pointing out that he himself gave no ordinary witness to the value of his theological synthesis through his whole life of prayer and contemplation, and also by his death which occurred just as he had sung the *Lumen Christi* in the Easter Vigil:

> Just as he had saluted with a loud voice the Light of Christ and was about to celebrate the Easter praise (*praeconium paschale*), our well-beloved Father in Christ, the devoted servant of the sacred mystery and initiator into its richness, Odo Casel, monk of Laach, made perfect in his holocaust and, passing over with his Lord during the holy night, entered into the blessed vision, being made perfect by means of the paschal mysteries which he himself had handed on to the initiates. *Deo gratias*!

This mortuary card, by any token, is one of the finest texts of the contemporary liturgical movement.

LITURGY, SPIRITUALITY AND DEVOTIONS

In our treatment of Dom Casel's teaching we quoted Fr Bouyer's account of it. We return to the same source for an introduction to the subject which it seemed appropriate to add at the end of this chapter.

In Chapter XVIII of *Liturgical Piety* Fr Bouyer gives the following rough sketch of the evolution of devotions in the Church:

> Formerly the liturgy comprehended the whole prayer-life of the Church and of all Christians; and therefore there was no problem [of the relation between liturgical life and spiritual life]. For the Christians of antiquity, the liturgy was not only a school of prayer, *the* school of prayer, but it *was* their prayer. In the collective prayer each took his own part and so made it his own most personal prayer; thus a prayer which was nourished by that of the whole community brought back to the prayer of the whole community the spiritual fruit which each person had derived.[4]

Fr Bouyer goes on to show how the liturgy began to grow fossilized at the turning point of the Middle Ages and how the people, unable to understand it, took no further interest in

[4] Bouyer, *op. cit.*, p. 243.

it. Then came the Franciscans and Dominicans who provided a vigorous evangelical impulse. They developed a type of piety centred on the humanity of Christ and the human feelings that such an emphasis could provoke. "The cleavage between liturgical and 'popular' piety had begun and could only continue to widen." There even occurred the development of a kind of neoplatonic mysticism which of its nature was completely uninterested in the strongly historical and factual aspect of the liturgical mystery; it was supplemented by the great and beautiful mysticism of the Rhenish school. At the same time, among the Benedictines and Cistercians occurred a decline of liturgical understanding which was exemplified by the accretions to the Office and, especially for the lay brothers, by the multiplication of devotions—Rosary, Way of the Cross and so on. Somewhat later came the "new worship in the Blessed Sacrament of a presence which was visualized more and more as an ordinary human kind of presence, increasingly separated from the Mass and even from communion" which threatened "to wipe out the whole idea of the sacramental order and of the presence of Christ *in mysterio*".

But what are we to do now? We must certainly not abolish at one stroke all forms of popular devotion, but, as *Mediator* and the Second Vatican Council both propose, we should endeavour gently and firmly to bring such practices back to the norm of authentic liturgy, to permeate them with its spirit and finally develop into an auxiliary of the liturgy what originated as a substitute for it. This indeed clearly seems to be the mind of the Council when it lays down that the popular devotions of Christian people are to be highly commended "provided that they are in agreement with the laws and norms of the Church, above all when they are ordered by the Holy See". Devotions proper to local churches, we are told, have a special dignity if they are "undertaken by mandate of the bishops according to customs or books lawfully approved", but they are to be so composed that they are "in harmony with the liturgical seasons in the sacred liturgy"; in addition they must in some sense be derived from the latter and so "lead the people to it", since of its very nature "the liturgy far surpasses any of them".

The devotional practice which above all others can be regenerated in the light of the liturgy is certainly the Rosary. But this is also the case with the more modern devotion to the Sacred Heart, without mentioning the Month of Mary of which Fr de Féligonde said, "But it is purely and simply Advent". Considerations such as these bring us

> finally to the truth which will give an organic unity to all our observations concerning ways in which devotions may be brought once more into the current of the liturgy rather than be cast aside by it. The fundamental approach to the problem of uniting personal, psychological and therefore subjective devotion with the objective discovery of the Mystery in the liturgical tradition must always be that of restoring that Christian culture apart from which liturgy must always fossilize and so become incapable of transmitting the life of which it is so full. This means that the first and fundamental condition for any liturgical revival which is truly a revival of piety must be a personal knowledge of the whole Bible and meditation on it, both to be achieved along the lines laid out for us by the liturgy; such a revival implies a full acceptance of the Bible as Word of God and as the framework and everliving source of authentic Christianity.[5]

As a conclusion to this section on liturgy, spirituality and devotions we set down here three principles:

1. The perspective revealed by this pastoral liturgical approach appears as the most comprehensive of all. Far from rejecting forms of spirituality and devotions which tended to supplant the liturgy, on the contrary it takes possession of them.

2. What makes the unity between liturgical and non-liturgical spirituality and devotion is on a last analysis the Word of God. It is in the Bible that the community celebration and personal prayer nourish each other, both feeding on this same Word of God. In these conditions, forms of spiritu-

---

[5] Bouyer, *op. cit.*, p. 253.

ality, devotion and various practices can be considered as
special approbations of revelation, liturgy itself being the
universal approbation (because belonging to the Mystery) for
all Christians gathered together in the unity of the faith.
Mysterium fidei.

3. But when this has been done, and agreement easily
reached on these points, it seems to us that the essential still
remains to be said. In fact the problem raised by this real
conflict between liturgy, spirituality and devotions goes beyond
the setting usually assigned to it. In fact, it is the whole problem
of Christian existence which is thus raised, in all its dimensions
of the sacred set within a profane world. For after all, what is it
that makes a Christian to be a Christian? Is it the liturgy? Is
it the practice of some devotion or other? Is it authentic incorporation in a certain school of spirituality or some branch of
Catholic Action?

In all the possible answers to these questions, what are we
to think of the place given to the sick, the poor, children?
Which is the most meritorious on Easter night, to sing in choir
at the vigil service or to remain at the door because someone
must look after the door, to look after a sick child because
it must be done . . . and so on?

To give the right answer to the questions raised it seems to
us that two notions require bringing into prominence once
more. In the first place, the notion of the "interior sacrifice", a
sacrifice finding its manifold expression in daily life and, finally,
its fulfilment in assimilation to the sacrifice of Christ. A passage from St Augustine on this subject, quoted by Fr Bouyer
at the end of his book *The Paschal Mystery*, is of capital importance in this context.[6] It can be asserted that this passage,
far more than the *Confessions*, inaugurates modern times with
the emergence of the human and religious person in the light
of God from a society still far too undifferentiated in the
objectivism of an insufficiently personalist worship. This passage offers also a true idea of the value of the whole of

[6] The passage in question is from *The City of God*, X, 5–6; see L.
Bouyer, *The Paschal Mystery* (London and Chicago, 1951), pp. 329–32.

existence, material and spiritual, at the level of faith and religious life.

But at the other end of the scale to this particular emphasis which can lead to individualism, subjectivism and an undue confusion of sacred and secular, the notion and the reality of the Church as the necessary mediation between man and God needs to be re-emphasized—the Church, the fraternal community outside which (its visible framework and invisible reality being clearly defined) no approach to God is possible.

If these two notions of interior sacrifice and ecclesial community are successfully harmonized, if with some realism we can speak of interior and ecclesial sacrifice, or, if it is preferred, of personalist and sacrificial community, then can be avoided not only all conflict but, also and especially, all danger of falling into those excesses frowned upon by upholders of the liturgy or of the schools of spirituality. Beyond all question it will be seen then that the liturgy occupies a special place in the Church as a manifestation, the only guarantee to the eyes of faith, of personal devotion which she does not reject but, on the contrary, takes for granted at the level of interior sacrifice in its community dimensions and realization.

At this level, it seems clear, the problem raised once more by the booklet by Jacques and Raïssa Maritain, *Liturgy and Contemplation*, a very proper answer to the excesses of a totalitarian liturgism in the devotion and spirituality of the Church, should no longer occur.

PART III

THE PRINCIPAL ADVANCES MADE
BY THE LITURGICAL RENEWAL

CHAPTER VII

THE DIVINE OFFICE

It may be a little paradoxical to begin this third part of the book on the principal advances of the liturgical renewal by speaking of the Divine Office; it has been done because the Office seems to be the least favoured part of the liturgy in this respect, and in this particular lack of emphasis there seems some danger of the whole movement becoming halted at one stage of its development. Speaking quite generally, it can be said that the liturgical renewal has been especially concerned with the Mass, or with the sacraments in general, but has entirely neglected the Office as a whole. Now in this, especially in regard to the faithful, there is serious danger of a too exclusive attachment to eucharistic celebrations, an attachment which in the long run must inevitably do harm to these very celebrations. A liturgy which was no longer anything but eucharistic (and that is in practice the case with numerous parishes where there is only Mass—Mass in the morning, at midday, in the evening—and nothing else) is a liturgy doomed to wither because it has thus been separated from the main trunk of the tree of worship whose roots are undeniably in the Divine Office.

The Mass is the flower at the summit of Christian worship. All the rest of Christian worship ought to be comparable to the worship of the synagogue, whence it originated, which continued to be practised by Christ and his apostles, finding in the readings from the Word of God and the singing of the psalms the clearest and commonest of the expressions that they used. And it is only in the practice of this worship that the faith of the congregation will be awakened, educated and nourished to enable them to participate at those times when all the requisite conditions for dignity, all the community dimensions of Christian prayer have been realized, in the eucharistic worship in the proper sense of the term.

The problem of the multiplication of Masses, particularly from the priest's point of view, is not touched on here. We return to it below in speaking of concelebration. Here we mention the problem from its pastoral aspect in view of the devotion of the faithful which we fear to see stunted because it will be reduced not only to the Mass, and cut off from its source of nourishment, but even to the Mass as one practice among others, or in preference to others.

We know, of course, that parish priests often have no choice and that people must be provided for as they come, and that generally means Mass. But to give a somewhat exaggerated picture, perhaps it can be said that in certain cases of the introduction of various methods of participation at Mass (dialogue, commentary etc.), in parishes where the liturgical renewal has taken root, to the ordinary member of the congregation these methods hardly differ from the adoption of some special devotion like the recitation of the Rosary or the introduction of the Nine First Fridays. The faithful indeed show themselves neither silent, surly, nor indifferent, as has too often been asserted, but docile. They have been told that now they must come to Mass rather than to the Rosary or Benediction; they obey and they come. But a time will arrive, and in many places it has already arrived, when presence at Mass, hardly having evolved from being regarded as the fulfilling of an obligation, falls into the routine of what is called religious practice without ever having really been integrated into the personal religious life of the faithful.

It is true that a revival of the Office is faced with very great difficulties which explains, without justifying it, the relative neglect which it has encountered in the liturgical movement. And it may not be out of place to recall at the outset the reaction of the Catholic Counter-Reformation in favour of sacrificial worship in opposition to the simple worship of preaching and the sacrifice of praise of early Protestantism.

In the next place, it is especially to be deplored that so great a confusion has arisen between worship of the Church and monastic worship, on the one hand, and between private recitation and public recitation on the other. It can even be asserted, with some exaggeration it is true, but it brings out more clearly the underlying truth, that even the reforms desired by some are vitiated by this twofold confusion and especially by the second. Thus a reform of the Office, drawn up in the first place with private recitation in view, runs the certain risk of starting on the wrong road at the outset since of its nature the Office, like the Mass, is a community activity and not private, even when in private recitation the intention of the Church comes to supply for the deficiency. A theatrical performance is never arranged on the supposition of there being only one spectator and it would be even more ridiculous to imagine his occupying the theatre all by himself. A theatrical performance is arranged with a full house in view. *Mutatis mutandis*, and granting of course the inadequacy of the comparison between the Office and a play, the process is the same. And indeed it is the same for Mass. No one yet has thought of a liturgical reform based on private celebration. On the contrary, it is agreed by all the promoters of the liturgical revival that Mass in its most solemn form must be envisaged, that is, pontifical high Mass, and that it is on the basis of this form that reforms will be made in the other legitimate types of celebration as required by the circumstances of time and place.[1]

---

[1] It seems not unlikely that the unfavourable reception by some of the new Latin translation of the Psalter was in part due to the fact that the Latin text, an imitation of Ciceronian Latin, hitherto unknown in the liturgical books, was obviously composed with private recitation in Second Vatican Council has decreed that the work of revising the "Psalter, already happily begun, is to be finished as soon as possible and is to take into account the style of Christian Latin".

Now it is as rearrangements or provisional modifications
that the recent changes[2] in the Office have been put forward;
they refer principally to private recitation by clerics and, when
the occasion arises, by laity. Meanwhile, until the thorough-
going reform takes place, and it can hardly do otherwise than
take into account various experiments made in different places
(hence the importance of paying attention to the non-eucharis-
tic Offices evolved in some communities, groups and parishes)
the following *desiderata* mentioned by Cardinal Lercaro at
the Assisi Congress are important. It is true, of course, that the
new rubrics issued in 1960, and the principles laid down in the
liturgical Constitution of the Second Vatican Council carry the
modifications in the Breviary further and so bring the Office
nearer to the form desired by Cardinal Lercaro, but his fundamental requirements need the full-scale reform of the Breviary
promised by the Council and a radical change in outlook on
the part of many who use it.

Taking as his starting-point that in a priest's life the Breviary
ought to be not a burden but a source of personal and pastoral
edification, a privileged task, the *opus Dei* (*psalterium meum,
gaudium meum*, as St Augustine said), Cardinal Lercaro raises
the problem of the coexistence of private prayer and spiritual
exercises on the one hand and public prayer and the Breviary
on the other. "The unity of spiritual life has everything to gain
from a certain harmonization which would simplify and reduce
the burdens and at the same time make more vital the whole
apostolic activity of the clergy."[3]

The following points, based on Cardinal Lercaro's paper, are
put forward as observations on the present state of affairs combined with suggestions for the future.

1. There must be a real rediscovery of the essential nature
of the Office—the sanctification of time, of the hours of the day
and of the year; prayer in union with the whole tradition of

[2] For a short account of the modifications introduced in the Roman
Breviary of recent years see, in The Twentieth Century Encyclopedia
of Catholicism, Volume 109, *The Liturgical Books* by Lancelot C.
Sheppard, pp. 85–108.

[3] *MD* 47/48, 299–315.

the Church, Scripture, the writings of the Fathers and Doctors down the ages. This prayer and praise should lead up to the Mass and enable it to be *lived* better.

2. With these points in mind the most urgent need is for the liturgical renewal, which has been centred on the Mass, to take more account of the Office and the need for reform of the Breviary both for the benefit of the clergy and of the laity.

With regard to the clergy, partial reforms of the Breviary have followed one another in the last half century—Pius X, simplification, new distribution of the Psalter, emphasis on the proper of the season; Pius XII, new Latin Psalter, simplification of rubrics; John XXIII, new code of rubrics with greater prominence given to the proper of the season by reform of the calendar and a new classification of feasts. The general trend of this simplification, particularly in the code of rubrics (1960), has been the pastoral emphasis and the return to the fundamental idea of the Office as the sanctification of time. The special prominence given to the temporal Office with a reduction of the sanctoral is also noteworthy. The liturgical Constitution of the Second Vatican Council has legislated for a reform of the Breviary.

What will be its principal points? There will certainly be a further reduction of the length of the Office by distribution of the Psalms over a longer period and the suppression in private recitation, perhaps, of what is specifically intended for choral celebration, a rearrangement and refashioning of the lectionary, with, certainly, further prominence given to the Office of the Season[4] and the suppression of feasts which celebrate an "idea" rather than an "event". This indeed has been the general trend since Pius X's reform in 1911.

With regard to the laity, certain steps have been taken which, though they have not yet received that official sanction which is

[4] While the 1960 rubrics go a long way in giving prominence to the Office of the Season, particularly of Advent and Lent, the point has not yet been reached outside these two seasons where it can be said that the the ferial Office is the rule rather than the exception. It remains to be seen how far the reform of the Breviary promised in the Constitution on Liturgy of the Second Vatican Council will affect the calendar.

required to make them fully liturgical, are worth noting here. A great number of Breviaries for lay people have been published in all languages. In English there are *The Short Breviary* (published by St John's Abbey, Collegeville) and *The Little Breviary* (London, 1958). Yet these lay Offices "raise a problem. Should the Office for the laity be fashioned on the model of that used by the clergy?" asks Cardinal Lercaro. Here again it seems that practice must decide and that the most successful examples will attract the attention of those entrusted with the reform of the Breviary who will thus be in a position to obtain the necessary official sanction. In any case, what is to be aimed at is the further (and normal) stage when, as at Mass, the Office, taking into account the present way of life among civilized peoples and the daily timetable of the active population, gathers together clergy and faithful for the praise of God and the hearing of his word.

The Sacerdotal Communities
of St. Séverin of Paris
and St. Joseph of Nice

CHAPTER VIII

THE LITURGICAL RENEWAL AND THE EUCHARIST

In the context of this third part of the book no mention is made of the advances achieved in theology as a result of the liturgical movement—biblical theology, the theology of the mystery of worship—since something has already been said of these matters in the second part. Here, on the subject of the Eucharist, we are concerned rather to detail a number of practical improvements with reference, not to understanding of the holy Sacrifice, but to its celebration. These improvements, none the less, are derived so directly from theological considerations that it is impossible not to refer to them summarily by way of introduction and as positive contributions made by the liturgical renewal.

Since the whole liturgical movement started from a rediscovery of the tradition of the Church, and more specially still from a rediscovery, not to say a discovery purely and simply, of the theology of the Church, the same holds good, right at the outset, for the Eucharist as sacrifice and sacrament. Thus, looking at the question on the level of theory, the direct inspiration of practice, the latter being the soil in which the former is made fruitful, we feel that at the present time the key to eucharistic worship is to be found in a better grasp of the relationship between Mass as a sacrament and Mass as a sacrifice, a relationship expressed in its simplest form as Mass-sacrificial meal.

It may well be asked why Christ chose bread and wine to symbolize and make effective his presence among us. If this presence was the ultimate purpose of his sacred institution, the transubstantiated bread and wine being reduced in fact to mere appearances, would it not have been better if his choice had fallen on a pearl, which does not corrupt or decay, or on a perfume, a more pervasive element, which would have rendered his presence more durable or more significant?

If Christ chose bread and wine it was, it seems, to show, at a given stage in civilization by the help of these elements of human communion, that by which his disciples could show and perpetuate the essence of his sacrifice. If, in fact, it is the essence of this sacrifice to be a total gift of absolute oblation to his Father, it can be said that Christ found no better way of expressing this divine gift than by means of elements which manifest, signify and effect a mutual gift among men. This can be said shortly by stating that Christ found perhaps no better expression of divine charity than human charity, since the latter is evidence of the former and is at the same time its consequence. In this way Christ reduced the twofold commandment of the Law to one alone.

That seems to be the meaning of the Johannine account of the Last Supper. Omitting the narrative of the institution, and in some sort substituting for it the account of the washing of feet as a gesture of friendly and brotherly welcome on the part of God himself, it dwells at length on the commandment of love among the disciples in relation to the revelation of the three divine Persons. This is also the meaning of the Pauline account which includes the institution narrative in a purely ecclesial context of love shared in daily life. And it is probably for the same reason that at this moment Luke inserts the dispute which arose between the disciples on the subject of who was greatest among them. In any case, it is the realization of two logia related by the Synoptics: "It is mercy that wins favour with me, not sacrifice," and "Where two or three are gathered together in my name, I am there in the midst of them".

Setting aside the former types of sacrifice in Judaism and the practices of worship surrounding them, Christ effectively reduced the worship of the new Alliance to the existence of the ecclesial community as such, as brotherly love: this love was both the witness and presence of Christ as the personified and incarnate expression of divine love, a love coming from God and given back to him in the highest way on the cross.

It is this which makes the Mass essentially communion, though this does not mean that the essence of sacrifice is confined to and is effected at the precise moment that bears this name, when the sacred species are consumed by the celebrant and the congregation. Rather is it all the Mass that is communion, in the gathering together of the congregation and the attitudes which manifest it, in the hearing of the Word and in the common expression of praise—all being accomplished over the bread and wine offered as symbols of this constant communion (this appears very clearly in the *Didache*). And the consecration is then the supreme moment of this brotherly communion which causes it to pass from symbol to reality. It is the moment when God answers fully the expectations of his faithful people in communion. It is the moment when God consecrates this brotherly communion by giving himself in his Son, really present under the species which make the communion manifest and effect the marvellous exchange, and the still more marvellous union, between this human brotherly love and its fulfilment in divine love by Christ, who is this Love in person.

And so there are no longer two loves. Just as substantially the bread and wine have disappeared, the brotherly communion which they symbolize is entirely merged in Christ's offering as a victim, the supreme expression of divine love, made really present on the altar under the species of bread and wine and at the precise moment of communion in the hearts of the faithful who share them. The "assumption" and as it were the "absorption" of the physical and human matter of the sacrifice are thus total. It is like the heat of the water mingled with the chalice after the consecration in the Byzantine rite, or like the fire from heaven which consumed the sacrifice of the prophet Elias. These symbols represent the real presence of Christ at Mass and the manner which, in him, priest and victim at the same time, God incarnate assuming in his person his whole mystical body, the love of God totally integrates the love of creation. The latter, in the communion of men with each other, is a figure here below, as nearly as it is possible for it to be, of the circumincession of the divine Persons which make them one in the holy Trinity.

This way of putting matters seems to place Trinitarian unity and ecclesial unity in a real and vital relationship in the sacrifice-meal and communion. It is founded on several scriptural contexts and is represented by a considerable tradition from the *Didache* to St Augustine.

This is also the way in which worship and life can be really coordinated, since worship, in accordance with the twofold commandment of love reduced to unity, is the sacred moment of life passed in charity—the special work of the disciples of Jesus and their *opus Dei*.

It is also the way really to explain, and not merely to acknowledge, the primitive and traditional doctrine of the common priesthood of the faithful, an idea so fundamental that, as Jungmann has shown, the terms which properly designate the priesthood were only used in the first two centuries in speaking of Christ or of the whole Church. We see here that the common priesthood of the faithful in the unity of the Church is not only a juridical function for the celebration of the sacrifice, it is, as mutual consent, brotherly communion before God, "body and soul" of the sacrament which, by the real presence, becomes the efficacious sign of divine love.

In the last place, to come to the real purpose of these considerations, it is what explains, at the starting-point of the liturgical movement, Pius X's insistence on *active* participation. If it is not just one method like another, laid down by the pope for the purpose of obtaining a better, technically more perfect celebration of the Eucharist, it must be thought that it goes much further and comes very near to the very essence of the Eucharist as ecclesial and Christocentric significant communion, in the sense of *ex opere operato*, of divine grace.

This participation and its most external forms of expression come near, according to the intention of the Church, to the very essence of the sacrifice-sacrament. And the active participation of the faithful, as of the celebrant and his ministers, in eucharistic worship is a way which is significant in itself of what this worship really effects. If such active participation is not absolutely required for validity, since one communicant, namely the celebrant, can by intention represent all the others (although the traditional insistence on the presence of at least a server is significant in this respect) it is no less evident that this validity itself requires active, congregational participation *in voto*, as every properly liturgical act is, *in voto*, an act of the whole Church. The need for participation by the congregation could not have been put more plainly than it is in the liturgical Constitution of the Second Vatican Council. In it participation (internal as well as external) is seen to be an essential part of public worship; indeed the reform of the books of the Roman rite is to be carried out with such participation in view so that the congregation may take part *scienter, actuose et fructuose*—that is, their participation is to be informed, active and fruitful.

This explains, without fully justifying it, the repugnance of some of the clergy for what are called "private" Masses,[1] and it is this, too, which inspires their desire for a return to the ancient custom, still practised in the Eastern Church, of concelebration. They are not, of course, thereby calling in question the legitimacy or the value of individual celebration, according to the circumstances of time and place (see below).

This whole way of rethinking and reordering the mystery of worship, cannot, without injustice, be taxed with a hankering after novelty, or with archeologism. It is certainly, and in the

---

[1] The new rubrics of the Roman Missal lay down that the expression "private Mass" is to be avoided: *Denominatio proinde Missae privatae vitetur* (n. 269).

present case indeed to a high degree, an authentic way of thinking with the Church, *sentire cum Ecclesia*. It is a question of the authentic expression in the very method of celebration, and in accordance with the sacramental order, of what it is really to effect. And that is brotherly communion in the name of Christ, the efficacious sign of his real presence as God's answer made to man—to man who, following Christ's example, in the unity of fellowship seeks God and finds him as a Father.

This renewal of the quest for eucharistic authenticity, which should find its counterpart in daily life, particularly in the practice of charity and of the missionary ideal, is in any case what appears to emerge most clearly from all that has been done at the practical, external level of eucharistic celebrations. It is now time to deal with this aspect of the question. In the following explanation account has been taken of the various episcopal directives for Mass as well as of the principal practices at the parochial level which these same directives have sanctioned. All that is said here is valid, *mutatis mutandis* of every kind of liturgical gathering, but it refers particularly to the Mass. And it is for this reason that it finds a place in this chapter.

PRINCIPAL INNOVATIONS OR REFORMS

The altar

The part played by the altar in the celebration and the doctrine concerning it need to be explained. The altar should stand free with its surroundings unencumbered. Its rôle as sacrificial table, particularly, should appear with the greatest possible clarity.[2]

The celebrant

The correctness, dignity and even elegance of the celebrant's gestures and attitudes are not superfluous extras. Like the altar, the celebrant, who really presides over the congregation, and is Christ's representative, must stand out clearly. Thus

[2] See Instruction on the Sacred Liturgy, V, 90–94 (pp. 261–262). Cf. *MD* 51, 132–45.

those Masses are inadmissible at which another priest from the pulpit, or from the middle of the nave, superimposes on the entire Mass an obtrusive commentary, relegating the celebrant to the background.

The congregation

As Fr Bouyer has shown, for a long time the idea of liturgy as a spectacle, like the grandiose ceremonies of the seventeenth-century French court, was everywhere current. We are in course of rediscovering nowadays that the liturgy is the work of the people, that there are not actors and "audience" since the congregation is in itself "mystery" of Christ.

From this general principle, which has been recalled and developed several times already in the course of this book, the following conclusions emerge:

The first way in which the congregation takes part is that it has gathered together. The primary quality of its participation, therefore, is to be found in the way that it has assembled. Its very material disposition should manifest its unity. But so far as possible (and this is a serious problem for huge urban parishes) this unity should be able to manifest itself by the parish Mass which should be the high Mass. Here we encounter the difficulty of several Masses; we shall refer to it again. There is also to be noted the danger of reserving the parish high Mass, either by reason of its inconvenient time or its archaic character, or else because even the clergy are not enthusiastic about it, to a handful of habitués scattered about the church—pensioners, old ladies who have already communicated at the seven o'clock Mass, sisters from the neighbouring home or institution who have already had their community Mass.

Total participation of the congregation is effected by sacramental communion. Hence the mitigation of the eucharistic fast and the recommendation that communion should be given from hosts consecrated during the Mass in question, as the Encyclical *Mediator* and the Constitution on liturgy of the Second Vatican Council requires; hence, too, the solemniza-

tion of communion by means of a procession and congregational singing.

Participation is also to be found in the ordinary attitudes in
church which enable the congregation to live the mystery
celebrated and knit them together in unity. The education of
the congregation in these matters is always necessary. But care
must be taken very patiently to offer reasons for the directions
given regarding the attitudes to be adopted for the different
parts of the Mass. It may be pointed out in this connection that
the normal attitude for Christian prayer is standing; beginning
with our Lady at the foot of the cross, it was the attitude of the
early Christians. The celebrant at the altar always stands. It is
important to observe, also, that apart from the aged and the
sick, it is the attitude that can be asked of the congregation
with the least difficulty.

Participation is expressed also by the' singing and the responses of the congregation. The schola or choir ought not to
prevent the faithful from making the responses or from singing. Its function is to execute certain anthems that the congregation does not know and it is legitimate on occasion for the
latter to listen (there are certain meditative chants, like the
gradual, which are intended for this purpose). In addition, it is
the function of the schola to sustain the singing of the congregation, but it ought not to take the place of the congregation
or require it to sing pieces that are too difficult.

In addition to these arrangements concerning attitudes, singing and responses, there are a certain number of laws governing
the congregation which confer on it its own essential nature.
They are here described summarily:

1. The Christian congregation is in the first place a festive
gathering. Joy is a necessary condition of a liturgy and of a
liturgical congregation; all forms of celebration share to a certain extent in the paschal joy in expectation of the Kingdom.

2. The Christian congregation is hierarchical. It forms a sort
of symphony in which there are different parts. "And this is
not merely to prevent confusion and disorder; it is rather, the
direct consequence of the fact that the Church, the *ecclesia*,
does not meet on its own initiative, or because its members

have spontaneously gathered together, but rather because it has been convoked by God's Word, speaking to it in the manner befitting that Word."[3]

3. Proclamation and hearing of the Word of God. "The reading of the Scripture that takes place in the framework of the Mass is not merely one among many types of reading the divine Word; it is the chief and fundamental type to which all the others refer as to their norm.   And, to penetrate still more deeply into this truth, it is in the living liturgical celebration alone, with all that this celebration ... implies for the living Church, that God's Word can be accepted as it desires to be accepted."[4]

4. Prayer. "The readings of the synagogal service and, still earlier, all the proclamations of the Word of God, have always been connected with the people's prayer and praise."[5]

5. The offering of the people in the one only sacrifice of Christ. "In this thanksgiving, the whole story of the redemption of Israel as proclaimed in the Bible was summed up in praise, the people thus created by God were dedicated anew to him, and a petition was made for a future and final intervention of God by which he would accomplish the work he had begun and himself bring to perfection the offering of the People."[6]

6. The Christian congregation is, in the last place, communion, as we have sufficiently shown at the beginning of this chapter. Here it need merely be recalled with Jungmann that the rôle of the congregation amounts to removing the veil of mist that in the later Middle Ages came down between the people in the nave and the worship at the altar. The faithful must realize that they are not strangers and sojourners, still less are they mere spectators of what Christ effects at the altar through the ministry of the priest. "The liturgy is the worship rendered by the mystical Body of Christ in the entirety of its Head and members."

[3] L. Bouyer, *Liturgical Piety* , p. 32.
[4] *Ibid.*, pp. 30–1.
[5] *Ibid.*, p. 115.
[6] *Ibid.*, pp. 115–16.

We give here an example of a celebration in the seventeenth century as a conclusion to this section on the rôle of the congregation. We are concerned here with the hero discovered by Fr Bouyer. His name was Jubé. In him we could see a precursor, if he had not gone much further than our own liturgical renewal, or even a prophet, if his example did not inspire with considerable modesty more than one contemporary liturgist.

The most famous among those liturgical pioneers of the seventeenth century was later denounced by Dom Guéranger as having been a living combination of heresies of all kinds, although, as a matter of fact, he can only be reproached for having signed the Appeal against the Bull *Unigenitus*, as did many of the most respectable churchmen of the time. This pioneer's name was Jubé, and he was the parish priest of Asnières, at that period a small place near Paris on the west bank of the Seine. Jubé insisted first of all on the public and collective character of the Mass. As a consequence, he never used the high altar in his church except on Sundays and feastdays when the congregation gathered together. He also restored the old Roman usage (which had endured longer in France than in Rome itself) of placing the linen cloth on the altar only just before Mass, and of having no other cross or lights on the altar than the processional cross and tapers, which were set in place at the beginning of Mass. Jubé began Mass by saying the Psalm *Judica* and the *Confiteor* along with the people; then he sat down at the Epistle side of the altar and listened to the Epistle and Gospel as they were sung by the assistant ministers, after having sung the collect himself. He sang the *Kyrie*, *Gloria* and *Credo* along with the people, instead of saying them in a low voice by himself. He also restored the offertory procession (which had never entirely disappeared from French churches), and had offerings of all kinds made in this procession which he later blessed at the *Per quem haec omnia* at the end of the canon, according to the original practice. He never began the canon before the *Sanctus* had been sung in full and he said the prayers of the canon loudly enough to be heard by the whole congregation in his small church. In other words, he wanted once more to make the readings, the singing, the prayers, the offertory real, rather than merely conventional acts; and he wanted to have the sacrifice offered with the full, though always hierarchically ordered, participation of the Christian people. Dom Guéranger later regarded all these practices of Jubé as so many reasons for horror and dismay. But we of today can see in most of them intelligent and healthy improvements, had they been introduced with the consent of proper authority.[7]

THE QUESTION OF CONCELEBRATION

The best introduction to this subject is that written by Dom Lambert Beauduin.[8] He establishes in the first place the legitimacy of the rite, taking into account the reservations of the canons and despite the discussions which took place on this subject in the later Middle Ages. And he shows what is the fundamental underlying theological idea; the unity of the priesthood which is made visible by this rite grouping around the bishop, the sole depositary of the fullness of the priesthood of the eternal Pontiff, the whole diocesan community, according to their various hierarchical functions. A third paragraph sketches the historical tradition, especially at Rome, down to the giving up of the rite by the Western Church towards the end of the thirteenth century.   Finally, noting the various traces of the practice still remaining, he respectfully expresses the desire for a restoration of concelebration which is so expressive of the Catholic spirit. That desire has now been granted by the liturgical Constitution promulgated on December 4th, 1963. Reference is made to this in the last chapter of this book, but it may be useful to mention here, however, certain matters which, although elementary, are too little known, and certain questions of a practical nature.

In the first place, it should be remembered that until a relatively late date (fourth century) there was only one Mass in Rome and that was the pope's; again, in St Thomas Aquinas's time, it was forbidden for two Masses to be celebrated at the same time in a church; that at the present time in the Byzantine

[7] *Ibid.*, pp. 53–4.
[8] See *MD* 7.

rite it is forbidden for two Masses to be celebrated at the same altar on the same day and that, if the practice of concelebration, in this and other oriental rites, is not usual it is entirely allowed and recognized; finally, that in the Roman rite there is concelebration at ordination Masses and at those of the consecration of a bishop, and that on Maundy Thursday only one Mass is celebrated in a church at which priests and faithful communicate.

It is true that with this last tradition, in fact evacuated of its substance, if it can be put thus, since there is no concelebration in the proper sense of the term by the priests, but only communion, can be compared the custom whereby a priest is allowed to celebrate three Masses on All Souls day and Christmas day. It can certainly be pointed out that it is here a question of permission (three Masses may be celebrated) whereas in the other case there is prohibition (it is forbidden on Maundy Thursday, as a general rule, to celebrate any other Mass than the community Mass). But this consideration would certainly not suffice to establish the principle of the multiplication of Masses and their frequency, and it is here that the real difficulty occurs.

What in fact is the reason that a priest celebrates one or several Masses, or that he does not celebrate at all in order to communicate and concelebrate? Is it the devotion of the priest and can one take as an example the case of the pope who celebrated several times a day, or the holy Jesuit priest who obtained an indult so that he could make his Mass last an hour and a half in order to satisfy his eucharistic devotion? Can it be the infinite value of the sacrifice of the Mass? But is this value, which in fact is infinite, since it is derived from the sacrifice consummated once for all upon the cross, subject to numerical considerations, to arithmetical calculations? If it is, why do not priests, whose principal function is to offer Mass, divest themselves of other obligations, to be able to celebrate several times a day and thus increase to the maximum number, as their devotion would lead them to do, the number of Masses celebrated uninterruptedly on earth?

We can see from these simple questions that considerations of devotion and those which take into account the infinite value of the Mass are not a sufficient explanation of the multiplication of Masses.   To put it more accurately, they cannot establish a norm for their frequency. How then can this be done?

In the absence of a clear and quick answer to unravel this complicated question a little, it can be advanced, firstly, that it is better provisionally to leave aside certain related questions like the precept obliging the faithful and priests to be present at Mass or to celebrate, the merits accruing to the celebration of Mass or presence at it and, *a fortiori*, the question of stipends. These questions are by no means secondary, but are nevertheless placed second in the sense that they ought not to influence the solution otherwise than as indications and should owe the recognition that they obtain to the fact that the question has already been solved.

In the next place, it is important to recall the difference of the "traditions" in the Church and their unequal value, not to mention their relative authenticity. In addition to Tradition (with a capital letter) and those traditions which are its expression at the dogmatic level, it is essential to place in their proper category those customs of a canonical and liturgical nature, sanctioned by usage and canon law, especially when, in another part of the Church, contrary customs are also legitimately established; in this way we shall cease to do wrong to our brethren in the faith and the same ecclesial communion by regarding as merely tolerated, or even as abuses, their customs which are contrary to our own.

Looking indeed at those customs and practices which are our own, we must take greater care to separate the chaff from the wheat. Thus it would have been possible to urge against Pius X's institution of frequent communion and that of children a "tradition" of many centuries standing in the opposite sense. In truth, it was not a tradition but rather the loss of the understanding of the tradition which has now been made clear, or more serious still, a lack of normal and necessary development in the life of the Church.

With these considerations in mind, it seems that to find a norm for the frequency of the celebration of Mass we must consider the eucharistic mystery as a whole. The principles established at the beginning of the present chapter can here be of some help to us. They amounted, in short, to bringing out clearly the essential link between what signifies and what is signified; what signifies is fundamentally the ecclesial community gathered together for the breaking of bread and symbolized before the consecration by the bread and wine as elements of communion; what is signified is the divine love which, in the Person of Christ made present on the altar at the moment of consecration, assumes and transfigures the communion in fellowship of the Church gathered together in his name.

If that is true it seems obvious that the ancient practice, shown by having only one Mass and by concelebration, is nearer to the primitive institution and the structure on which it is founded. The fact of the gathering together of the community being an essential in what signifies, it seems that the frequency of Mass ought to be regulated, in principle, on this. In practice account would be taken of legitimately related elements.

If then in a particular place the whole congregation can be gathered together for a Mass, this will be the Mass and there will be only one. And the Mass will be celebrated as often as reasonably and with due dignity the community can be gathered anew. Thus what has hitherto been precept could also become the norm. The Sunday precept could also be the norm for the parochial celebration as the custom of conventual Mass could be the norm of the frequency of celebration in a community of monastic type. In that case it would be necessary to be very careful to determine not only the types of community but their real diversification. It is certain that at the present time, within the boundaries of an urban parish, there are in fact several communities. It can be said indeed that there are as many parish communities as there are Masses. In ecclesiastical parlance it is common to hear mention of the "eleven o'clock congregation".

And in fact these are different sections of the public that require to be sociologically determined and to be integrated afresh in the unity of the community and of the parochial Mass. In this respect the multiplicity of Masses in a parish will no longer be a derogation to the principle, any more than the existence of these Masses is in relation to the bishop's Mass.

A similar procedure would make it easy to determine the frequency of Masses during the week and Masses for special groups. In this respect the decree on evening Masses contains certain useful indications. On the other hand, the celebration of "private" Masses apart from, and *a fortiori* during community celebrations, as well as the multiplicity of Masses in a monastery, raises a real problem and it seems that if this problem is to be solved by concelebration it is equally true that a necessary preliminary is the solution of the problem of the multiplication of the priestly office, according to the needs of places and periods. But that is another problem.

As a conclusion to this section, and in case one point or another raised above has been misunderstood, there is added here a word on the solitary Eucharist. It is obvious, indeed, that a celebration in isolation is not *per se* implicated in what was said above since it was put forward as a suggestion on the norm to be established for the frequency of Masses. This will easily be seen from the following comparison between celebration by a priest who is a passenger on a liner and celebration by Fr de Foucauld in the desert. Many priests have had experience of celebration on board ship, especially with pilgrimage groups when there are several priests present. Conditions, it can be said, are, at the very least, summary. On the other hand, it is certain that the intention of the isolated celebrant makes up for the significance of the ecclesial congregation. But more than that, in the case of Fr de Foucauld in the Sahara or of Fr Peyriguère in the Berber mountains, or again in the case of a priest explorer in the Arabian desert or Central Asia, the intention of the priest celebrating with the whole Church and in her name assumes an entirely different meaning. In the name of the universal Church, he celebrates, alone, for that local Church which only exists in himself. And this can be true also of an isolated priest in a Christian country as in missionary territory. In the suburbs of a great dechristianized city, or in the depths of the country, it can be said that, following the diversity and the impenetrability of classes and peoples, the priest by himself is the Church. And his Eucharist is then in a very special way what indeed it is, the desire, previously expressed by fasting, of a divine presence which in the end will triumph over human impenetrability and obtain, by virtue of the words of the Gospel, perfect union of strangers and sojourners in the humanity of Jesus, priest and victim. This solitary Eucharist is then like that which is celebrated in brotherly union with a soul in danger, in the keen suffering of being unable to share with this soul the eucharistic communion. It is the bread of fellowship which is then broken and the fact that it is eaten alone does not impair within us the desire for others, a loved one or some special section of humanity, the sustenance of the essential desire for God and for his kingdom, *donec veniat*.

A religious who for long years experienced the fact of the Eucharist in solitude can express far better than we can these things and restore for us, if we have lost them, the legitimacy and the profound meaning of such solitary celebrations. Fr Charles-André Poissonier, a Franciscan hermit at Tazert in South Morocco, who died in 1938 and was an almost immediate disciple of Fr de Foucauld, wrote in his private notebook:

> When I celebrate Mass alone in my little chapel which on one side dominates Tazert and on the other clings to the mountainside in which it is embedded; when at night I recite my Office alone with our Lord present before me, it is then that I feel, it is then that I live my missionary life, for it is in the name of all those surrounding me that I pray, that I adore, that I render to God the homage due to him. As I have in some sort become a Moroccan, by my incorporation among this people with whom I live in close relations, and on the other hand, having become a member of Christ by my faith, I have the impression that in me Christ has become a Moroccan and desires to pray himself

for his Moroccan brothers. It is in that especially that I feel myself to be a missionary, far more than in my medical work which is and must remain secondary. And so it is of little importance if the harvest is not yet even beginning to grow, if perhaps, and even probably, I shall not see it with my eyes. I shall nevertheless have fulfilled my missionary rôle by bringing the prayer of Christ to a place where it was not hitherto.... Christ will have taken possession of a part of his Kingdom which he did not previously possess....

In another context Pierre Teilhard de Chardin said the same thing no less admirably in "The Mass on the world" (see at the end of *The Milieu divin*).

The Sacerdotal Communities
of St. Séverin of Paris
and St. Joseph of Nice

CHAPTER IX

PASTORAL PRACTICE AND THE SACRAMENTS

FUNDAMENTAL REQUIREMENTS

Ever since the Council of Trent, and in reaction against Protestant moralism, Catholic theology has felt itself obliged to insist on the principle of *opus operatum*. But if, from this point of view, it is true that in the celebration of Mass or the administration of the sacraments, "one priest is as good as another", from the canonical point of view the problem of validity does not exclude that of licitness. It must also be remembered that the spiritual movement of the post-Tridentine period was concerned far more greatly than in previous times to promote a sacerdotal spirituality, to insist, that is, on the moral and religious dispositions of the minister of the sacraments and of the celebrant of the Eucharist. And yet it is true, perhaps, that until recently less consideration was given to the pastoral problem raised by the dispositions of the faithful. The first important sign of a renewal in this field is to be found, probably, at the beginning of this century in the measures taken by Pius X for the promotion of frequent communion and the admission of children to the holy table. It required this action of the supreme authority for Christian people no longer to regard themselves as excommunicated to all intents and purposes. The movement thus set on foot by Pius X forms the starting-point for a more acute awareness of all that is required of us by the sacrament that is offered to us.

It is clear in fact that our faith in the *opus operatum* of the sacraments in no wise allays the uneasiness that we experience when confronted by those who from routine, or from an attachment, founded on a species of folklore rather than on faith, to ceremonies whose real significance has been lost to sight, continue to have recourse to the priest for the baptism of their children and for marriage. It is difficult to ascertain how far genuine faith subsists beneath this quasi-superstitious attachment to traditional institutions. It could be the still smoking flax that we must be careful not to quench. But obviously that is not enough. The question is to discover what can be done to revive the flame and bring these nominal Christians to an understanding of what in the eyes of the Church is the meaning of the act that they ask of her.

The primary concern will therefore be to lead those who thus present themselves for the reception of a sacrament to dispositions of actual faith. The Council of Trent, and those who worked to render effective the reform that it promulgated, attached great importance to children's catechism. But at a dechristianized period like our own the problem of the instruction of adults has become increasingly urgent. Since some of those who still ask the Church to bless their marriages and baptize their children scarcely ever go to Mass and are thus deprived of the instruction that is given in the liturgy of the Word, it can hardly be considered strange to wonder what is the real significance for them of the marriage or the baptism that they ask of the Church.

In those countries where these religious acts are quite distinct from the corresponding civil formalities it would seem to be relatively easy to make it clear to people that these sacraments have in fact no significance other than a religious one. And so on these occasions a purely administrative attitude must be avoided; the priest must not confine himself merely to registering a baptism or a marriage but take the trouble to make these events the basis of a real adult catechesis.

So far as marriage is concerned, the increasingly precise canonical prescriptions regarding the preliminary inquiries provide the priest, responsible for this investigation, with the basis for instruction, which must lead those with whom he is dealing to a realization that they are not undergoing a tiresome formality, but that they can obtain real spiritual benefit from this living contact with their pastor. And he, provided that he does not lose sight of the spirit informing the letter of the regulations, can be led to a genuine concern for the religious education of the betrothed couple who come to him.

In this way new institutions arise to meet new needs. Retreats are organized for engaged couples and even a sort of catechumenate during which a series of instructions is spread over a fairly long period. Aid is sought from various quarters, from doctors, from couples with some experience of married life. In short, the dialogue between priest and faithful is broadened to the dimension of the Christian community, of an institution of the Church in which each individual according to his own particular competence, his own particular gifts, has his positive contribution to offer. By his presence the priest must ensure that these meetings become real liturgies, preparing for the sacramental liturgy which is now incorporated with the baptismal liturgy.

Moreover, the whole of the fervent community must be concerned with those whose faith is obscured by prejudice and misunderstandings and should strive to lead them, especially on the occasion of marriage, to clearer awareness of the Gospel message that perhaps they have not troubled to study since childhood. For this purpose, systematic explanations of the Christian faith have been organized, in addition to the special preparation for marriage, for those who have come to this important turning-point of their vocation.

Something of the same sort should be done for baptisms. If the practice of infant baptism can be justified by the principle of *opus operatum*, from the pastoral point of view a real catechumenate ought to be instituted for the benefit of the parents and godparents who have taken the step of asking for baptism for a child. It can take shape quite naturally by informal instructions, visits to families, etc., and normally should last some time according to the needs of the Christian education of the neophyte, until the age when he can regularly attend catechism lessons. In this way baptism will no longer be a mere formality and the occasion of a celebration that is entirely of worldly inspiration; thus too, the primary meaning of the baptismal liturgy can be rediscovered by those who previously were present at its rites as passive spectators without seeking to understand their meaning.

Something like two years before the voting of the Constitution on liturgy at the Second Vatican Council the Congregation of Rites gave permission for the rite of baptism of adults to be performed in stages during the instruction of the convert. This virtual restoration of the catechumenate has been followed by the instruction in the Constitution on liturgy of the Second Vatican Council which lays down that "the catechumenate for adults is to be restored; it is to comprise several distinct steps, and to be taken into use as and when the Ordinary may see fit".

Lastly, the same concern for adult catechesis is to be found in assistance of the sick and dying. By instructing the faithful about the real meaning of the prayers of the Church and the rites of the sacrament of the sick the priest will combat the prevailing prejudice about this sacrament and accustom Christians no longer to regard it as the sacrament of the dying but as an appeal to God for the recovery of the sick person: "Stretch out your right hand and set him on his feet again, put strength into him, and keep him safe under your powerful protection, give him back again to your holy Church..." (liturgy of the sick).

In this way by a concern to lead the candidate for the sacraments to dispositions of faith an attempt will be made to make the sacrament intelligible. Bilingual rituals have already been adopted in many countries. Obviously, when it is a question of certain rites which have, so to say, become a trifle stale in the course of time under the influence of routine or misunderstood practical necessities, the matter is one of some delicacy. Thus the exorcisms at baptism have not been translated in the bilingual rituals in English-speaking countries. But it is clear that there is a problem here. In the Nestorian Church the exorcisms have been eliminated from the baptismal liturgy; this, in the view of all other Christian Churches of East and West, is the effect of the Pelagian heresy, whose influence, rejected everywhere else, has been successful among Nestorians. In the state of mind provoked by the liturgical movement we shall experience increasingly, no doubt, a rediscovery of those values of faith which formed the foundation of all our traditional rites, and increasingly, too, we shall apreciate their authentic savour. Now that the whole ritual of the sacraments, including the sacramental forms, may be in the vernacular and the rites themselves are to be reformed as a result of the liturgical Constitution, this rediscovery and greater appreciation are likely to be easier and to occur more quickly.

THE SACRAMENTS AND THE PASCHAL MYSTERY

The liturgical reform of the Easter vigil is undoubtedly one of the most important events of the history of the liturgical renewal. From the outset it was allowed to incorporate in it the administration of baptism which gives its full significance to this vigil. The present liturgy provides that all the faithful should be associated with this baptismal emphasis by a solemn renewal each year on this occasion of their baptismal promises and profession of faith; this allusion to baptism is maintained even in the case when there is no neophyte in the congregation.

As we know, in the time of St Augustine certain considerations caused the administration of baptism to be postponed until after the age of reason and even until adulthood, thus prolonging the catechumenate throughout youth, except of course in danger of death when baptism was always given to infants. Thus there is a certain opposition between considerations of a pedagogical nature and those of a theological nature which urge that children should be admitted at an early age not only to baptism but to the fullness of sacramental life according to the custom that has been preserved in the Churches of the East.

The same opposition between the pedagogical and theological points of view is encountered again with confirmation. In the traditional enumeration of the sacraments we begin by mentioning the three sacraments of Christian initiation which formerly were all three conferred during the Easter vigil—baptism, confirmation, Eucharist—and this is still the Eastern custom. In the Latin Church, since confirmation as a general rule is normally reserved to the bishop, more often than not there would be an insurmountable practical difficulty in including it in the Easter vigil. On the other hand, if it is more normal, from the theological point of view, to confer confirmation before first Communion, from the pedagogical point of view there is a temptation to postpone the age of confirmation which is here regarded as the sacrament of Christian maturity. This is the custom which has become fairly well established in the Protestant Churches. In fact, among most Catholics confirmation does not stand out very clearly. The liturgical Constitution of the Second Vatican Council has, however, made it clear that confirmation forms part of the rites of Christian initiation and has said that it may be given within Mass when convenient. The rite is to be revised in order to show the "intimate connection of this sacrament with the whole process of Christian initiation" and to make it emerge more clearly; for the same reason, the Constitution continues, it is fitting that "candidates should renew their baptismal promises just before they are confirmed".

At the end of the Middle Ages, and in the seventeenth and eighteenth centuries in most Western countries, the point was reached of omitting entirely to confer confirmation. The present practice of the Catholic Church is in sharp reaction against such a tendency, but if, in practice, all children are confirmed and the present law of the Church even allows all parish priests to administer the sacrament to children of school age in danger of death, it certainly cannot be said that this sacrament is better understood and stands out more clearly in the memories of the majority of Christians. We have here, then, a concrete situation, which will no doubt call for further development since, in the prevailing climate of the liturgical renewal it is increasingly felt to be abnormal.

In any case, the restoration of the Easter vigil to its fundamental and primary significance has made a valuable contribution to showing more clearly the community character of the sacraments conferred on this occasion.

PENANCE

The sacrament of penance gave every appearance at one time of being the indisputable condition for the reception of communion. In the stages of a child's religious life the following steps were commonly regarded as usual—baptism, penance, Eucharist, confirmation. This was an order very different from the traditional order of the sacraments which preserves the idea of the unity of the three sacraments of Christian initiation, the sacrament of penance only being mentioned afterwards, together with the sacrament of the sick, which was regarded in a similar way.

Under the influence of the liturgical renewal, and especially of the practice of frequent communion, which has increasingly restored among the faithful the desire to communicate whenever they take part in Mass, the sacrament of penance has recovered its own particular value. If in the early Church it was essentially the rite of reconciliation of those who had been excommunicated and, as such, the condition in effect for their admission to communion, the practice of frequent confession, of confessions of devotion, which began to be introduced into the Church at an early date under the influence of monasticism, ought logically to contribute to a consideration of this sacrament in itself and independently of the Eucharist.

In fact, it is exactly the opposite which has occurred. The distinction between confession of devotion and the sacrament of reconciliation of the excommunicated has become blurred in the minds of the faithful who in the end have come to regard themselves in practice as "excommunicated". Hence those Masses celebrated at which no one dares to communicate because they have not been to confession immediately beforehand.

Hence also in the minds of very many Christians, the idea of fulfilling the Easter precept is primarily one of going to confession.

This confession, moreover, is less and less regarded as a sacrament. The "confessional" is the last stage of an evolution which has succeeded in conferring on it a private character. The liturgy of the sacrament for this very reason has become increasingly rudimentary. A biologist would be tempted to say that nowadays it was scarcely more than a "vestigial organ". In the view of the ordinary Christian it is a question, fundamentally, of giving an exact account of all his sins to the priest. The insistence laid, even lately, on the integrity of the confession, is of particular significance in this respect. Hence, also, the importance attached increasingly to the freedom of choice of confessor by the penitent, a slender palliative to the repugnance that he can feel at undergoing this disagreeable formality. But all this contributes to making confession much more an interview with a priest, which can turn into direction of conscience, than a sacrament, that is, an encounter with God in the joy of redemption.

The last remaining memory of Christian feeling subsisting among dechristianized masses is the idea that a sacrament is a celebration. There is a celebration on the occasion of a marriage, a baptism. The one sacrament that seems to have lost this particular note is the sacrament of penance. Yet "there is more rejoicing in heaven over one sinner who repents...." The sacrament of penance, like the other sacraments, is a sacrament of redemption, an invention of the redemptive love of Christ. It seems that to bring back the general run of Christians to greater awareness of the reality of faith, the sacrament of penance must be restored, in one form or another, to its ecclesial and community dimensions. If, in considering our sins, we feel the need to invoke the intervention of the authorities of the Church, it is because we have become aware of everything that can have impaired our relationship with the Church at the same time as with God; in these conditions, the priest would not be regarded so much as the one who is charged with the resolution of cases of conscience but as the minister of a sacrament.

But to do that it would also be necessary to restore the whole penitential liturgy. Certain essays of this sort have been made. It may well be thought that the state of mind from which the liturgical renewal of our times derives, as it becomes increasingly more marked, will furnish a major contribution towards the creation of a climate of opinion that will bring about the disappearance of certain misconceptions and ensure a better understanding of the function of penance in Christian life. And it is possible that the reformed rite of penance, called for by the Second Vatican Council will reflect some of the *desiderata* mentioned above.

MARRIAGE

The same liturgical problem is raised by marriage and the need for liturgical renewal is felt also in this field.

That this is so illustrates obviously one of the characteristics of our times. In a civilization in which the frequency of divorce cases causes one to think of a real collapse of the family as an institution, where social customs evolve under the pressure of a world where the distribution of work between the sexes is very different from what it formerly was, it is hardly surprising that a vigorous and healthy reaction should provoke the formation of family movements, of communities of families and of a thorough re-examination of the whole concept of family spirituality. In this context, which is peculiar to our own period, must be situated the investigation into the pastoral problems of marriage.

Traditionally, the rites of marriage were so to say embedded in a whole context of customs and usages varying from one region to another wherein were mingled together the sacred and the profane. But all this social structure has today suddenly broken down. A great gap has appeared which requires to be filled at the very time when the problem of the family appears with a clarity and a gravity that are entirely new. Here, once more, the spirit of the liturgical renewal must normally find expression in parallel investigations and endeavours in the different countries. The United States, Belgium, Germany and Ireland have obtained approval for a new rite of marriage. Here again, it is when marriage is no longer considered solely as a contract between two individuals that the rite takes on its full meaning: it is a moment in the life of the whole parochial community and the nuptial Mass is therefore no longer a "private" Mass, but the community as a whole shares in it. A time will come no doubt when, as in the young communities of missionary countries, the succession of marriages, one after another in the same church throughout a whole morning, each with its "own" Mass, attended only by those who have come out of social habit or regard for the families who have "ordered" it, will be unknown.

CONCLUSION

If we attempt to state clearly the general characteristics of this liturgical renewal, as they are shown on the different occasions that we have just considered, one thing seems to emerge very clearly: this is the striking importance attached to the rôle of the community as a whole. In certain country parishes where there is only one Mass on Sundays the custom has been introduced of administering baptism in the presence of the congregation gathered for this Mass. The community character of the sacrament is brought out particularly at the Easter vigil and the catechumenate for adults will certainly take this into account: preparation for baptism in fact to be efficacious presupposes that the catechumen is in touch not only with the priest and godparents but also with the Christian community which is to receive him in its midst. The rite of the baptism of adults, indeed, makes provision for these three contingencies. The extent to which its real significance is realized will lead to proportionate emphasis being given to the different stages of the catechumenate, by the scrutinies required by the Ritual which will be carried out in the presence of the assembled community where the priest and godparents have both their own rôles to play.

This question of godparents and of entry into the community recurs in connection with confirmation. Here again the spirit of authenticity which is a characteristic of the liturgical renewal is in opposition to the unmeaning formality which consists in designating more or less arbitrarily a collective "godparent" for a whole number of candidates. If on principle the godparent at confirmation should be different from that of baptism, in accordance with a custom still mentioned expressly in canon law (can. 796, §1), there is some advantage in letting the child, who could not be consulted at the time of his baptism, freely ratify at this stage the choice then made in his name or, on the other hand, without of course ignoring the advice of his natural educators, in allowing him to choose another godparent in a position to help him more effectively. Ordinarily this problem should arouse the conscience of the Christian community as a whole in the case of children who cannot find in their own families that climate of faith which they need; in these very frequent cases it is through the child and on the occasion of his confirmation that the whole family should be taken into sponsorship by a member of the community who fully realizes his missionary rôle as a witness to the faith.

A similar problem occurs in connection with marriage. Allusion has already been made to the pre-marriage courses in which certain married couples are called on to give the benefit of their experience to the engaged couples. In certain cases, could not the official witness to a marriage act as a sort of godparent whose rôle might find expression in the rite of marriage? Those educators who are closely in touch with the psychological difficulties of the victims of marital or family instability in the modern world, are fully aware how important it is to show them, in their immediate surroundings, really successful marriages. Frequentation of a genuinely happy home can very often exert a decisive influence on the development of young couples in difficulties of one sort or another. We have here, indeed, an example of how older couples can assume some responsibility for younger ones—a state of affairs which should be regarded as quite normal and which, when it is done with the necessary tact and respect, should find its clear expression in the liturgical and pastoral renewal of the Church in our days. Here again, sponsorship by individuals is in direct relationship with the concern of the whole community for the special needs of each of its members.

The Sacerdotal Communities
of St. Séverin of Paris
and St. Joseph of Nice

CHAPTER X

LITURGICAL CHANGES IN THE ENGLISH-SPEAKING WORLD

THE UNITED STATES

In the United States, as presumably elsewhere, the reception of the Constitution on the Sacred Liturgy has varied from jubilation to grudging obedience. There is strong evidence that this diversity is closely related to two factors which have been operating on behalf of the liturgy in the country for some decades—where their influence has been welcomed there was a readiness for the Constitution; where this had not been the case the Council's decree fell on less fertile soil. These good works are the magazine *Worship,* originally *Orate Fratres,* and the Liturgical Conference, the outgrowth of the Benedictine Liturgical Conference. No attempt to speak of the implementation of the Council's action in behalf of the liturgy can fail to take these into consideration.

The periodical, since its first appearance on November 28th, 1926, has fulfilled the promise voiced by its first editor, Virgil Michel, O.S.B., of Saint John's Abbey, Collegeville, Minnesota, in that first issue, "Our general aim is to develop a better understanding of the spiritual import of the liturgy". As liturgical awareness has grown and needs have expanded the magazine has consistently shown itself to be strongly contemporary. Under its present editor, Godfrey Diekmann, O.S.B., it has been for years an example of that constant reformation to which all in the Church are called.

The main preoccupation of the Liturgical Conference for the past quarter century has been the sponsorship of yearly Liturgical Weeks, national meetings in various cathedral cities which have provided education and liturgical experience to thousands upon thousands. In recent years the Conference has expanded its service extensively. Since the establishment of a national office in Washington in January 1960 with Mr John B. Mannion as Executive Secretary, in addition to the ever more demanding work connected with the Liturgical Weeks, the Conference has been able to fill other needs. Its most significant undertaking since the Constitution has been the inauguration of the Parish Worship Programme. The purpose of this project has been described by Fr Frederick R. McManus as "the fulfilment, without delay or hesitation, of the great Council's commitment to a sincere and living worship of the Father in heaven. It attempts to translate into the practical situations of parish life what the council has taught with force and eloquence." To date, two sections of the programme have been completed and include the following titles: *Priest's Guide to Parish Worship, Training Program for Commentators and Lectors, The Bible Service, What is the Liturgical Renewal? Preaching the Liturgical Renewal, Leaflet Lessons in the Liturgy, Manual for Church Musicians, Programs for Lay Education.*

At the annual meeting of the American hierarchy in November 1958, there was established the Bishops' Commission on the Liturgical Apostolate. In 1965 the secretariat of the commission opened an office in Washington under the direction of Fr Frederick R. McManus of the Catholic University as Executive Secretary.

On April 2nd, 1964, the Bishops' Commission issued a decree on the use of English in the liturgy. This became effective on November 29th, the first Sunday in Advent. It provides for the use of English for the entire Divine Office under the conditions specified in the Constitution and for the entire rite of the sacraments other than the Eucharist, including their essential forms, and the sacramentals. In the celebration of Mass English was authorized for the lessons, the prayer of the faithful, the ordinary and proper parts which belong to the people. The decree also provides for the proclamation of the lessons facing the people and for the use of English in chants between the lessons, at the introit, offertory and communion provided such pieces are appropriate to these respective parts of the Mass.

Since the proclamation of the Constitution the majority of bishops have appointed diocesan liturgical commissions to promote the aims of the Council relative to liturgical education and celebration. Several of the diocesan commissions have issued directories among which the most extensive is that of the archdiocese of Chicago. These commissions have been involved to a great extent with acquainting the clergy, religious and faithful with the pertinent provisions of the Instruction of September 26th, 1964, implementing the Constitution which went into effect March 7th, 1965, the first Sunday in Lent.

To aid those appointed to responsibility on diocesan commissions, at the invitation of Bishop Charles Helmsing the Liturgical Conference sponsored a programme in Kansas City, April 27-30th, 1964. At the conclusion of the meeting a draft of observations was adopted by the general body which were forwarded to the bishops of the country. These included the necessity of close co-operation between diocesan liturgical commissions and those in charge of art, music, architecture and ecclesiastical building as well as with the school department and the Confraternity of Christian Doctrine office. The resolutions detailed the need of educational programmes for all, the advisability of specialized training for some in each diocese, and need for the incorporation of the theology of the Constitution into all retreats and missions for clergy, religious and laity. They also called for the appointment on a national level of an advisory committee of experts on all pertinent matters, the use of the Liturgical Conference and other competent agencies in the preparation of materials to assist in the implementation of the Constitution and the establishment of a national Institute of higher studies in pastoral liturgy. Lastly, a plea in favour of fuller use of the vernacular was included. This is quoted later in this paper.

In June 1964 the Bishops' Commission sponsored a three-day meeting for representatives of the country's major seminaries at St John Seminary, Detroit. Archbishop John Deardon was host and chairman of the meeting, the purpose of which was the exploration of the implementation of the Constitution in seminaries as ordered by the Council. At this meeting a committee was formed to arrange an institute for seminary professors of liturgy; one such was held in St Louis, August 28th-31st. The discussions centred round the following points: a syllabus for seminary liturgy courses, the basic themes of liturgical theology and liturgical celebrations in the seminary. Over one hundred seminary rectors and professors attended and it was their unanimous opinion that the institute should continue in the future.

The Liturgical Week of 1964, the twenty-fifth of the series, was held in St Louis. Its theme was "The Challenge of the Council: Person, Parish, World". The vernacular was employed in the daily community Masses, to the extent permitted by the legislation which was to become universal in Advent. It is estimated that the number of persons who attended one or more sessions was over twenty thousand. This gathering has been described as "*the* great Catholic meeting of the United States". One hundred and eighty representatives of other faiths registered and there is evidence that there were many others who attended. In the main the form taken by the meeting was that of its predecessors and included a special theological programme at which Dr Arthur Piepkorn of the Lutheran Concordia Theological Seminary delivered a paper entitled "The Eucharist and its Ecumenical Dimensions". As in the past there were in addition to the general sessions, specialized meetings dealing with all areas of liturgical interest.

In various cities throughout the country since the Constitution regional Liturgical Days have been held. These have been modelled on the National Liturgical Weeks.

On February 23rd-25th at Cleveland the Liturgical Conference sponsored a workshop to which were invited architects, those concerned with the construction of churches, artists and members of diocesan liturgical commissions. About six hundred availed themselves of this opportunity to learn and discuss the implications of the Constitution pertinent to their responsibilities in the renewal.

In answer to the call of the Council, diocesan conferences for the clergy have been held throughout the country. In addition, institutes for teachers and religious have been inaugurated. In some cases these have consisted of a day or two of concentrated study but in others regular courses meet weekly over a period of several months.

At least one bishop, Cardinal Cushing of Boston, has issued a pastoral letter to encourage implementation of the action of the Council.

With the information available at present, it is impossible to present any comprehensive evaluation of reaction to the *Constitution* among our people. There are, however, certain indications of opinion, reflected in the press, secular and religious, which point to several general trends. The action of the Council has been received with enthusiasm by those already liturgically formed. They have seen the document as a point of no return on the way to a more deeply understood, sincerely celebrated and more fruitful worship. Understandably, these are in the minority. For the rest, reaction must be measured by their degree of acceptance of the celebration of those liturgical actions in which they have had experience. These are mainly the sacraments and, first of all, the Eucharist. Since the most striking change has been the introduction of the vernacular, this is the more common aspect for comment rather than the other changes in the rites. The only exception to this is the practice of celebrating Mass facing the people. For although this is not strictly an innovation in the Roman rite, it has become far commoner in conjunction with the reforms of the Council. There is some strong resistance in this matter but it does not seem to characterize most of our people. Both clergy and laity in general have found in this type of eucharistic celebration an obvious sign of the nature of the Mass as a family banquet and have experienced a more intense sharing in common worship than ever before. The generally favourable clerical response came as a surprise to some but the evident pastoral good involved has triumphed over even strong reluctance.

The complaint most commonly heard has to do with the constant change from Latin to vernacular and *vice versa*. The principle on which decisions were reached in this area —that presidential prayers and their introductions remain in Latin—is unknown to most of the faithful who view the changes back and forth as confusing and pointless. Even those to whom the matter has been explained are slow to accept it with enthusiasm. The very least for which the majority hope in the near future is the use of the vernacular for the collect, the prayer over the gifts and the postcommunion prayer. But most will not be satisfied with this and express themselves as desirous of having in their own language all those parts which are said aloud and to which the congregation responds. There does seem to be a growing conviction that the full potential of the rite's meaning will not be attainable until there is an entirely vernacular celebration as in the other sacraments. Among those priests who have rejoiced in the vernacular, that is, the greater part, there is great disappointment in its denial on those occasions when circumstances necessitate celebration with only a server.

In this connection it is interesting to note one of the recommendations made by the body attending the meeting for diocesan liturgical commissions held in Kansas City: "To help us achieve an intelligent and unified worship throughout the Mass, and to express more fully the proclamation of our Lord's saving death and resurrection, it is the hope of the commission members that the American bishops will in due time seek the use of the English language for the complete Mass." In this and other matters regarding the rite of Mass there is considerable dissatisfaction with the principle of gradualism.

There is deep concern among knowledgeable people, both lay and clerical, that education in the reform of the liturgy should not be neglected, especially on the parochial level. It is felt that explanation of the meaning of the changes and the theological basis of the renewal have often been far behind the obedient adoption of the actual changes in the manner of celebration.

J. Richard Quinn

OTHER COUNTRIES

Though a committee of bishops from the various English-speaking countries was formed in Rome during October 1963 for the purpose of making plans for a uniform translation of Mass texts acceptable to all, the intrinsic difficulties of this task are so great that no definite outcome can be expected for a long time. In consequence, each hierarchy has adopted for the time being a different version of the ordinary of the Mass. There has been some borrowing as regards the proper of the Mass and the Ritual for the Sacraments.

It is a sad fact that in most English-speaking countries the liturgical movement has made far less progress than in Europe. Until the second session of the Council it was still regarded with suspicion by authorities, and thought to be but a passing fad of a minority of enthusiasts, rather than "a providential disposition of God for the present time" and "movement of the Holy Ghost in the Church", as Pius XII declared it to be after the Assisi Congress in 1956. Hence the English-speaking countries have been less well prepared for liturgical changes than have others, and bishops returning from the Council in 1963 had a difficult situation to face when planning to put the liturgical Constitution into effect.

Press reports have tended to concentrate upon one point above all, namely, the introduction of English into the liturgy. If the following paragraphs appear to deal too exclusively with this matter, the explanation is that the press has given little or no information about other things which, in themselves, are really more important and fundamental. Such are the appointment of national and diocesan commissions for liturgy and for sacred music and art, the foundation of institutes of pastoral liturgy, steps taken for the training of liturgy professors in seminaries, the reform of the curricula of the seminaries, and the provision for the liturgical enlightenment of "those already working in the Lord's vineyard". If anything has, in fact, been done about all these things, one cannot learn much about them from the English Catholic press. That is why they are barely mentioned here.

Of the countries to be reviewed Australia comes first alphabetically and also in the extent of its progress. The Australian bishops, even before they left Rome in December 1963, had decided to approve the Collegeville Breviary translation, and were giving individual permissions for its use as early as February 1964. Immediately, also, they appointed a National Liturgical Commission which, under the inspiring leadership of Archbishop Guilford Young of Hobart, Tasmania, set to work on a version of the ordinary of the Mass. The bishops met in Sydney on March 3rd, 1964, to examine this and to hear proposals from the Commission, about implementing the liturgical Constitution; within three days they had sent their proposals to Rome for confirmation. After two months of waiting they received approval both of their *acta* and of their texts, and they met again in June to plan details.

By that time the bishops had gleaned far more information about which points of Mass-reform Rome was likely to grant if asked. They decided, therefore, to draw up a new set of *acta* which went far beyond their previous proposals. They asked for the elimination of Psalm 42 and of the Last Gospel, for the Secret, the doxology at the end of the Canon and the embolism to be said or sung aloud, and for the use of English in everything which the people were to say or sing, as also for everything they would hear except the Preface and doxology. By the end of that same month they had obtained all the needed permissions from Rome, and, with astonishing speed and efficiency, they promulgated their decree, printed and distributed their texts and briefed their clergy. It was left to each bishop to decide the date on which these changes would take effect in his diocese; some of them had already done so by the middle of July.

Then an event occurred which caused a sensation. Cardinal Gilroy received a last-minute request, signed by a secretary of the Congregation of Rites, that the permissions granted should not be put into effect until the publication of an Instruction even then being planned in Rome. So in Sydney and some of the dioceses all the orders that had been given were reversed; priests and people, to their confusion and dismay, were told to resume the use of Psalm 42, the

Last Gospel, the inaudible Secret and embolism and even, it seems, the Latin language. But other bishops decided that this Roman intervention had come too late. The disturbance and bewilderment which would be caused by a reversal of policy would, they felt, do more harm than a temporary lack of uniformity, and that it would be better to let things take their course. When the Instruction did at last come out (on September 26th.) those dioceses which had suffered the shock of a reversed policy came, of course, into line with the rest.

There are a few small local differences of application; but in general one may say that the Australians have carried through with admirable success the most advanced liturgical reform to be found in the entire English-speaking world. They have even begun sung Masses in English, using adaptations of Gregorian chant prepared by experts and approved by the bishops. They are preparing their own Ritual, and meanwhile are using the one from the United States.

Canada also came into action at once. On February 19th the hierarchy announced that "having consulted with authorities in Rome since the *motu proprio* was issued", they would introduce vernacular epistles and gospels into the Mass by March 7th, 1964, and also vernacular versions of the ordinary for which they had Roman approval. The proper would have to wait until altar Missals were printed, but these were expected (and were in fact taken into use) by the end of the year. The Canadian plan was almost the same as that of the Australians though, at this early date, they had not asked for vernacular Secret and embolism. They introduced these and all other changes indicated in the Instruction of September 26th as soon as the altar Missals were ready. They approved the Collegeville Breviary and the American Ritual; they granted Communion under both kinds to the bridal couple at nuptial Masses.

The bishops of the Caribbean Islands have several languages to deal with, but one of them is English. They, too, began without any delay and had sent their *acta* to Rome before Christmas of 1963. The *motu proprio* of January 25th, 1964, had, of course, not been issued and so no texts were sent with the *acta*. In April, Rome answered the Caribbean bishops asking for their texts. These were duly sent, together with further *acta* which contained requests for audible Secret, doxology and embolism, omission of Psalm 42 and the Last Gospel, and almost as much vernacular as in the Australian plan. They had to wait until October 1964 (after the Instruction) before they could carry out all that they had desired. From the very beginning, however, they had approved the Collegeville Breviary and both the American and the English Rituals.

In England nothing happened until February 1964, when the bishops issued a statement that they had met to consider liturgical changes, that no details could be made known, and that they were awaiting an Instruction from Rome. In Low Week the bishops met again and issued another statement which, in effect, was a repetition of what they said in February; they added a caution that no changes were to be made at present. In June they announced that Rome had confirmed their *acta* and their text of the ordinary which would be published shortly. (This was not the work of the literary committee set up later to translate the propers.) This ordinary, together with English Epistles and Gospels, was introduced on November 29th, 1964. When published the ordinary had Greek Kyrie, Latin *Sanctus, Pater, Agnus,* dismissal and blessing. Until a definitive version of the proper had been prepared, only the Epistles and Gospels were to be in English. The Collegeville Breviary and the English "Small Ritual" were approved for use.

On October 20th, 1964, the bishops issued fresh decrees which added to their previous decisions those ritual changes ordered by the Instruction of the Congregation of Rites of September 26th. And they would now permit the Lord's Prayer to be in English.

This plan went into effect on November 29th and was received by clergy and laity with general approval. But a great many criticisms were voiced concerning the official version of the ordinary and the frequent changes from one language to another in the course of the Mass. In January 1965 the hierarchy instructed their priests to find out what their people thought of the liturgical changes, and to submit reports. These were considered at a hierarchy meeting on February 3rd, 1965; afterwards it was announced that the bishops had decided to send to Rome for approval certain existing missals, so that the translations of the proper given in these might be used *ad interim* until the literary committee had worked out a final version.

Of New Zealand nothing was reported in the Catholic press except that they were using English in the Mass by August 16th, 1964.

Of India it is known that the *acta* and translations submitted by the bishops had been confirmed by July; and that all parts of the Mass which are audible will be in English excepting those of the great eucharistic prayer. No general date was settled for the implementation of the decrees; each bishop was to introduce the changes when he thought fit. English was to be used in low Mass only.

Of Ireland too there is little news available. In October 1964 the bishops announced that they had sent their *acta* and translations to Rome and were awaiting their confirmation. By January 1965 the confirmation must have been given, since booklets containing the texts for the ordinary were then being printed. The epistles and gospels are in English (or in Irish in certain parts of the country), but no other parts of the proper were in the vernacular by March 7th (when changes took place). The Irish have their own trilingual Ritual already; presumably those parts of it which hitherto have remained in Latin will be translated.

Scotland was unusually well prepared for the changes introduced on March 7th. The Scottish hierarchy met in

December 1963 and decided to have in English everything that the people say or hear excepting only the great eucharistic prayer. They appointed a liturgical commission of bishops, priests and laity to work out a version of the ordinary of the Mass. They decided on the O'Connell-Finberg version of the proper and placed orders for the printing of altar missals. By the autumn of 1964 a syllabus of sermons for priests to deliver to their people had been prepared, and conferences were held for clergy in several dioceses. At these the clergy heard lectures by liturgical experts and then took part in a Mass according to the "new rite", celebrated facing the people by the bishop. Exactly the same thing was done for selected laity—parties sent from each parish to take part in the "experimental Mass". Similar conferences were held also for teachers associations of some larger cities.

By this means public opinion was effectively mobilized in favour of the changes; for there returned to the parishes from these conferences many priests and laity who felt that they were "in the know", had been consulted, and were eager to spread enthusiasm among others. For, after all these experimental Masses, opinions were solicited concerning intelligibility, euphony and rhythm of the ordinary proposed for use; suggestions were considered by the liturgical commission and a number of improvements were made in the text. The next stage in the preparations was the organization of similar days (lectures with experimental Mass) in each of the deaneries, for crowds of several hundred people at a time.

In this way a spirit of enthusiasm and of widespread expectancy was created; clergy and people looked forward eagerly to the introduction of the changes, and at its inception the new rite was accounted a triumphant success. Everything specified in the Instruction of September 26th is, of course, included in the Scottish "form" which is to have, in addition, the restored Prayer of the Faithful.

Finally, a few words concerning South Africa. The bishops met in January of 1964 soon after returning from the Council, and sent their *acta* together with the St Andrew Bible Missal to Rome for approval. After receiving confirmation, they introduced English Epistles and Gospels in July, and authorized experiments in various places with newly devised versions of the ordinary. They set up a liturgical Commission to supervise these, to organize local conferences for clergy and people, to collate the results of inquiries and decide on a final version for the ordinary. The amount of English to be used is the same as that decided on by the Australians and Canadians—that is, everything possible. Each bishop is free to advance from one stage to another as and when he thinks fit; nearly every diocese had everything that was permissible by early September. The ritual changes ordered by the Instruction of September 26th have since been introduced, and work is being done on a version for the proper destined ultimately to replace that of the Bible Missal which is regarded as a temporary expedient. South African bishops have given Communion under both kinds to nuns on profession days and to the bridal couples at nuptial Masses. They have approved the Collegeville Breviary and are using the American Ritual.

With the encouragement of the Consilium for the implementation of the Liturgical Constitution of the Second Vatican Council international committees are now at work on providing uniform liturgical texts for all the major languages. The committee for the English-speaking world has already agreed on principles of translation and have produced two versions of the order of Mass which have been given wide circulation in all the countries concerned; comments and criticisms have been invited. Meanwhile as a temporary measure an agreed common version for the British Isles will be in use by the end of 1966.

Clifford Howell, S.J.

CHAPTER XI

THE FUTURE OF THE
LITURGICAL MOVEMENT

If it is forbidden to envisage a religious syncretism at the doctrinal level, is it allowed to envisage a liturgical syncretism? At a period of extreme political and administrative centralization like our own, in which the phenomenon of acculturation is no less manifest, is a universal liturgy out of the question— a liturgy which would be the reduction to a common denominator and to the best of their elements of the principal Christian liturgies in existence? Can we dream of such a universal liturgy which would be adapted and presented to each human group in accordance with its cultural differences, in its own language, with those elements common to all in one language, Latin the language of the Roman Church, Greek or Hebrew as languages of the Revelation, Aramaic as our Lord's own language?

Such a dream, which some will not fail to find utopian, could not in any case be realized by a team of scholars, specialists in the ancient and modern history of the liturgy, nor by a central administrative body, even if it were composed of the various qualified representatives of all the Churches of the East and West. These artificial methods of work have never, in the whole history of Christian worship, furnished anything but mediocre and somewhat negative results, to the detriment of a natural development as diversified as the beliefs which have been its cause.

And so we believe that in this natural movement of religious evolution, and so far as we can dare to foretell the future, the liturgical movement will go forward in a twofold direction, at once divergent and complementary, despite the inherent contradiction in this statement.

It will go forward in the direction of a certain freedom which, there is no denying it and whatever certain grumbling critics may think, is one of the fundamental advances of our times. And so the liturgical movement must lead to the evolution of greatly diversified forms following the various countries and human groups, since to express its faith and worship religious inspiration must draw even on popular folklore and, of course, on the different cultures.

On the other hand, in the context of an ever more rapid internationalization, this faith and worship, while respecting legitimate local forms of expression, must come to common expressions which will not be a synthesis of local forms. Culture has never been a collection of local folklores cunningly put together by certain talented persons for whom the whole is formed by a simple addition of the parts. In the same way, a universal expression of divine worship can very well be based on a vital sense of tradition—and this has nothing to do with an archeological inventory of the same tradition. No more than religious thought can develop on the basis of Denzinger's *Enchiridion*, the universal liturgy of the future Church will not be built up on the basis of a synthesis of the liturgical renewal even extended to the whole Church.

In the establishment of this liturgy the principal rôle will obviously fall to the Roman Church, considered not only as the mistress of all other Churches, but as developing within herself as a local Church (the diocese of Rome) forms of worship suitable as formerly (for example, the Roman liturgy of the fourth century) to be adopted into the framework of a genuinely Catholic liturgy. But history has witnessed more than one example of a local liturgy, one, so to say, without authority at the beginning, spreading to the whole of the Church, or to a large part of the Church. Not to mention the apostolic Churches of the East, even in the West there are examples of liturgies which have not only preserved their local customs but have passed them on to other communities.

It seems likely that the future will respect and develop this beneficial ecclesial tradition. In a legitimate diversification of liturgies (it is obvious that at the present time the dispute over the Chinese rites would be unthinkable) the liturgy of the Church will be the realization, under the authority of Rome, of a harmonized synthesis of what "the Spirit will say to the Churches".

Outstanding in the liturgical Constitution of the Second Vatican Council are the provisions for the adaptation of the liturgy to different peoples and cultures. The relevant paragraphs, some of which have already been mentioned, dealing with the use of the vernacular and the reform of the liturgical books, carry the proposed adaptation to a certain stage, but it is paragraph 40 under the general heading of "Principles for the adaptation of the liturgy to the culture and tradition of nations" which is particularly to the point in this connection: "In certain places and circumstances, however, an even more radical adaptation of the liturgy is needed." It does not disguise the difficulties facing such an endeavour and, consequently, lays down careful rules to be followed and allows experiments to be undertaken for a limited period of time among groups specially suited for the purpose.

EASTERN RITES

In the ecumenical sphere and following the general lines of the movement, the attention given to non-Latin Christian Churches is an important factor of the liturgical renewal. This has already been mentioned in Part II of this book. To the extent that ecumenism consists, for all Churches, in the rediscovery of a certain Christian authenticity, the liturgy, which is a privileged means for this return to authenticity, must itself be inspired by it.

Here we may mention more particularly the family of Eastern Churches in the Near and Middle East in communion with Rome. These Churches, which have their own liturgical and national languages and employ living languages in their eucharistic celebrations, use French as their principal cultural language. Since all the seminaries in the Middle East for the past two generations or more have been under the direction of French religious, the principal review concerning these communities (*Proche-Orient Chrétien*) is published by the White Fathers of St Anne's seminary in Jerusalem, that concerning more especially the Churches of Syrian (liturgical) language (*L'Orient Syrien*) is published in Paris and, a fact of particular significance, the first Byzantine "Missal" for the use of the faithful, which was recently published at Alexandria, was in French; an Arabic translation appeared afterwards.

None of the foregoing affects the fact that these various communities really belong, at the cultural and ethnical levels, to the world in which they live, in which they seek not only not to be submerged but to contribute to its opening to the rest of mankind. On the other hand, sufficient advantage has not been taken of the phenomenon of acculturation, which is being emphasized here. This applies to both sides, to the East and the West; it could lead to a better communion between the Churches and more fruitful mutual aid in what concerns us here, that is, the liturgical field. If we are no longer in that period when Eastern liturgies, celebrated on the occasion of the weeks of prayer for Christian unity, provided an attractive and perhaps somewhat exotic spectacle for some of the faithful of the Roman rite, it does not appear that serious consideration has been given to the liturgical traditions of the East, despite the efforts of the White Fathers at St Anne's or the Benedictines of Amay-Chevetogne. These traditions, in fact, have made little progress among the liturgists of the present period. What the Eastern Churches desire is no longer to be regarded as if they were, so to say, dependents on the "Colonial Office" but to be treated as if they were fully allied States. It is certainly to be hoped that the tradition on this point represented by Dom Guéranger (see chapter I, footnote 2, p. 20) will no longer prevail anywhere and that comparative liturgy, as revived scientifically by Baumstark, will gain a large following.

Fr Bouyer deplores the practical non-existence of canonical study of the liturgy. He does so very rightly on the basis of the theological content, the spiritual structure and the pastoral setting of the liturgy. There are, he says, a number of rubrical commentaries on the liturgy, but these, however useful they may be,

> bear about the same relation to a canonical study of the liturgy that cook-books bear to a treatise on the chemistry of food. Indeed, cook-books have a great advantage over handbooks of ceremonies—when you have some practical experience in cooking and follow their advice quite blindly, you can produce very good dishes even though you do not know why; but blindly following handbooks of ceremonies—because of their purely logical and superficial way of solving questions—will give you only a worship which is apparently correct but may be intrinsically dead.[1]

Here may be added a complementary desideratum in connection with the elaboration of this canonical study of the liturgy that is necessary. For the universal Church it could only be the fruit, at the starting-point, of a systematic comparison extended to all the traditions of worship in existence in the Church and of methodical examination of the concept of the sacred and the constants of the religious mind, both individual and communal.

Secondly, without taking into account questions of law, missionaries have reached the conclusion that knowledge of rites different from those of the Latin Church could be of great use for those among them who intend to establish the Church in places that have not yet, or only partially, been evangelized. They have even come to advocate the adoption of this or that oriental rite in a region where it has already been in use for a long time (as in India) or its extension to another region which by political circumstances is placed in, or has returned to,

---

[1] Bouyer, *op. cit.*, p. 280.

a cultural sphere also endowed with one or several rites (the case of North Africa in relationship with the Arab world as a whole is relevant here). The variation in political conditions, on the one hand, and the variety of rites, which entails disadvantages, on the other, calls for very great circumspection in this field.

Nevertheless, there can only be praise and gratitude for all those, priests, isolated religious or entire religious communities, who, according to local circumstances, have adopted a rite different from their own. This attitude is an undeniable manifestation of a genuinely spiritual and ecclesial point of view. The Christian East has nothing analogous, or so little to propose, in answer to the Western Church that can prove so living and valuable, except for the fact that the Eastern tradition accommodates itself more easily than does the Latin tradition to the countries to which it spreads, and thus, after all, can offer comparison with the principle which appears to inspire the passage of a Latin to an Eastern rite—that is, to pray in the language and rites of the communities among whom we are or, in the absence of these rites, with those of the communities nearest to them.

In any case, great caution is needed here; the natural play of sympathies and affinities must be given free rein and a watchful eye must be kept on the evolution of peoples and societies as we look towards a future which depends on the Church, to the extent that we believe that she alone is capable of building up on the ruins of present nationalisms and imperialisms a new civilization for a humanity reconciled together at last.

THE PROBLEM OF AFRICANIZATION

The problem of adaptation occurs particularly, as we have seen, in missionary countries, and it is in these that the radical adaptation foreseen by the liturgical Constitution will probably take place. In this connection, a report drawn up by Dom Thierry Maertens, a few years before the Council met, is relevant here. He was describing a journey of liturgical research undertaken in Africa. He writes:

> The problem of Africanization of the liturgy is certainly one of those which gives most concern to the Church in Africa, particularly to the African priests. It is a delicate problem and presupposes that those who study it have an accurate idea of what is God's part and what is man's in the liturgy. Everywhere I held study sessions or lectures I was concerned, in order to determine the limits of Africanization, to distinguish between the *biblical* rites, giving expression to God's primordial and untouchable plan, and the *cultural* or *catechetical* elements which constitute the setting for the former. The liturgy is primarily a supernatural work whose expression must be sought in the will of God as it is principally to be found in Scripture. This supernatural work encounters and transforms a human psychology; it is therefore only normal that this supernatural psychology should also find its expression in the liturgy. From this twofold form of expression—supernatural and human— in the liturgy springs a pastoral method which is in a state of continual tension between two poles and the balance is not always easy to achieve. Before the more recent Roman directives Europe experienced certain tendencies which emphasized the supernatural, even to the point of neglecting the pastoral side, and also tendencies urging a form of adaptation in which man and his complexes became the final criterion of liturgical symbolism. The same tension occurs in Africa and I have often been tempted to label some experiment that I have encountered as being excessively human or excessively supernatural. On occasion Africanization runs the risk of falling into the former category. It is important then for agreement to be reached on the limits of Africanization.
>
> In the first place, a clear distinction must be made between work of liturgical Africanization and the present national movements. Both are good and praiseworthy and it is quite right that Christians and their priests should be simultaneously concerned about both problems. But it is not suitable that the liturgical problem should be presented in the nationalist context. Africanization is a cause with arguments at its disposal which are far more theological and ecclesial. In all truth I feel

bound to say how greatly I was impressed by the excellent judgment of the African clergy in this matter.

Then, Africanization is not, and cannot be merely a question of ritual. It is no part of the Church's mission to save customary rites from disappearance, as if her liturgy were a museum full of fine pieces. An African rite can have a chance of incorporation only to the extent that it remains expressive of a living community that can be supernaturalized. Now in many regions several rites have been carefully recorded by ethnologists that are gradually disappearing under the influence of Europeanization and modernization, especially in the cities which will control the form taken by the future face of Africa.

At the present time there is a considerable urge towards "negritude". It should be encouraged and fostered. But it will encounter such difficulties in the Europeanized centres that the Church can only commit herself to this trend with infinite prudence. She will probably limit, for the time being at any rate, the possibilities of Africanization to paraliturgical ceremonies.

Lastly, Africanization will demand the undertaking of numerous works of research and important pastoral experiments. A too enthusiastic approach might lead to it being thought that the whole of the liturgical renewal in Africa consisted in this work. It would be a grievous error excessively to "humanize" the work of Christ. It is desirable, therefore, that those who are concerned with the Africanization of rites should also be those who develop the biblical catechesis of these same rites, thus "initiating" the African to liturgical life at the same time as they "adapt" certain elements of the liturgy to the African religious mind. Priests trained in this twofold task will be really able to do useful work in pastoral liturgy. . . .

The whole of this report is worthy of quotation and particularly the part which follows on the possibilities in the way of Africanization together with what is said, in speaking of general principles, of everything concerning the community work of liturgy in Negro Africa, the importance of the proclamation of the Word of God within the act of worship and finally the special possibilities that seem to be offered to the

African Church in the matter of singing, following the special gifts of their peoples.

SOUTH AMERICA

It is also important to point out what is being done in one part of the Church where the ecumenical problem crops up in terms different from Europe and where missionary needs are felt as acutely, and sometimes more acutely, than in missionary countries in the proper sense of the term. The importance of Latin America, in the eyes of the universal Church and in a general view of the present evolution of the world, hardly requires emphasis.

In a paper read at the Nijmegen missionary conference in 1955, Mgr Larrain, bishop of Talca in Chile, speaking on the urgency for liturgical renewal in Latin America, examined the situation there in some detail. His conclusion was that for the faith to be revitalized there the missionary must be prepared to face widespread religious ignorance, lack of understanding of the Church and an alarming shortage of priests. The source of these troubles, he considered, might well lie in not having given sufficient emphasis to liturgical life among Latin Americans.

It was Geoffrey Kurth who said fifty years ago that the liturgy lived is a solution to the social problems of men. In it we find the organic and vital sense of the collective. In it we come to understand the meaning of *social* when we say "we" and not "me". In it and by it we enter into communion with our brothers in Jesus Christ. In it we overcome the individualistic view of human affairs in favour of the value of the social outlook. But if such values are to be inculcated in Latin America then we must have a liturgical renewal. The liturgy, without losing any of its traditional richness where our own lives and the history of the Church express themselves, must be adapted to our contemporary lives.[2]

Mgr Larrain called for a threefold adaptation, and in doing

[2] Johannes Hofinger, S.J. (Editor), *Liturgy and the Missions* (London and New York, 1960), pp. 93–5.

so anticipated the liturgical Constitution. In the first place the liturgy must be adapted to the present historical situation. If the Christian tradition of the Middle Ages, especially in what concerns active participation in liturgical life, poses a problem for Latin America whose culture stems from Western civilization, how much greater is the problem in Asia and Africa where no such Western tradition has influenced the native cultures. How impersonal and remote must liturgy be that is unadapted to such peoples. Secondly, there must be psychological adaptation, adaptation, that is, to the mentality of the people. And lastly there must be adaptation of language. Mgr Larrain called for a far greater use of the vernacular. Despite its name, in Latin America there is unfortunately no Latin tradition. . . . Latin is taught only in the seminaries. Even the cultured classes, to say nothing of the average people, know nothing of Latin as a language. Such adaptation, Mgr Larrain concluded, "will contribute much to the missionary's work of evangelization, and restore to the Catholic faith in Latin America the vitality and dynamism it needs".

The Sacerdotal Communities
of St. Séverin of Paris
and St. Joseph of Nice

PART IV

FUNDAMENTAL DOCUMENTS
OF THE LITURGICAL RENEWAL

THE CONSTITUTION
ON THE SACRED LITURGY

INTRODUCTION

1. This sacred Council has several aims in view: it desires to impart an ever increasing vigour to the Christian life of the faithful; to adapt more suitably to the needs of our own times those institutions which are subject to change; to foster whatever can promote union among all who believe in Christ; to strengthen whatever can help to call the whole of mankind into the household of the Church. The Council therefore sees particularly cogent reasons for undertaking the reform and promotion of the liturgy.

2. For the liturgy, "through which the work of our redemption is accomplished",[1] most of all in the divine sacrifice of the Eucharist, is the outstanding means whereby the faithful may express in their lives, and manifest to others, the mystery of Christ and the real nature of the true Church. It is of the essence of the Church that she be both human and divine, visible and yet invisibly equipped, eager to act and yet intent on contemplation, present in this world and yet not at home in it; and she is all these things in such wise that in her the human is directed and subordinated to the

---

[1] Secret of the ninth Sunday after Pentecost.

divine, the visible likewise to the invisible, action to contemplation, and this present world to that city yet to come, which we seek.[2] While the liturgy daily builds up those who are within into a holy temple of the Lord, into a dwelling place for God in the Spirit,[3] to the mature measure of the fullness of Christ,[4] at the same time it marvellously strengthens their power to preach Christ, and thus shows forth the Church to those who are outside as a sign lifted up among the nations[5] under which the scattered children of God may be gathered together[6] until there is one sheepfold and one shepherd.[7]

3. Wherefore the sacred Council judges that the following principles concerning the promotion and reform of the liturgy should be called to mind, and that practical norms should be established.

Among these principles and norms there are some which can and should be applied both to the Roman rite and also to all the other rites. The practical norms which follow, however, should be taken as applying only to the Roman rite, except for those which, in the very nature of things, affect other rites as well.

4. Lastly, in faithful obedience to tradition, the sacred Council declares that holy Mother Church holds all lawfully acknowledged rites to be of equal right and dignity; that she wishes to preserve them in the future and to foster them in every way. The Council also desires that, where necessary, the rites be revised carefully in the light of sound tradition, and that they be given new vigour to meet the circumstances and needs of modern times.

[2] Cf. Heb. 13. 14.
[3] Cf. Eph. 2. 21-22.
[4] Cf. Eph. 4. 13.
[5] Cf. Isa. 11. 12.
[6] Cf. John 11. 52.
[7] Cf. John 10. 16.

CHAPTER I: GENERAL PRINCIPLES FOR THE RESTORATION AND PROMOTION OF THE SACRED LITURGY

I. The nature of the sacred liturgy and its importance in the church's life

5. God who "wills that all men be saved and come to the knowledge of the truth" (1 Tim. 2. 4), "who in many and various ways spoke in times past to the fathers by the prophets" (Heb. 1. 1), when the fullness of time had come sent his Son, the Word made flesh, anointed by the Holy Spirit, to preach the gospel to the poor, to heal the contrite of heart,[8] to be a "bodily and spiritual medicine",[9] the Mediator between God and man.[10] For his humanity, united with the person of the Word, was the instrument of our salvation. Therefore in Christ "the perfect achievement of our reconciliation came forth, and the fullness of divine worship was given to us".[11]

The wonderful works of God among the people of the Old Testament were but a prelude to the work of Christ the Lord in redeeming mankind and giving perfect glory to God. He achieved his task principally by the paschal mystery of his blessed passion, resurrection from the dead, and glorious ascension, whereby "dying, he destroyed our death and, rising, he restored our life".[12] For it was from the side of Christ as he slept the sleep of death upon the cross that there came forth "the wondrous sacrament of the whole Church".[13]

[8] Cf. Isa. 61. 1; Luke 4. 18
[9] St Ignatius of Antioch; *To the Ephesians*, 7. 2.
[10] Cf. 1 Tim. 2. 5
[11] *Sacramentarium Veronese* (ed. C. Mohlberg), n. 1265; cf. also n. 1241, 1248.
[12] Easter Preface of the Roman Missal.
[13] Cf. Prayer before the second lesson for Holy Saturday, as it was in the Roman Missal before the restoration of Holy Week.

6. Just as Christ was sent by the Father, so also he sent the apostles, filled with the Holy Spirit. This he did that, by preaching the gospel to every creature,[14] they might proclaim that the Son of God, by his death and resurrection, had freed us from the power of Satan[15] and from death, and brought us into the kingdom of his Father. His purpose also was that they might accomplish the work of salvation which they had proclaimed, by means of sacrifice and sacraments, around which the entire liturgical life revolves. Thus by baptism men are plunged into the paschal mystery of Christ: they die with him, are buried with him, and rise with him;[16] they receive the spirit of adoption as sons "in which we cry: Abba, Father" (Rom. 8. 15), and thus become true adorers whom the Father seeks.[17] In like manner, as often as they eat the supper of the Lord they proclaim the death of the Lord until he comes.[18] For that reason, on the very day of Pentecost, when the Church appeared before the world, "those who received the word" of Peter "were baptized". And "they continued steadfastly in the teaching of the apostles and in the communion of the breaking of bread and in prayers . . . praising God and being in favour with all the people" (Acts 2. 41-7). From that time onwards the Church has never failed to come together to celebrate the paschal mystery: reading those things "which were in all the scriptures concerning him" (Luke 25. 27), celebrating the eucharist in which "the victory and triumph of his death are again made present",[19] and at the same time giving thanks "to God for his unspeakable gift" (2 Cor. 9. 15) in Christ Jesus,

[14] Cf. Mark 16. 15.
[15] Cf. Acts 26. 18.
[16] Cf. Rom. 6. 4; Eph. 2. 6; Col. 3. 1; 2 Tim. 2. 11.
[17] Cf. John 4. 23.
[18] Cf. 1 Cor. 11. 26.
[19] Council of Trent, Session XIII, Decree on the Holy Eucharist, c. 5.

"in praise of his glory" (Eph. 1. 12), through the power of the Holy Spirit.

7. To accomplish so great a work, Christ is always present in his Church, especially in her liturgical celebrations. He is present in the sacrifice of the Mass, not only in the person of his minister, "the same now offering, through the ministry of priests, who formerly offered himself on the cross",[20] but especially under the eucharistic species. By his power he is present in the sacraments, so that when a man baptizes it is really Christ himself who baptizes.[21] He is present in his word, since it is he himself who speaks when the holy scriptures are read in the Church. He is present, lastly, when the Church prays and sings, for he promised: "Where two or three are gathered together in my name, there am I in the midst of them" (Matt. 18. 20).

Christ indeed always associates the Church with himself in this great work wherein God is perfectly glorified and men are sanctified. The Church is his beloved Bride who calls to her Lord, and through him offers worship to the Eternal Father.

Rightly, then, the liturgy is considered as an exercise of the priestly office of Jesus Christ. In the liturgy the sanctification of man is signified by signs perceptible to the senses, and is effected in a way which corresponds with each of these signs; in the liturgy the whole public worship is performed by the mystical body of Jesus Christ, that is, by the head and his members.

From this it follows that every liturgical celebration, because it is an action of Christ the priest and of his body which is the Church, is a sacred action surpassing all others; no other action of the Church can equal its efficacy by the same title and to the same degree.

[20] Council of Trent, Session XXII, Doctrine on the Holy Sacrifice of the Mass, c. 2.
[21] Cf. St. Augustine, *Tractatus in Ioannem*, VI, n. 7: P.L. 35, 1428.

8. In the earthly liturgy we take part in a foretaste of that heavenly liturgy which is celebrated in the holy city of Jerusalem towards which we journey as pilgrims, where Christ is sitting at the right hand of God, a minister of the holies and of the true tabernacle;[22] we sing a hymn to the Lord's glory with all the warriors of the heavenly army; venerating the memory of the saints, we hope for some part and fellowship with them; we eagerly await the Saviour, our Lord Jesus Christ, until he, our life, shall appear and we too will appear with him in glory.[23]

9. The sacred liturgy does not exhaust the entire activity of the Church. Before men can come to the liturgy they must be called to faith and to conversion: "How then are they to call upon him in whom they have not yet believed? But how are they to believe him whom they have not heard? And how are they to hear if no one preaches? And how are men to preach unless they be sent?" (Rom. 10. 14-15)

Therefore the Church announces the good tidings of salvation to those who do not believe, so that all men may know the true God and Jesus Christ whom he has sent, and may be converted from their ways, doing penance.[24] To believers also the Church must ever preach faith and penance; she must prepare them for the sacraments, teach them to observe all that Christ has commanded,[25] and invite them to all the works of charity, piety, and the apostolate. For all these works make it clear that Christ's faithful, though not of this world, are to be the light of the world and to glorify the Father before men.

10. Nevertheless the liturgy is the summit toward which the activity of the Church is directed; at the same time it is the fount from which all her power flows. For the aim and

[22] Cf. Apoc. 21. 2; Col. 3. 1; Heb. 8. 2.
[23] Cf. Phil. 3. 20; Col. 3. 4.
[24] Cf. John 17. 3; Luke 24. 27; Acts 2. 38.
[25] Cf. Matt. 28, 20.

object of apostolic works is that all who are made sons of God by faith and baptism should come together to praise God in the midst of his Church, to take part in the sacrifice, and to eat the Lord's supper.

The liturgy in its turn moves the faithful, filled with "the paschal sacraments", to be "one in holiness";[26] it prays that "they may hold fast in their lives to what they have grasped by their faith";[27] the renewal in the eucharist of the covenant between the Lord and man draws the faithful into the compelling love of Christ and sets them on fire. From the liturgy, therefore, and especially from the eucharist, as from a fount, grace is poured forth upon us; and the sanctification of men in Christ and the glorification of God, to which all other activities of the Church are directed as towards their end, is achieved in the most efficacious possible way.

11. But in order that the liturgy may be able to produce its full effects, it is necessary that the faithful come to it with proper dispositions, that their minds should be attuned to their voices, and that they should cooperate with divine grace lest they receive it in vain.[28] Pastors of souls must therefore realize that, when the liturgy is celebrated, something more is required than the mere observation of the laws governing valid and licit celebration; it is their duty also to ensure that the faithful take part fully aware of what they are doing, actively engaged in the rite, and enriched by its effects.

12. The spiritual life, however, is not limited solely to participation in the liturgy. The Christian is indeed called to pray with his brethren, but he must also enter into his chamber to pray to the Father in secret;[29] yet more, accord-

---

[26] Postcommunion for both Masses of Easter Sunday.
[27] Collect of the Mass for Tuesday of Easter Week.
[28] Cf. 2 Cor. 6. 1.
[29] Cf. Matt. 6. 6.

ing to the teaching of the Apostle, he should pray without ceasing.[30] We learn from the same Apostle that we must always bear about in our body the dying of Jesus, so that the life also of Jesus may be made manifest in our bodily frame.[31] This is why we ask the Lord in the sacrifice of the Mass that, "receiving the offering of the spiritual victim", he may fashion us for himself "as an eternal gift".[32]

13. Popular devotions of the Christian people are to be highly commended, provided they accord with the laws and norms of the Church, above all when they are ordered by the Apostolic See.

Devotions proper to individual Churches also have a special dignity if they are undertaken by mandate of the bishops according to customs or books lawfully approved.

But these devotions should be so drawn up that they harmonize with the liturgical seasons, accord with the sacred liturgy, are in some fashion derived from it, and lead the people to it, since, in fact, the liturgy by its very nature far surpasses any of them.

II. The Promotion of Liturgical Instruction and Active Participation

14. Mother Church earnestly desires that all the faithful should be led to that full, conscious, and active participation in liturgical celebrations which is demanded by the very nature of the liturgy. Such participation by the Christian people as "a chosen race, a royal priesthood, a holy nation, a redeemed people" (1 Peter 2. 9; cf. 2. 4. 5), is their right and duty by reason of their baptism.

In the restoration and promotion of the sacred liturgy, this full and active participation by all the people is the aim to be considered before all else; for it is the primary and

[30] Cf. 1 Thess. 5. 17.
[31] Cf. 2 Cor. 4. 10-11.
[32] Secret for Monday of Pentecost Week.

indispensable source from which the faithful are to derive the true Christian spirit; and therefore pastors of souls must zealously strive to achieve it, by means of the necessary instruction, in all their pastoral work.

Yet it would be futile to entertain any hopes of realizing this unless the pastors themselves, in the first place, become thoroughly imbued with the spirit and power of the liturgy, and undertake to give instruction about it. A prime need, therefore, is that attention be directed, first of all, to the liturgical instruction of the clergy. Wherefore the sacred Council has decided to enact as follows:

15. Professors who are appointed to teach liturgy in seminaries, religious houses of study, and theological faculties must be properly trained for their work in institutes which specialize in this subject.

16. The study of sacred liturgy is to be ranked among the compulsory and major courses in seminaries and religious houses of studies; in theological faculties it is to rank among the principal courses. It is to be taught under its theological, historical, spiritual, pastoral, and juridical aspects. Moreover, other professors, while striving to expound the mystery of Christ and the history of salvation from the angle proper to each of their own subjects, must nevertheless do so in a way which will clearly bring out the connection between their subjects and the liturgy, as also the unity which underlies all priestly training. This consideration is especially important for professors of dogmatic, spiritual, and pastoral theology and for those of holy Scripture.

17. In seminaries and houses of religious, clerics shall be given a liturgical formation in their spiritual life. For this they will need proper direction, so that they may be able to understand the sacred rites and take part in them wholeheartedly; and they will also need personally to celebrate the sacred mysteries, as well as popular devotions which are imbued with the spirit of the liturgy. In addition they must

learn how to observe the liturgical laws, so that life in seminaries and houses of religious may be thoroughly influenced by the spirit of the liturgy.

18. Priests, both secular and religious, who are already working in the Lord's vineyard are to be helped by every suitable means to understand ever more fully what it is that they are doing when they perform sacred rites; they are to be aided to live the liturgical life and to share it with the faithful entrusted to their care.

19. With zeal and patience, pastors of souls must promote the liturgical instruction of the faithful, and also their active participation in the liturgy both internally and externally, taking into account their age and condition, their way of life, and standard of religious culture. By so doing, pastors will be fulfilling one of the chief duties of a faithful dispenser of the mysteries of God; and in this matter they must lead their flock not only in word but also by example.

20. Transmissions of the sacred rites by radio and television shall be done with discretion and dignity, under the leadership and direction of a suitable person appointed for this office by the bishops. This is especially important when the service to be broadcast is the Mass.

III. The Reform of the Sacred Liturgy

21. In order that the Christian people may more certainly derive an abundance of graces from the sacred liturgy, holy Mother Church desires to undertake with great care a general restoration of the liturgy itself. For the liturgy is made up of immutable elements divinely instituted, and of elements subject to change. These not only may but ought to be changed with the passage of time if they have suffered from the intrusion of anything out of harmony with the inner nature of the liturgy or have become unsuited to it.

In this restoration, both texts and rites should be drawn up so that they express more clearly the holy things which they signify; the Christian people, so far as possible, should be enabled to understand them with ease and to take part in them fully, actively, and as befits a community.

Wherefore the sacred Council establishes the following general norms:

(A) General norms

22. (i) Regulation of the sacred liturgy depends solely on the authority of the Church, that is, on the Apostolic See and, as laws may determine, on the bishop.

(ii) In virtue of power conceded by the law, the regulation of the liturgy within certain defined limits belongs also to various kinds of competent territorial bodies of bishops legitimately established.

(iii) Therefore no other person, even if he be a priest, may add, remove, or change anything in the liturgy on his own authority.

23. That sound tradition may be retained, and yet the way remain open to legitimate progress, a careful investigation is always to be made into each part of the liturgy which is to be revised. This investigation should be theological, historical, and pastoral. Also the general laws governing the structure and meaning of the liturgy must be studied in conjunction with the experience derived from recent liturgical reforms and from the indults conceded to various places. Finally, there must be no innovations unless the good of the Church genuinely and certainly requires them; and care must be taken that any new forms adopted should in some way grow organically from forms already existing.

As far as possible, notable differences between the rites used in adjacent regions must be carefully avoided.

24. Sacred Scripture is of the greatest importance in the celebration of the liturgy. For it is from Scripture that lessons are read and explained in the homily, and psalms are sung; the prayers, collects, and liturgical songs are scriptural

in their inspiration, and it is from the Scriptures that actions and signs derive their meaning. Thus to achieve the restoration, progress, and adaptation of the sacred liturgy, it is essential to promote that warm and living love for Scripture to which the venerable tradition of both eastern and western rites gives testimony.

25. The liturgical books are to be revised as soon as possible; experts are to be employed on the task, and bishops are to be consulted, from various parts of the world.

(B) *Norms drawn from the hierarchic and communal nature of the liturgy*

26. Liturgical services are not private functions, but are celebrations of the Church, which is the "sacrament of unity", namely, the holy people united and ordered under their bishops.[33]

Therefore liturgical services pertain to the whole body of the Church; they manifest it and have effects upon it; but they concern the individual members of the Church in different ways, according to their differing rank, office, and actual participation.

27. It is to be stressed that whenever rites, according to their specific nature, make provision for communal celebration involving the presence and active participation of the faithful, this way of celebrating them is to be preferred, so far as possible, to a celebration that is individual and quasi-private.

This applies with especial force to the celebration of Mass and the administration of the sacraments, even though every Mass has of itself a public and social nature.

28. In liturgical celebrations each person, minister or layman, who has an office to perform, should do all of, but

[33] St. Cyprian, *On the Unity of the Catholic Church*, 7; cf. Letter 66, n. 8, 3.

only, those parts which pertain to his office by the nature of
the rite and the principles of liturgy.

29. Servers, lectors, commentators, and members of the
choir also exercise a genuine liturgical function. They ought,
therefore, to discharge their office with the sincere piety and
decorum demanded by so exalted a ministry and rightly expected of them by God's people.

Consequently they must all be deeply imbued with the
spirit of the liturgy, each in his own measure, and they must
be trained to perform their functions in a correct and orderly
manner.

30. To promote active participation, the people should
be encouraged to take part by means of acclamations, responses, psalmody, antiphons, and songs, as well as by actions, gestures, and bodily attitudes. And at the proper times
all should observe a reverent silence.

31. The revision of the liturgical books must carefully
attend to the provision of rubrics also for the people's parts.

32. The liturgy makes distinctions between persons according to their liturgical function and sacred Orders, and
there are liturgical laws providing for due honours to be given
to civil authorities. Apart from these instances, no special
honours are to be paid in the liturgy to any private persons
or classes of persons, whether in the ceremonies or by external display.

(C) *Norms based upon the didactic and*
pastoral nature of the liturgy

33. Although the sacred liturgy is above all things the
worship of the divine Majesty, it likewise contains much
instruction for the faithful.[34] For in the liturgy God speaks
to his people and Christ is still proclaiming his gospel. And
the people reply to God both by song and prayer.

[34] Cf. Council of Trent, Session XXII, Doctrine on the holy sacrifice of the Mass, c. 8.

Moreover, the prayers addressed to God by the priest who presides over the assembly in the person of Christ are said in the name of the entire holy people and of all present. And the visible signs used by the liturgy to signify invisible divine things have been chosen by Christ or the Church. Thus not only when things are read "which were written for our instruction" (Rom. 15. 4), but also when the Church prays or sings or acts, the faith of those taking part is nourished and their minds are raised to God, so that they may offer him their rational service and more abundantly receive his grace.

Wherefore, in the revision of the liturgy, the following general norms should be observed:

34. The rites should be distinguished by a noble simplicity; they should be short, clear, and unencumbered by useless repetitions; they should be within the people's powers of comprehension, and normally should not require much explanation.

35. That the intimate connection between words and rites may be apparent in the liturgy:

(i) In sacred celebrations there is to be more reading from holy Scripture, and it is to be more varied and suitable.

(ii) Because the sermon is part of the liturgical service, the best place for it is to be indicated even in the rubrics, as far as the nature of the rite will allow; the ministry of preaching is to be fulfilled with exactitude and fidelity. The sermon, moreover, should draw its content mainly from scriptural and liturgical sources, and its character should be that of a proclamation of God's wonderful works in the history of salvation, the mystery of Christ, ever made present and active within us, especially in the celebration of the liturgy.

(iii) Instruction which is more explicitly liturgical should also be given in a variety of ways; if necessary, short directives to be spoken by the priest or proper minister should be provided within the rites themselves. But they should occur only at the more suitable moments, and be in prescribed or similar words.

(iv) Bible services should be encouraged, especially on the vigils of the more solemn feasts, on some weekdays in Advent and Lent, and on Sundays and feast days. They are particularly to be commended in places where no priest is available; when this is so, a deacon or some other person authorized by the bishop should preside over the celebration.

36. (i) Particular law remaining in force, the use of the Latin language is to be preserved in the Latin rites.

(ii) But since the use of the mother tongue, whether in the Mass, the administration of the sacraments, or other parts of the liturgy, frequently may be of great advantage to the people, the limits of its employment may be extended. This will apply in the first place to the readings and directives, and to some of the prayers and chants, according to the regulations on this matter to be laid down separately in subsequent chapters.

(iii) These norms being observed, it is for the competent territorial ecclesiastical authority mentioned in Art. 22, ii, to decide whether, and to what extent, the vernacular language is to be used; their decrees are to be approved, that is, confirmed, by the Apostolic See. And, whenever it seems to be called for, this authority is to consult with bishops of neighbouring regions which have the same language.

(iv) Translations from the Latin text into the mother tongue intended for use in the liturgy must be approved by the competent territorial ecclesiastical authority mentioned above.

(D) *Norms for adapting the liturgy to the culture and traditions of peoples*

37. Even in the liturgy, the Church has no wish to impose a rigid uniformity in matters which do not implicate the faith or the good of the whole community; rather does she respect and foster the genius and talents of the various races and peoples. Anything in these peoples' way of life which is not

indissolubly bound up with superstition and error she studies with sympathy and, if possible, preserves intact. Sometimes in fact she admits such things into the liturgy itself, so long as they harmonize with its true and authentic spirit.

38. Provisions shall also be made, when revising the liturgical books, for legitimate variations and adaptations to different groups, regions, and peoples, especially in mission lands, provided that the substantial unity of the Roman rite is preserved; and this should be borne in mind when drawing up the rites and devising rubrics.

39. Within the limits set by the typical editions of the liturgical books it shall be for the competent territorial ecclesiastical authority mentioned in Art. 22, ii, to specify adaptations, especially in the case of the administration of the sacraments, the sacramentals, processions, liturgical language, sacred music and the arts, but according to the fundamental norms laid down in this Constitution.

40. In some places and circumstances however, an even more radical adaptation of the liturgy is needed, and this entails greater difficulties. Wherefore:

(i) The competent territorial ecclesiastical authority mentioned in Art. 22, ii, must, in this matter, carefully and prudently consider which elements from the traditions and culture of individual peoples might appropriately be admitted into divine worship. Adaptations which are judged to be useful or necessary should then be submitted to the Apostolic See, by whose consent they may be introduced.

(ii) To ensure that adaptations may be made with all the circumspection which they demand, the Apostolic See will grant power to this same territorial ecclesiastical authority to permit and to direct, as the case requires, the necessary preliminary experiments over a determined period of time among certain groups suited for the purpose.

(iii) Because liturgical laws often involve special difficulties with respect to adaptation, particularly in mission lands, men who are experts in these matters must be employed to formulate them.

IV. *Promotion of liturgical life in diocese and parish*

41. The bishop is to be considered as the high priest of his flock, from whom the life in Christ of his faithful is in some way derived and dependent.

Therefore all should hold in great esteem the liturgical life of the diocese centred around the bishop, especially in his cathedral church; they must be convinced that the pre-eminent manifestation of the Church consists in the full active participation of all God's holy people in these liturgical celebrations, especially in the same Eucharist, in a single prayer, at one altar, at which there presides the bishop surrounded by his college of priests and by his ministers.[35]

42. But because it is impossible for the bishop always and everywhere to preside over the whole flock in his Church, he cannot do other than establish lesser groupings of the faithful. Among these the parishes, set up locally under a pastor who takes the place of the bishop, are the most important; for in some manner they represent the visible Church constituted throughout the world.

And therefore the liturgical life of the parish and its relationship to the bishop must be fostered theoretically and practically among the faithful and clergy; efforts also must be made to encourage a sense of community within the parish, above all in the common celebration of the Sunday Mass.

V. *The promotion of pastoral-liturgical action*

43. Zeal for the promotion and restoration of the liturgy is rightly held to be a sign of the providential dispositions of God in our time, as a movement of the Holy Spirit in his Church. It is today a distinguishing mark of the Church's

---

[35] Cf. St. Ignatius of Antioch, *To the Smyrnians*, 8; *To the Magnesians*, 7; *To the Philadelphians*, 4.

life, indeed of the whole tenour of contemporary religious thought and action.

So that this pastoral-liturgical action may become even more vigorous in the Church, the sacred Council decrees:

44. It is desirable that the competent territorial ecclesiastical authority mentioned in Art. 22, ii, set up a liturgical commission, to be assisted by experts in liturgical science, sacred music, art, and pastoral practice. So far as possible the commission should be aided by some kind of Institute for Pastoral Liturgy, consisting of persons who are eminent in these matters, and including laymen as circumstances suggest. Under the direction of the above-mentioned territorial ecclesiastical authority the commission is to regulate pastoral-liturgical action throughout the territory, and to promote studies and necessary experiments whenever there is question of adaptations to be proposed to the Apostolic See.

45. For the same reason every diocese is to have a commission on the sacred liturgy under the direction of the bishop, for promoting the liturgical apostolate.

Sometimes it may be expedient that several dioceses should form between them one single commission which will be able to promote the liturgy by common consultation.

46. Besides the commission on the sacred liturgy, every diocese, as far as possible, should have commissions for sacred music and sacred art.

These three commissions must work in closest collaboration; indeed it will often be best to fuse the three of them into one single commission.

CHAPTER II: THE MOST SACRED MYSTERY OF THE EUCHARIST

47. At the Last Supper, on the night when he was betrayed, our Saviour, instituted the eucharistic sacrifice of his body and blood. He did this in order to perpetuate the sacri-

fice of the Cross throughout the centuries until he should come again, and so to entrust to his beloved spouse, the Church, a memorial of his death and resurrection: a sacrament of love, a sign of unity, a bond of charity,[36] a paschal banquet in which Christ is eaten, the mind is filled with grace, and a pledge of future glory is given to us.[37]

48. The Church, therefore, earnestly desires that Christ's faithful, when present at this mystery of faith, should not be there as strangers or silent spectators; on the contrary, through a good understanding of the rites and prayers they should take part in the sacred action conscious of what they are doing, with devotion and full collaboration. They should be instructed by God's word and be nourished at the table of the Lord's body; they should give thanks to God; by offering the immaculate victim, not only through the hands of the priest, but also with him, they should learn also to offer themselves; through Christ the Mediator,[38] they should be drawn day by day into ever more perfect union with God and with each other, so that finally God may be all in all.

49. For this reason the Sacred Council, having in mind those Masses which are celebrated with the assistance of the faithful, especially on Sundays and feasts of obligation, has made the following decrees in order that the sacrifice of the Mass, even in the ritual forms of its celebration, may become pastorally efficacious to the fullest degree.

50. The rite of the Mass is to be revised in such a way that the intrinsic nature and purpose of its several parts, as also the connection between them, may be more clearly manifested, and that devout and active participation by the faithful may be more easily achieved.

For this purpose the rites are to be simplified, due care

[36] Cf. St. Augustine, *Tractatus in Ioannem*, VI, n. 13.
[37] Roman Breviary, feast of Corpus Christi, Second Vespers, antiphon to the Magnificat.
[38] Cf. St. Cyril of Alexandria, *Commentary on the Gospel of John,* book XI, chap. XI-XII: Migne, *Patrologia Graeca,* 74, 557-564.

being taken to preserve their substance; elements which, with the passage of time, came to be duplicated, or were added with but little advantage, are now to be discarded; other elements which have suffered injury through accidents of history are now to be restored to the vigour which they had in the days of the holy Fathers, as may seem useful or necessary.

51. The treasures of the Bible are to be opened up more lavishly, so that richer fare may be provided for the faithful at the table of God's word. In this way a more representative portion of the holy Scriptures will be read to the people in the course of a prescribed number of years.

52. By means of the homily the mysteries of the faith and the guiding principles of the Christian life are expounded from the sacred text, during the course of the liturgical year; the homily, therefore, is to be highly esteemed as part of the liturgy itself; in fact, at those Masses which are celebrated with the assistance of the people on Sundays and feasts of obligation, it should not be omitted except for a serious reason.

53. Especially on Sundays and feasts of obligation there is to be restored, after the Gospel and the homily, "the common prayer" or "the prayer of the faithful". By this prayer, in which the people are to take part, intercession will be made for holy Church, for the civil authorities, for those oppressed by various needs, for all mankind, and for the salvation of the entire world.[39]

54. In Masses which are celebrated with the people, a suitable place may be allotted to their mother tongue. This is to apply in the first place to the readings and "the common prayer", but also, as local conditions may warrant, to those parts which pertain to the people, according to the norm laid down in Art. 36 of this Constitution.

Nevertheless steps should be taken so that the faithful may

[39] Cf. 1 Tim. 2. 1-2.

also be able to say or to sing together in Latin those parts of the Ordinary of the Mass which pertain to them.

And wherever a more extended use of the mother tongue within the Mass appears desirable, the regulation laid down in Art. 40 of this Constitution is to be observed.

55. That more perfect form of participation in the Mass whereby the faithful, after the priest's communion, receive the Lord's body from the same sacrifice, is strongly commended.

The dogmatic principles which were laid down by the Council of Trent remaining intact,[40] communion under both kinds may be granted when the bishops think fit, not only to clerics and religious, but also to the laity, in cases to be determined by the Apostolic See, as, for instance, to the newly ordained in the Mass of their sacred ordination, to the newly professed in the Mass of their religious profession, and to the newly baptized in the Mass which follows their baptism.

56. The two parts which, in a certain sense, go to make up the Mass, namely, the liturgy of the word and the eucharistic liturgy, are so closely connected with each other that they form but one single act of worship. Accordingly this sacred Synod strongly urges pastors of souls that, when instructing the faithful, they insistently teach them to take their part in the entire Mass, especially on Sundays and feasts of obligation.

57. (i) Concelebration, whereby the unity of the priesthood is appropriately manifested, has remained in use to this day in the Church both in the east and in the west. For this reason it has seemed good to the Council to extend permission for concelebration to the following cases:

(a) on the Thursday of the Lord's Supper not

[40] Session XXI, July 16, 1562. Doctrine on Communion under Both Species, chap. 1-3: *Concilium Tridentinum. Diariorum, Actorum, Epistolarum, Tractatuum nova collectio,* ed. Soc. Goerresiana, vol. VIII (Freiburg in Br., 1919), 698-699.

only at the Mass of the Chrism, but also at the evening Mass;

(b) at Masses during councils, bishops' conferences, and synods;

(c) at the Mass for the blessing of an abbot.

Also, with permission of the ordinary, to whom it belongs to decide whether concelebration is opportune:

(a) at conventual Mass, and at the principal Mass in churches when the needs of the faithful do not require that all the priests available should celebrate individually;

(b) at Masses celebrated at any kind of priests' meetings, whether the priests be secular clergy or religious.

(ii) The regulation, however, of the discipline of concelebration in the diocese pertains to the bishop.

Nevertheless, each priest shall always retain his right to celebrate Mass individually, though not at the same time in the same church as a concelebrated Mass, nor on Thursday of the Lord's Supper.

58. A new rite for concelebration is to be drawn up and inserted into the Pontifical and into the Roman Missal.

CHAPTER III: THE OTHER SACRAMENTS AND THE SACRAMENTALS

59. The purpose of the sacraments is to sanctify men, to build up the body of Christ, and, finally, to give worship to God; because they are signs they also instruct. They not only presuppose faith, but by words and objects they also nourish, strengthen, and express it; that is why they are called "sacraments of faith". They do indeed impart grace, but, in addition, the very act of celebrating them most effectively disposes the faithful to receive this grace in a fruitful manner, to worship God duly, and to practice charity.

It is therefore of the highest importance that the faithful should easily understand the sacramental signs, and should frequent with great eagerness those sacraments which were instituted to nourish the Christian life.

60. Holy Mother Church has, moreover, instituted sacramentals. These are sacred signs which bear a resemblance to the sacraments: they signify effects, particularly of a spiritual kind, which are obtained through the Church's intercession. By them men are disposed to receive the chief effect of the sacraments, and various occasions in life are rendered holy.

61. Thus, for well-disposed members of the faithful, the liturgy of the sacraments and sacramentals sanctifies almost every event in their lives; they are given access to the stream of divine grace which flows from the paschal mystery of the passion, death, and resurrection of Christ, the fount from which all sacraments and sacramentals draw their power. There is hardly any proper use of material things which cannot thus be directed towards the sanctification of men and the praise of God.

62. With the passage of time, however, there have crept into the rites of the sacraments and sacramentals certain features which have rendered their nature and purpose far from clear to the people of today; hence some changes have become necessary to adapt them to the needs of our own times. For this reason the sacred Council decrees as follows concerning their revision.

63. Because the use of the mother tongue in the administration of the sacraments and sacramentals can often be of considerable help to the people, this use is to be extended according to the following norms:

(a) The vernacular language may be used in administering the sacraments and sacramentals, according to the norm of Art. 36.

(b) In harmony with the new edition of the Roman Ritual, particular rituals shall be prepared without delay by the competent territorial ecclesiastical authority mentioned in Art. 22, ii, of this Constitution. These rituals, which are to be adapted, also as regards the language employed, to the needs of the different regions, are to be reviewed by the Apostolic See and then introduced into the regions for which they have been prepared. But in drawing up these rituals or particular collections of rites, the instructions prefixed to the individual rites in the Roman Ritual, whether they be pastoral and rubrical or whether they have special social import, shall not be omitted.

64. The catechumenate for adults, comprising several distinct steps, is to be restored and to be taken into use at the discretion of the local ordinary. By this means the time of the catechumenate, which is intended as a period of suitable instruction, may be sanctified by sacred rites to be celebrated at successive intervals of time.

65. In mission lands it is found that some of the peoples already make use of initiation rites. Elements from these, when capable of being adapted to Christian ritual, may be admitted along with those already found in Christian tradition, according to the norm laid down in Art. 37-40 of this Constitution.

66. Both of the rites for the baptism of adults are to be revised: not only the simpler rite, but also the more solemn one, which must take into account the restored catechumenate. A special Mass "for the conferring of baptism" is to be inserted into the Roman Missal.

67. The rite for the baptism of infants is to be revised, and it should be adapted to the circumstance that those to be baptized are, in fact, infants. The rôles of parents and godparents, and also their duties, should be brought out more clearly in the rite itself.

68. The baptismal rite should contain variants, to be used at the discretion of the local ordinary, for occasions when a very large number are to be baptized together. Moreover, a shorter rite is to be drawn up, especially for mission lands, to be used by catechists, but also by the faithful in general

when there is danger of death, and neither priest nor deacon is available.

69. In place of the rite called the "Order of supplying what was omitted in the baptism of an infant," a new rite is to be drawn up. This should manifest more fittingly and clearly that the infant, baptized by the short rite, has already been received into the Church.

And a new rite is to be drawn up for converts who have already been validly baptized; it should indicate that they are now admitted to communion with the Church.

70. Except during Eastertide, baptismal water may be blessed within the rite of baptism itself by an approved shorter formula.

71. The rite of confirmation is to be revised and the intimate connection which this sacrament has with the whole of Christian initiation is to be more clearly set forth; for this reason it is fitting for candidates to renew their baptismal promises just before they are confirmed.

Confirmation may be given within the Mass when convenient; when it is given outside the Mass, the rite that is used should be introduced by a formula to be drawn up for this purpose.

72. The rite and formulas for the sacrament of penance are to be revised so that they more clearly express both the nature and effect of the sacrament.

73. "Extreme unction", which may also and more fittingly be called "Anointing of the Sick", is not a sacrament for those only who are at the point of death. Hence, as soon as any one of the faithful begins to be in danger of death from sickness or old age, the fitting time for him to receive this sacrament has certainly already arrived.

74. In addition to the separate rites for anointing of the sick and for viaticum, a continuous rite shall be prepared according to which the sick man is anointed after he has made his confession and before he receives viaticum.

75. The number of the anointings is to be adapted to the occasion, and the prayers which belong to the rite of anointing are to be revised so as to correspond with the varying conditions of the sick who receive the sacrament.

76. Both the ceremonies and texts of the ordination rites are to be revised. The address given by the bishop at the beginning of each ordination or consecration may be in the mother tongue.

When a bishop is consecrated, the laying on of hands may be done by all the bishops present.

77. The marriage rite now found in the Roman Ritual is to be revised and enriched in such a way that the grace of the sacrament is more clearly signified and the duties of the spouses are taught.

"If any regions are wont to use other praiseworthy customs and ceremonies when celebrating the sacrament of matrimony, the sacred Synod earnestly desires that these by all means be retained." [41]

Moreover the competent territorial ecclesiastical authority mentioned in Art. 22, ii, of this Constitution is free to draw up its own rite suited to the usages of place and people, according to the provision of Art. 63. But the rite must always conform to the law that the priest assisting at the marriage must ask for and obtain the consent of the contracting parties.

78. Matrimony is normally to be celebrated within the Mass, after the reading of the gospel and the homily, and before "the prayer of the faithful". The prayer for the bride, duly amended to remind both spouses of their equal obligation to remain faithful to each other, may be said in the mother tongue.

But if the sacrament of matrimony is celebrated apart from Mass, the epistle and gospel from the nuptial Mass are to be

[41] Council of Trent, Session XXIV, November 11th, 1563, On Reform, chap. I .Cf. Roman Ritual, title VIII, chap. II, n. 6.

read at the beginning of the rite, and the blessing should always be given to the spouses.

79. The sacramentals are to undergo a revision which takes into account the primary principle of enabling the faithful to participate intelligently, actively, and easily; the circumstances of our own days must also be considered. When rituals are revised, as laid down in Art. 63, new sacramentals may also be added as the need for these becomes apparent.

Reserved blessings shall be very few; reservations shall be in favour only of bishops or ordinaries.

Let provision be made that some sacramentals, at least in special circumstances and at the discretion of the ordinary, may be administered by qualified lay persons.

80. The rite for the consecration of virgins at present found in the Roman Pontifical is to be revised.

Moreover, a rite of religious profession and renewal of vows shall be drawn up in order to achieve greater unity, sobriety, and dignity. Apart from exceptions in particular law, this rite should be adopted by those who make their profession or renewal of vows within the Mass.

Religious profession should preferably be made within the Mass.

81. The rite for the burial of the dead should express more clearly the paschal character of Christian death, and should correspond more closely to the circumstances and traditions found in various regions. This holds good also for the liturgical colour to be used.

82. The rite for the burial of infants is to be revised, and a special Mass for the occasion should be provided.

CHAPTER IV: THE DIVINE OFFICE

83. Christ Jesus, high priest of the new and eternal covenant, taking human nature, introduced into his earthly exile that hymn which is sung throughout all ages in the halls of

heaven. He joins the entire community of mankind to himself, associating it with his own singing of this canticle of divine praise.

For he continues his priestly work through the agency of his Church—which is ceaselessly engaged in praising the Lord and interceding for the salvation of the whole world. She does this, not only by celebrating the eucharist, but also in other ways, especially by praying the divine Office.

84. By tradition going back to early Christian times, the divine Office is devised so that the whole course of the day and night is made holy by the praises of God. Therefore, when this wonderful song of praise is rightly performed by priests and others who are deputed for this purpose by the Church's ordinance, or by the faithful praying together with the priest in the approved form, then it is truly the voice of the bride addressed to her bridegroom; it is the very prayer which Christ himself, together with his body, addresses to the Father.

85. Hence all who render this service are not only fulfilling a duty of the Church, but also are sharing in the greatest honour of Christ's spouse, for by offering these praises to God they are standing before God's throne in the name of the Church their Mother.

86. Priests who are engaged in the sacred pastoral ministry will offer the praises of the hours with greater fervour the more vividly they realize that they must heed St Paul's exhortation: "Pray without ceasing" (1 Thess. 5. 17). For the work in which they labour will effect nothing and bring forth no fruit except by the power of the Lord who said: "Without me you can do nothing" (John 15. 5). That is why the apostles, instituting deacons, said: "We will devote ourselves to prayer and to the ministry of the word" (Acts 6. 4).

87. In order that the divine Office may be better and more perfectly prayed in existing circumstances, whether by priests or by other members of the Church, the sacred Council,

carrying further the restoration already so happily begun by the Apostolic See, has seen fit to decree as follows concerning the Office of the Roman rite.

88. Because the purpose of the Office is to sanctify the day, the traditional sequence of the hours is to be restored so that once again they may be genuinely related to the time of the day when they are prayed, as far as this may be possible. Moreover, it will be necessary to take into account the modern conditions in which daily life has to be lived, especially by those who are called to labour in apostolic works.

89. Therefore, when the Office is revised, these norms are to be observed:

(a) By the venerable tradition of the universal Church, Lauds as morning prayer and Vespers as evening prayer are the two hinges on which the daily Office turns; hence they are to be considered as the chief hours and are to be celebrated as such.

(b) Compline is to be drawn up so that it will be a suitable prayer for the end of the day.

(c) The hour known as Matins, although it should retain the character of nocturnal praise when celebrated in choir, shall be adapted so that it may be recited at any hour of the day; it shall be made up of fewer psalms and longer readings.

(d) The hour of Prime is to be suppressed.

(e) In choir the minor hours of Terce, Sext, and None are to be observed. But outside choir it will be lawful to select any one of these three, according to the respective time of the day.

90. The divine Office, because it is the public prayer of the Church, is a source of piety and nourishment for personal prayer. And therefore priests and all others who take part in the divine Office are earnestly exhorted in the Lord to attune their minds to their voices when praying it. The better to achieve this, let them take steps to improve their

understanding of the liturgy and of the bible, especially of the psalms.

In revising the Roman Office, its ancient and venerable treasures are to be so adapted that all those to whom they are handed on may more extensively and easily draw profit from them.

91. So that it may really be possible in practice to observe the course of the hours proposed in Art. 89, the psalms are no longer to be distributed throughout one week, but through some longer period of time.

The work of revising the psalter, already happily begun, is to be finished as soon as possible, and is to take into account the style of Christian Latin, the liturgical use of psalms, also when sung, and the entire tradition of the Latin Church.

92. As regards the readings, the following shall be observed:

(a) Readings from sacred Scripture shall be arranged so that the riches of God's word may be easily accessible in more abundant measure.

(b) Readings excerpted from the works of the fathers, doctors, and ecclesiastical writers shall be better selected.

(c) The accounts of martyrdom or the lives of the saints are to accord with the facts of history.

93. To whatever extent may seem desirable, the hymns are to be restored to their original form, and whatever smacks of mythology or ill accords with Christian piety is to be removed or changed. Also, as occasion may arise, let other selections from the treasury of hymns be incorporated.

94. That the day may be truly sanctified, and that the hours themselves may be recited with spiritual advantage, it is best that each of them be prayed at a time which most closely corresponds with its true canonical time.

95. Communities obliged to choral Office are bound to

celebrate the Office in choir every day in addition to the conventual Mass. In particular:

(a) Orders of canons, of monks and of nuns, and of other regulars bound by law or constitutions to choral Office must celebrate the entire Office.

(b) Cathedral or collegiate chapters are bound to recite those parts of the Office imposed on them by general or particular law.

(c) All members of the above communities who are in major orders or who are solemnly professed, except for lay brothers, are bound to recite individually those canonical hours which they do not pray in choir.

96. Clerics not bound to Office in choir, if they are in major orders, are bound to pray the entire Office every day, either in common or individually, as laid down in Art. 89.

97. Appropriate instances are to be defined by the rubrics in which a liturgical service may be substituted for the divine Office.

In particular cases, and for a just reason, ordinaries can dispense their subjects wholly or in part from the obligation of reciting the divine Office, or may commute the obligation.

98. Members of any institute dedicated to acquiring perfection who, according to their constitutions, are to recite any parts of the divine Office are thereby performing the public prayer of the Church.

They too perform the public prayer of the Church who, in virtue of their constitutions, recite any short Office, provided this is drawn up after the pattern of the divine Office and is duly approved.

99. Since the divine Office is the voice of the Church, that is, of the whole mystical body publicly praising God, those clerics who are not obliged to Office in choir, especially priests who live together or who assemble for any purpose, are urged to pray at least some part of the divine Office in common.

All who pray the divine Office, whether in choir or in common, should fulfill the task entrusted to them as perfectly as possible; this refers not only to the internal devotion of their minds but also to their external manner of celebration.

It is, moreover, fitting that the Office, both in choir and in common, be sung when possible.

100. Pastors of souls should see to it that the chief hours, especially Vespers, are celebrated in common in church on Sundays and the more solemn feasts. And the laity, too, are encouraged to recite the divine Office, either with the priests, or among themselves, or even individually.

101. (i) In accordance with the centuries-old tradition of the Latin rite, the Latin language is to be retained by clerics in the divine Office. But in individual cases the ordinary has the power of granting the use of a vernacular translation to those clerics for whom the use of Latin constitutes a grave obstacle to their praying the Office properly. The vernacular version, however, must be one that is drawn up according to the provisions of Art. 36.

(ii) The competent superior has the power to grant the use of the vernacular in the celebration of the divine Office, even in choir, to nuns and to members of institutes dedicated to acquiring perfection, both men who are not clerics and women. The version, however, must be one that is approved.

(iii) Any cleric bound to the divine Office fulfills his obligation if he prays the Office in the vernacular together with a group of the faithful or with those mentioned in (ii) above, provided that the text of the translation is approved.

CHAPTER V: THE LITURGICAL YEAR

102. Holy Mother Church is conscious that she must celebrate the saving work of her divine Spouse by devoutly recalling it on certain days throughout the course of the year. Every week, on the day which she has called the Lord's

day, she keeps the memory of the Lord's resurrection, which she also celebrates once in the year, together with his blessed passion, in the most solemn festival of Easter.

Within the cycle of a year, moreover, she unfolds the whole mystery of Christ, from the incarnation and birth until the ascension, the day of Pentecost, and the expectation of blessed hope and of the coming of the Lord.

Recalling thus the mysteries of redemption, the Church opens to the faithful the riches of her Lord's powers and merits, so that these are in some way made present for all time, and the faithful are enabled to lay hold upon them and become filled with saving grace.

103. In celebrating this annual cycle of Christ's mysteries, holy Church honours with especial love the Blessed Mary, Mother of God, who is joined by an inseparable bond to the saving work of her Son. In her the Church holds up and admires the most excellent fruit of the redemption, and joyfully contemplates, as in a faultless image, that which she herself desires and hopes wholly to be.

104. The Church has also included in the annual cycle days devoted to the memory of the martyrs and the other saints. Raised up to perfection by the manifold grace of God, and already in possession of eternal salvation, they sing God's perfect praise in heaven and offer prayers for us. By celebrating the passage of these saints from earth to heaven the Church proclaims the paschal mystery achieved in the saints who have suffered and been glorified with Christ; she proposes them to the faithful as examples drawing all to the Father through Christ, and through their merits she pleads for God's favours.

105. Finally, in the various seasons of the year and according to her traditional discipline, the Church completes the formation of the faithful by means of pious practices for soul and body, by instruction, prayer, and works of penance and of mercy.

Accordingly the sacred Council has seen fit to decree as follows.

106. By a tradition handed down from the apostles which took its origin from the very day of Christ's resurrection, the Church celebrates the paschal mystery every eighth day; with good reason this, then, bears the name of the Lord's day or Sunday. For in this day Christ's faithful should come together into one place so that, by hearing the word of God and taking part in the Eucharist, they may call to mind the passion, the resurrection, and the glorification of the Lord Jesus, and may thank God who "has begotten them again, through the resurrection of Jesus Christ from the dead, unto a living hope" (1 Peter 1. 3). Hence the Lord's day is the original feast day, and it should be proposed to the piety of the faithful and taught to them so that it may become in fact a day of joy and of freedom from work. Other celebrations, unless they be truly of greatest importance, shall not have precedence over the Sunday which is the foundation and kernel of the whole liturgical year.

107. The liturgical year is to be revised so that the traditional customs and discipline of the sacred seasons shall be preserved or restored to suit the conditions of modern times; their specific character is to be retained, so that they duly nourish the piety of the faithful who celebrate the mysteries of Christian redemption, and above all the paschal mystery. If certain adaptations are considered necessary on account of local conditions, they are to be made in accordance with the provisions of Art. 39 and 40.

108. The minds of the faithful must be directed primarily towards the feasts of the Lord whereby the mysteries of salvation are celebrated in the course of the year. Therefore, the proper of the time shall be given the preference which is its due over the feasts of the saints, so that the

entire cycle of the mysteries of salvation may be suitably recalled.

109. The season of Lent has a twofold character: primarily by recalling or preparing for baptism and by penance, it disposes the faithful, who more diligently hear the word of God and devote themselves to prayer, to celebrate the paschal mystery. This twofold character is to be brought into greater prominence both in the liturgy and by liturgical catechesis. Hence:

(a) More use is to be made of the baptismal features proper to the Lenten liturgy; some of them, which used to flourish in bygone days, are to be restored as may seem good.

(b) The same is to apply to the penitential elements. As regards instruction it is important to impress on the minds of the faithful not only the social consequences of sin but also that essence of the virtue of penance which leads to the detestation of sin as an offense against God; the rôle of the Church in penitential practices is not to be passed over, and the people must be exhorted to pray for sinners.

110. During Lent penance should not be only internal and individual, but also external and social. The practice of penance should be fostered in ways that are possible in our own times and in different regions, and according to the circumstances of the faithful; it should be encouraged by the authorities mentioned in Art. 22.

Nevertheless, let the paschal fast be kept sacred. Let it be celebrated everywhere on Good Friday and, where possible, prolonged throughout Holy Saturday, so that the joys of the Sunday of the resurrection may be attained with uplifted and clear mind.

111. The saints have been traditionally honoured in the Church and their authentic relics and images held in venera-

tion. For the feasts of the saints proclaim the wonderful works of Christ in his servants, and display to the faithful fitting examples for their imitation.

Lest the feasts of the saints should take precedence over the feasts which commemorate the very mysteries of salvation, many of them should be left to be celebrated by a particular Church or nation or family of religious; only those should be extended to the universal Church which commemorate saints who are truly of universal importance.

CHAPTER VI: SACRED MUSIC

112. The musical tradition of the universal Church is a treasure of inestimable value, greater even than that of any other art. The main reason for this pre-eminence is that, as sacred song united to the words, it forms a necessary or integral part of the solemn liturgy.

Holy scripture, indeed, has bestowed praise upon sacred song,[42] and the same may be said of the fathers of the Church and of the Roman pontiffs who in recent times, led by St Pius X, have explained more precisely the ministerial function supplied by sacred music in the service of the Lord.

Therefore sacred music is to be considered the more holy in proportion as it is more closely connected with the liturgical action, whether it adds delight to prayer, fosters unity of minds, or confers greater solemnity upon the sacred rites. But the Church approves of all forms of true art having the needed qualities, and admits them into divine worship.

Accordingly, the sacred Council, keeping to the norms and precepts of ecclesiastical tradition and discipline, and having regard to the purpose of sacred music, which is the glory of God and the sanctification of the faithful, decrees as follows.

[42] Cf. Eph. 5. 19; Col. 3. 16.

113. Liturgical worship is given a more noble form when the divine offices are celebrated solemnly in song, with the assistance of sacred ministers and the active participation of the people.

As regards the language to be used, the provisions of Art. 36 are to be observed; for the Mass, Art. 54; for the sacraments, Art. 63; for the divine Office, Art. 101.

114. The treasury of sacred music is to be preserved and fostered with great care. Choirs must be diligently promoted, especially in cathedral churches; but bishops and other pastors of souls must be at pains to ensure that, whenever the sacred action is to be celebrated with song, the whole body of the faithful may be able to contribute that active participation which is rightly theirs, as laid down in Art. 28 and 30.

115. Great importance is to be attached to the teaching and practice of music in seminaries, in the novitiates and houses of study of religious of both sexes, and also in other Catholic institutions and schools. To impart this instruction, teachers are to be carefully trained and put in charge of the teaching of sacred music.

It is desirable also to found higher institutes or sacred music whenever this can be done.

Composers and singers, especially boys, must also be given a genuine liturgical training.

116. The Church acknowledges Gregorian chant as specially suited to the Roman liturgy: therefore, other things being equal, it should be given pride of place in liturgical services.

But other kinds of sacred music, especially polyphony, are by no means excluded from liturgical celebrations, so long as they accord with the spirit of the liturgical action, as laid down in Art. 30.

117. The typical edition of the books of Gregorian chant is to be completed; and a more critical edition is to be pre-

pared of those books already published since the restoration
by St Pius X.

It is desirable also that an edition be prepared containing simpler melodies, for use in small churches.

118. Religious singing by the people is to be skillfully
fostered, so that in devotions and sacred exercises, as also
during liturgical services, the voices of the faithful may
ring out according to the norms and requirements of the
rubrics.

119. In certain parts of the world, especially mission
lands, there are peoples who have their own musical traditions, and these play a great part in their religious and social
life. For this reason due importance is to be attached to their
music, and a suitable place is to be given to it, not only in
forming their attitude towards religion, but also in adapting
worship to their native genius, as indicated in Art. 39 and 40.

Therefore, when missionaries are being given training
in music, every effort should be made to see that they become competent in promoting the traditional music of these
peoples, both in schools and in sacred services, as far as may
be practicable.

120. In the Latin Church the pipe organ is to be held
in high esteem, for it is the traditional musical instrument
which adds a wonderful splendour to the Church's ceremonies and powerfully lifts up man's mind to God and to
higher things.

But other instruments also may be admitted for use in
divine worship, with the knowledge and consent of the competent territorial authority, as laid down in Art. 22, ii, 37,
and 40. This may be done, however, only on condition that
the instruments are suitable, or can be made suitable, for
sacred use, accord with the dignity of the temple, and truly
contribute to the edification of the faithful.

121. Composers, filled with the Christian spirit, should

feel that their vocation is to cultivate sacred music and increase its store of treasures.

Let them produce compositions which have the qualities proper to genuine sacred music, not confining themselves to works which can be sung only by large choirs, but providing also for the needs of small choirs and for the active participation of the entire assembly of the faithful.

The texts intended to be sung must always be in conormity with Catholic doctrine; indeed they should be drawn chiefly from holy Scripture and from liturgical sources.

CHAPTER VII: SACRED ART AND SACRED FURNISHINGS

122. Very rightly the fine arts are considered to rank among the noblest activities of man's genius, and this applies especially to religious art and to its highest achievement, which is sacred art. These arts, by their very nature, are oriented towards the infinite beauty of God which they attempt in some way to portray by the work of human hands; they achieve their purpose of redounding to God's praise and glory in proportion as they are directed the more exclusively to a single aim of turning men's minds devoutly towards God.

Holy Mother Church has therefore always been the friend of the fine arts and has ever sought their noble help, with the special aim that all things set apart for use in divine worship should be truly worthy, becoming, and beautiful, signs and symbols of the supernatural world, and for this purpose she has trained artists. In fact, the Church has, with good reason, always reserved to herself the right to pass judgement upon the arts, deciding which of the works of artists are in accordance with faith, piety, and cherished traditional laws, and thereby fitted for sacred use.

The Church has been particularly careful to see that sacred furnishings should worthily and beautifully serve the dignity of worship, and has admitted changes in materials, style, or ornamentation prompted by the progress of the technical arts with the passage of time.

Wherefore it has pleased the Fathers to issue the following decrees on these matters.

123. The Church has not adopted any particular style of art as her very own; she has admitted styles from every period according to the natural talents and circumstances of peoples, and the needs of the various rites. Thus, in the course of the centuries, she has brought into being a treasury of art which must be very carefully preserved. The art of our own days, coming from every race and region, shall also be given free scope in the Church, provided that it adorns the sacred buildings and holy rites with due reverence and honour; thereby it is enabled to contribute its own voice to that wonderful chorus of praise in honour of the Catholic faith sung by great men in times gone by.

124. Ordinaries, by the encouragement and favour they show to art which is truly sacred, should strive after noble beauty rather than mere sumptuous display. This principle is to apply also in the matter of sacred vestments and ornaments.

Let bishops carefully remove from the house of God and from other sacred places those works of artists which are repugnant to faith, morals, and Christian piety, and which offend true religious sense either by depraved forms or by lack of artistic worth, mediocrity and pretence.

And when churches are to be built, let great care be taken that they be suitable for the celebration of liturgical services and for the active participation of the faithful.

125. The practice of placing sacred images in churches so that they may be venerated by the faithful is to be maintained. Nevertheless their number should be moderate and

their relative positions should reflect right order. For otherwise they may create confusion among the Christian people and foster devotion of doubtful orthodoxy.

126. When passing judgement on works of art, local ordinaries shall give a hearing to the diocesan commission on sacred art and, if needed, also to others who are especially expert, and to the commissions referred to in Art. 44, 45, and 46.

Ordinaries must be very careful to see that sacred furnishings and works of value are not disposed of or dispersed; for they are the ornaments of the house of God.

127. Bishops should have a special concern for artists, so as to imbue them with the spirit of sacred art and of the sacred liturgy. This they may do in person or through suitable priests who are gifted with a knowledge and love of art.

It is also desirable that schools or academies of sacred art should be founded in those parts of the world where they would be useful, so that artists may be trained.

All artists who, prompted by their talents, desire to serve God's glory in holy Church, should ever bear in mind that they are engaged in a kind of sacred imitation of God the Creator, and are concerned with works destined to be used in Catholic worship, to edify the faithful, and to foster their piety and their religious formation.

128. Along with the revision of the liturgical books, as laid down in Art. 25, there is to be an early revision of the canons and ecclesiastical statutes which govern the provision of material things involved in sacred worship. These laws refer especially to the worthy and well planned construction of sacred buildings, the shape and construction of altars, the nobility, placing, and safety of the eucharistic tabernacle, the dignity and suitability of the baptistery, the proper ordering of sacred images, embellishments, and vestments. Laws which seem less suited to the reformed liturgy

are to be brought into harmony with it, or else abolished; and any which are helpful are to be retained if already in use, or introduced where they are lacking.

According to the norm of Art. 22 of this Constitution, the territorial bodies of bishops are empowered to adapt such things to the needs and customs of their different regions; this applies especially to the materials and form of sacred furnishings and vestments.

129. During their philosophical and theological studies, clerics are to be taught about the history and development of sacred art, and about the sound principles governing the production of its works. In consequence they will be able to appreciate and preserve the Church's venerable monuments, and be in a position to aid, by good advice, artists who are engaged in producing works of art.

130. It is fitting that the use of pontificals be reserved to those ecclesiastical persons who have episcopal rank or some particular jurisdiction.

APPENDIX: A DECLARATION OF THE SECOND ECUMENICAL COUNCIL OF THE VATICAN ON REVISION OF THE CALENDAR

The Second Ecumenical Sacred Council of the Vatican, recognizing the importance of the wishes expressed by many concerning the assignment of the feast of Easter to a fixed Sunday and concerning an unchanging calendar, having carefully considered the effects which could result from the introduction of a new calendar, declares as follows:

1. The sacred Council would not object if the feast of Easter were assigned to a particular Sunday of the Gregorian Calendar, provided that those whom it may concern, espe-

---

Reprinted through the courtesy of the National Catholic Welfare Conference.

cially the brethren who are not in communion with the Apostolic See, give their assent.

2. The sacred Council likewise declares that it does not oppose efforts designed to introduce a perpetual calendar into civil society.

But, among the various systems which are being suggested to stabilize a perpetual calendar and to introduce it into civil life, the Church has no objection only in the case of those systems which retain and safeguard a seven-day week with Sunday, without the introduction of any days outside the week, so that the succession of weeks may be left intact, unless there is question of the most serious reasons. Concerning these the Apostolic See shall judge.

A COMMENTARY ON
THE LITURGICAL
CONSTITUTION

THE INTRODUCTION

The aims of the Second Vatican Council, stated by Pope John XXIII in his Encyclical *Ad Petri Cathedram,* are summarized at the beginning of this, its first Constitution, as being: *to impart an ever increasing vigour to the Christian life of the faithful; to adapt more suitably to the needs of our times those institutions which are subject to change; to foster whatever can promote union among all who believe in Christ; to strengthen whatever can help to call the whole of mankind into the household of the Church* (n. 1).

The reform of the liturgy which the Constitution sets in progress is a very important means for the achievement of these ends, for the liturgy is, of its very nature, the epiphany of the Church. It manifests her true nature by showing her engaged in the most important of her activities. It reveals her attributes, paradoxical on the rational plane but making wonderful sense on the plane of divine revelation. For those things in the Church which are human, active, visible, and mundane are signs and symbols and transitory means of attaining the everlasting qualities which belong to her: divine, contemplative, invisible and celestial. By manifesting the Church both to those within her fold and to those without, the liturgy builds up its members into a holy dwelling-place for God in the Spirit, it equips them to preach the Gospel to the nations and makes of the Church a standard raised among the Gentiles under which the scattered children of God may be gathered (n. 2). This, at least, is the function it should have and which the Council has determined to restore to it.

Accordingly, the Constitution lays before us certain basic principles which are valid for all liturgy, and establishes certain norms for application to the Roman rite (n. 3).

Whatever may have been the attitude of Roman authorities in the past, the Council takes this opportunity to declare unequivocally that all the rites of the Church are of equal dignity and no one of them is to be deemed a model for the others, all are to be preserved and fostered, and *where necessary also to be reformed in the light of sound tradition that they may be given new vigour to meet the needs of modern times* (n. 4).

GENERAL PRINCIPLES FOR THE RESTORATION AND PROMOTION OF THE SACRED LITURGY

The first chapter of the Constitution is by far the most important of its seven chapters and takes up a third of the whole text. It is to this chapter that the largest part of this commentary will be devoted, because it is only in the light of what is said here that the reforms indicated in the rest of the Constitution can be appreciated. It is necessary to understand what the Church is doing in this matter and why she is doing it, before true obedience can be given to the often painful measures of reform which will gradually be imposed.

The chapter opens with the most remarkable doctrinal statement on the nature of the sacred liturgy and its importance in the Church's life. No other Council has ever made such a statement; the classic textbooks of the seminaries are silent on the subject; only in most recent times have theologians applied themselves to working out a theology of worship. The result is that what the Council has to say here is fresh and full of weighty consequences not only for the theology of the Church and of the sacraments, for catechetics and pastoral work, but for the very life of the faithful.

The Constitution makes use of one basic concept which, though frequently found in the Fathers of the Church, has been neglected for many centuries and has only recently begun once more to appear in the writings of theologians. This is the concept of "mystery-sacrament." For a long time the word "sacrament" was reserved for the seven rites of the Church by which grace is conferred *ex opere operato* or by the very performance of the rite. But it also has a wider sense designating a person or thing which reveals to us the mysterious plan of God for our salvation in a manner attuned to our understanding, and reveals it in the act of being realized. The Council has decided to return to this ancient usage of the word, since the concept for which it stands is of great use for our understanding of the mystery of the Church and of her liturgy.

The chapter opens with the following statement:

> God who "wills that all men be saved and come to knowledge of the truth" (1 Tim. 2. 4), "who in divers manners spoke in times past to the Fathers by the prophets" (Hebr. 1. 1), when the fullness of time had come, sent his Son, the Word made flesh, anointed by the Holy Spirit, to preach the Gospel to the poor and heal the broken-hearted, as a physician of flesh and spirit, the mediator between God and man. For his humanity in the unity of the person of the Word was the instrument of our salvation. Thus in Christ the perfect achieve-

ment of our reconcilation appeared, and the fullness of divine worship entered among us.[1]

In this paragraph the key theme of the whole Constitution is clearly announced. Christ's coming forth into the world brings not only the perfect achievement of our reconciliation, but the fullness of divine worship. The one is subordinate to the other. Redemption, like creation itself, is orientated to the glory of the Father. For in this God's glory is manifest: that he has not only created the world and man in it, a creature endowed with freedom, but that he is powerful to save mankind from the disastrous results which follow from the abuse of that freedom. Christ's act of redemption is therefore a supreme act of the worship of God. "I have glorified you upon earth; I have completed the work which you gave me to perform. . . . I have manifested your name to the men whom you have taken from the world to give to me" (John 17. 4.6). The act of redemption includes both revelation and the divine saving action. God wishes all men to be *saved* and to come to a *knowledge of the truth*. In different ways he spoke of old to the people of Israel through the prophets, but now he speaks to us in his Word made flesh, his incarnate Son who by his life and by his very being speaks of his Father, manifesting his name and the purpose of his loving kindness which is our salvation. He is *anointed by the Spirit to preach the Gospel to the poor and heal the broken-hearted, a physician, as St Ignatius says,*[2] *of flesh and spirit,* bringing salvation in the spiritual sphere by his proclamation of forgiveness, and also in the material creation by uniting it with his divinity. Christ is in fact the mediator between God and man, bringing God's gifts to men and offering to his Father the worship of a redeemed human race. His human nature *anointed by the Spirit* is the *instrument of our salva-*

[1] Constitution n. 5.
[2] Epistle to the Ephesians 7. 2.

tion as St Thomas Aquinas had taught following in the steps of St John Damascene. For, by the suffering and the deeds of the man Jesus Christ, God brings about the salvation of the human race.

Composed of flesh and Spirit, belonging, that is, both to this world and to the divine sphere, Christ is the sacrament of God's saving plan, revealing it in terms that we can understand, and at the same time bringing it about. But, again as St Thomas taught, the sacraments are not merely remedies to heal our fallen nature, they are also ordered to divine worship. Christ as the mediator between God and man brings divine life to moribund humanity in order to bring to his Father a holy people to declare the wonderful deeds of him who called them out of darkness into his marvellous light (cf. 1 Peter 2. 9). He brought about our salvation by presenting in our name a worship acceptable to God; this act of worship consists of his making redeemed humanity a pure oblation to his Father.

It will not be out of place here to remark that most of the errors about the nature of the liturgy, from which priests and the laity have suffered in the past—and which continue to obstruct the liturgical movement—spring from a failure to appreciate this double rôle, common both to Christ's mystery and the liturgical activity of the Church by which it is represented and applied to individuals over the ages. On the one hand, the liturgy is seen as a pure act of praise which has no immediate reference to the spiritual welfare of those who perform it; on the other, the sacraments are regarded as purely medicinal acts of God for our salvation in which only the objective validity of the rite is important. The principles set out by the Constitution with regard to the work of Christ ought to prevent us from opposing liturgy and sacraments, salvation and worship, the sanctification of man and the glory of God.

Christ's work of giving glory to God by the salvation of men was accomplished first and foremost, the Constitution says, in the paschal mystery. This name is given to the unique tripartite event of the passion, the resurrection from the dwelling place of the dead and the glorious ascension to God. This is the event in which, as the Church sings in the Preface for Easter, by dying Christ destroyed our death and by rising restored us to life. It was in this event that the Church was formed from the side of Christ as he slept the sleep of death upon the cross. For many hundreds of years Christians in the West have not thought in terms of the paschal mystery; that is, they have forgotten that the passion and death, resurrection, and ascension of Christ are but three aspects of a single act by which Jesus Christ, "passing over" from the sinful world to the kingdom of his Father, accomplished our salvation. Until recently most emphasis was placed upon the passion seen in isolation as the act by which Christ paid the debt due on our sins and thus redeemed us. No causal significance was commonly attributed to the resurrection and ascension but they were regarded merely as proofs of Christ's divinity. The New Testament, the Fathers and the Eastern Churches see the whole event in a very different light: the death and resurrection of Christ means for them the destruction of all the old creation corrupted by sin and doomed to die, the death of human nature estranged from God and the beginning of a new creation, a restored human nature reconciled to God, participating in his divine life, incapable of suffering, immortal and glorious. The passion is but the way that leads to salvation achieved in the resurrection. This notion has been the constant theme of the champions of the liturgical movement over the last fifty years; the Council has now adopted it to express the faith of the Church.

From the pierced side of Christ on the cross *came forth the*

From the pierced side of Christ on the cross *came forth the wonderful sacrament of the whole Church,* for, like the man Jesus Christ and in succession to him, the Church has the sacramental function of proclaiming the redemption wrought by Christ's paschal mystery and of bringing that salvation to all creatures even to the end of the world. This idea of the Church as a sacrament appears again in the Dogmatic Constitution on the Church promulgated on November 21st, 1964. There it is stated that the Church is in Christ as a sacrament and sign and instrument of close union with God and of the unity of the whole human race.[3] In the Church the mystery of salvation is manifested to the world; and through her activity it becomes a reality in the lives of individuals, bringing them to an intimate union with the Father and the Son in the Holy Spirit.

6. Christ sends his apostles out into the world just as he was sent forth by the Father. They are to preach the Gospel announcing the good news of salvation. But their function is not only to announce and to preach; they are to bring about through the sacraments the salvation they proclaim. Around these sacraments and especially the sacrifice of the Eucharist revolves the whole liturgy with which all the Constitution is concerned. Taken as a whole the liturgy, like Christ himself, and like the Church who performs it, is sacramental: it manifests to men the mystery of salvation, it is the instrument through which this salvation becomes a reality for the different generations of believers, in it the Church as the holy people which Christ has acquired offers to God in union with her head that worship which is his due.

This is exemplified by the two great sacraments. In baptism *men are plunged into the paschal mystery of Christ,*

[3] Chapter 1.

and are thus constituted the true worshippers in spirit and truth which the Father seeks. Baptism not only initiates us into the community in which the graces of salvation are poured out; it involves us in the society of the priestly people, in the worship which Christ continues to offer his Father through the members of his body on earth. In the Eucharist this community is nourished with Christ's body and blood and strengthened with his divine grace-life, while at the same time it proclaims the salvific mystery of its Lord returning thanks to God.

From the day of Pentecost on which the Church, born from the side of Christ on Calvary, appeared before the world in the power of the Holy Spirit, the spiritual reality which it contains and communicates was made manifest in its sacramental activity. *From that time forward the Church has never ceased to come together to celebrate the paschal mystery.* This she does by reading what the Scriptures have to say of Christ, by celebrating the Eucharist *in which the victory and triumph of his death are represented* and by giving praise to God for his ineffable gifts.

7. These community acts of the Church are the outward manifestation of a supernatural mystery. Christ is always present in his Church in order through her to bring to perfection his work of salvation; and he is especially present in her liturgical actions. What the Council has to say about this presence marks a very important step forward in Western theology, where the presence of Christ in the Blessed Sacrament has caused the other ways in which he is present in the liturgy to be forgotten. In the sacrifice of the Mass the Constitution first mentions Christ's presence in the person of his minister, for as the Council of Trent says he is "the same now offering through the ministry of priests who formerly offered himself on the cross." [4] If the Church is now the

visible body of Christ on earth, the bishop or priest who
presides when the Church is assembled to celebrate the
Eucharist manifests the invisible presence of Christ her head.
He is especially present in the bread and the wine of the
sacrifice as being the Church's offering, and uniting in his
body which once hung upon the cross all those who offer.
"One loaf, we who are many are one body, all who share
the one bread" (1 Cor. 10. 17). He is present also in the
other sacraments, not in the substantial way in which he is
present in the Eucharist, but by his power: when the Church
administers baptism it is Christ who baptizes and similarly
all the other sacraments are acts of Christ himself. To receive the sacraments is to encounter Christ who, through the
corporate acts of his Church, himself applies to individuals
the effects of his salvation according to their need. The
Constitution then lists a fourth mode of Christ's presence not
mentioned before by any document of the magisterium: *He
is present in his word since it is he himself who speaks when
the holy scriptures are read in church.* Lastly, as he promised
in the Gospel (Matt. 18. 20) he is present in the midst of
his faithful when they are gathered together in his name to
pray and to sing.

These are five modes of real presence. But, since the
whole structure of the liturgy is sacramental, they differ in
nature as the various significative elements in the whole
signify different aspects of the mystery. Among them the
Eucharist is pre-eminent since it *is* the body of Christ which
was born of the Virgin Mary in a symbolic form which manifests the unity of the mystical body and Christ's presence in
his Church.

It would be false, however, to suppose that in all this the
Church in any way compels Christ to act through his sacraments. Rather it is Christ who has the initiative and deigns

⁴ Session XXLL, c. 2 (Denzinger 1743 [1940]).

to associate the Church with himself in that great work by which men are sanctified and God receives perfect glory. It is because he has chosen to use the Church as an instrument for the perfecting of this work, that her communal acts of worship are the outward manifestations of the mystery of salvation as it takes effect over the centuries. *The Church is his beloved bride who calls to her Lord, and through him offers worship to the eternal Father.*

The doctrinal exposition comes to a climax with a definition of liturgy. This is not a superfluous growth marring the purity of a spiritual and interior religion, nor is it merely the ceremonial frills which lend mystery and majesty to the rites by which divine grace is conferred; it is the *exercise of the priestly office of Jesus Christ, in which the sanctification of man is signified by signs perceptible to the senses and brought about in a manner which corresponds with each of these signs, and in which a complete public worship is performed by the mystical body of Jesus Christ, by the head, that is, and by the members.*

The liturgy is the exercise of the priestly office of Jesus Christ in which he accomplished the sanctification of men in order that he may offer them united in himself as an acceptable oblation to the Father. Christ exercises his priestly function through the members of his body, the Church, in which his saving work is made manifest to the world. The community acts of this Church serve as the signs or sacraments by which the spiritual effects of Christ's priestly activity are rendered intelligible and realized in differing ways according to the various needs of the individual members. But the system of outward religious acts serves not only to manifest the saving grace of God, it is also the symbolic ritual through which the sanctified community offers to the Father its worship in spirit and truth; it is the human vehicle of the sanctification and the worship brought about by Christ in union with his body on earth. Hence it follows that among all the activity of the Church the liturgy is the sacred action surpassing all others.

From this definition the principles of reform, to be elaborated in the rest of the document, are already clear: the faithful have a right and a duty to take part actively in the liturgy in which *the whole public worship is performed . . . by the head . . . and by the members;* because the rites have the sacramental function of signifying the spiritual realities they bring about, the people ought to be able to understand what they are doing.

8. But a right emphasis on intelligibility and communal action should not blind us to the majesty of the supernatural reality. The earthly liturgy is a shadow and a foretaste of the heavenly liturgy in the celestial Jerusalem, for the priest of both is the same Lord of glory and in our earthly rites we join with all the warriors of the heavenly army. The reality which is manifested on earth in visible signs belongs of itself to the new creation of the perfected kingdom of God: it is truly eschatological. This perspective has always been dear to the Oriental Churches. So far from making us move further away from the viewpoint of our Eastern brethren, the reforms of the Roman liturgy should bring us closer together.

9. Although the liturgy is the highest and most sacred of all the activities of the Christian society, it does not exhaust this activity. Before men can come to the liturgy, *they must be called to faith and conversion.* Before liturgy is possible the Church must proclaim the kerygma, the *praeconium salutis* as the Latin text puts it, the simple message of salvation through the passion and resurrection of Christ. All through their lives Christians need to be confronted with this message, and to be taught all that Christ has commanded, to be encouraged to deeper faith, to penance, charity, and apostolic labours. All these works, though they do not form part of the liturgy, help to manifest the mystery of salvation

at work in the Christian community, and through them also Christ gives glory to the Father.

10-12. The liturgy is the fountainhead from which all the life of the body flows and into which it returns. As a source of power and grace it enables Christians to live lives in imitation of Christ; as the ritual act in which they offer to God the worship of their Christian lives united with the sacrifice of his Son, it is the summit towards which all their effort is directed.

The liturgy, through which Christ acts in his Church, possesses an efficacy which does not originate with the worshippers, but those who take part in it will only be able to receive its full effect if they are properly disposed. On the one hand the liturgy is there to aid this disposition. Pastors must see to it that the celebration is not only valid and licit; it is their duty also to ensure that the faithful take part, being fully aware of what *they are doing, actively engaged in the rite and enriched by its effects* (11). The faithful themselves, on the other hand, must make sure that their liturgical actions are not the empty expressions of a spiritual life that they do not lead. What is expressed in church must be lived outside. The Christian life must first and foremost be a life of prayer. Private prayer in the chamber must first exist if the public liturgy in the assembly is to be truthful. Only this will enable them more and more *to bear about in their bodies the dying of Christ* which in sacramental form they proclaimed at baptism, *so that the life of Jesus may be made manifest in their bodily frame.*[5] There is no opposition between private prayer and public liturgy; though the latter is not the same as the former. It presupposes it and depends upon it (12).

13. Just as the Christian cannot survive without an interior life of private prayer, so to foster this it has become necessary over the centuries to institute certain forms of worship which are something between private prayer and the official liturgy.

[5] cf. II Cor. 4. 10-11.

These are called popular devotions or *pia exercitia*. They are of two types: gatherings for prayer of a more popular nature than that provided by the liturgy, like the Stations of the Cross or the Holy Hour, and celebrations in conformity with local traditions or circumstances. The ancient liturgy provided for all the devotional needs of the Christian people in a way which centred on the essentials of the faith; and had sufficient adaptability to respond to all popular and local requirements. This is still largely the case with the Eastern rites. In the West the use of a liturgical language that was not generally understood, on the one hand, and a more rigid conception of liturgy which was the outcome of centralization, on the other, led to the proliferation of popular and local devotions which would provide for the faithful what they could not find in the official worship of the Church. Some of them tended to concentrate on inessentials and to express a religious sentiment which lacked both the universal appeal and the deep doctrinal relevance of the more discreet liturgical prayer. They have, however, taken deep root in the life of Christian communities and therefore the Constitution says that they are to be highly commended so long as they conform with the laws and norms of the Church, and especially when they are ordered by the Holy See. But they are to harmonize with the liturgical seasons—it would be wrong, for instance, if the people were distracted from the observances of Lent by devotions for the month of St Joseph. They should be so constructed as to accord with the liturgy by being properly related to the paschal mystery and other central Christian realities. Nor should they supplant the liturgy which the Church is engaged in renewing as the staple form of worship accommodated to all—the Stations of the Cross should not supplant the celebration of the passion and death of our Lord on Good Friday or evening devotions the parish celebration of Vespers in English on a Sunday evening. They should take their inspiration from the forms of the liturgy and be of such a nature as to assist the faithful to understand and make their own the official prayer of the Church, *for the liturgy by its very nature far surpasses any of them.*

II. THE PROMOTION OF LITURGICAL INSTRUCTION AND ACTIVE PARTICIPATION

The Church *earnestly desires that all the faithful should be led to that full conscious and active participation in the liturgical celebrations which is demanded by the very nature of the liturgy.* This is their right and duty as baptized members of Christ, for they are, as St Peter says, "a chosen race, a royal priesthood, a holy nation, a redeemed people" (1 Peter 2. 9; cf. 2. 4-5). The liturgy is the *primary and indispensable source* from which they should receive a sound apprehension of the mysteries of faith and the grace to live a life deeply committed to Christ. Therefore, full and active participation by all the faithful is the aim to be considered before all else in the restoration of the liturgy, and all pastors must strive to achieve it by means of the necessary instruction.

Before this is possible, of course, the priests themselves must become *thoroughly imbued with the spirit and power of* the liturgy. This is the great difficulty. Clauses 15-20 lay down the means that must be taken to ensure that it is brought about.

III. THE RESTORATION OF THE LITURGY

If the liturgy is once more to play its proper rôle in building up the Church to the stature that is demanded by the difficulties of our times, it is not sufficient to set out with clarity the teaching about its nature nor to legislate for the instruction of the clergy and laity; the Church must undertake a radical reform of the liturgy itself. She has not only the right but the duty to do this. For the liturgy, like the Church who celebrates it and, indeed, like Christ himself, is both divine and human. It is divine because it brings to us the grace of salvation, but by its human elements it reveals to us and to the world the saving mystery in which we are involved. The divinely instituted elements are immutable, but the human elements have grown slowly through the course of the ages and should be changed when it is perceived that something out of harmony with the inner nature of the liturgy has been intruded, or when they have in any way become unsuited to the times and ill adapted to fulfill their important rôle. On such a restoration the Council has resolved.

The only basis on which such a reform can be carried out is a clear understanding of the nature of the liturgy such as has been set out in the first section of this chapter. The liturgy is sacramental: its function is to manifest, to reveal in human terms the mystery of salvation which Christ brings about by its means. It must speak to men of this mystery, not only in its remedial aspects, but in its Godward aspect as the glory which Christ offers his Father by the redemption of men. The restoration must then ensure that the rites and texts are drawn up so as to *express more clearly the holy things which they signify* for only when all the members of the Church can understand the liturgy with ease and take part in it fully, actively and as befits a community will it be able to achieve its full effect in their lives and be truly a medium in which they can express the worship of their Christian lives.

As the liturgy took shape over the centuries there has been a constant tension between its rôle of signification and the reverence men felt for the divine mystery which it contains. Churchmen have been acutely aware that through the rites of the liturgy we are associated with the angelic ministers around the throne of God and assist at the heavenly altar.

The thought is awe-inspiring and has led them to hedge the sacred rite about with pomp and ceremony which obscured its symbolic nature and made of it a cloud of awesome ritual separating the sacred from the profane lest familiarity should breed contempt. The history of religions shows that such is the universal reaction of men brought in contact with sacred things. It is a natural reaction and not one to be despised. Both the sacredness of the invisible mystery and the meaningfulness of the visible rites must be respected but the highest authority of the Church has now declared that the rôle of signification must take unchallenged precedence.

22. The Constitution then proceeds to set out the norms which must govern the reform, and, in the first place, some general principles.

The first point to be established is the authority on which the reform should depend. For many centuries the diocesan bishops exercised great control over the liturgical tradition, but ever since the Council of Trent this power has, in increasing degrees, been reserved to the pope.[6] By conceding authority to the various kinds of legitimately established bishops' conferences, the Council is returning to an older discipline which will make for a liturgy better adapted to the local needs of peoples differing in custom, language and culture. This power is strictly limited in the various sections of the Constitution. The organization of the sacred liturgy belongs to the authority of the Church. No private person has any right to make changes according to his own taste or ideas precisely because the liturgy is not the act of this or that congregation but of the whole body of Christ; frequently it is linked with the integrity of the Catholic faith itself. The faithful have the right that the liturgy they take part in should be the liturgy of the Church and not that of an individual

[6] See *Mediator Dei,* n. 62.1.

priest or master of ceremonies, however enlightened he may be. The nature of the territorial authority which is to regulate, within certain limits, the practice of the liturgy in different parts of the world is described by the Instruction *Inter oecumenici* of September 26th, 1964, nn. 23-31, which also lays down that the acts of these assemblies should not be promulgated till they have been ratified by the Apostolic See.

23. Restoration does not in any sense imply that the Church wishes to invent anew the forms of her worship. These she has had from the time of the apostles and they have developed without a break in the centuries that followed. The first step must be to understand these traditional forms and the path of their development. Those elements which may have become unsuited to the present situation can be adapted, but one should not change or destroy what one does not understand. Historical, theological and pastoral studies should be made by people competent in the subject before changes are proposed so that nothing is spoiled that may be of value to pastoral efforts.

Great use has always been made in the liturgy of holy Scripture; the great majority of the prayers and chants are taken from it or inspired by it and this is one of the reasons why modern Catholics who have become so unfamiliar with the sacred text find the imagery and language of the liturgy so difficult. But the answer to this problem does not lie in abandoning the use of Scripture for it was written for our instruction; it lies rather in a return to the Bible, and that primarily through the liturgy, so that its thought and images become once more the staple diet of every Christian mind.

25. To ensure that the principles which it lays down will be observed the Council orders that the liturgical books are to be revised by an international group of bishops with knowledge of the present pastoral needs assisted by experts in the

liturgical sciences drawn from all over the world. The members of this commission have already been appointed and are hard at work upon their task.

The Constitution now turns to the consideration of the norms which are to govern the restoration itself. These must derive from the nature of the liturgy which is the chief activity of the Christian community and, like the activity of all communities, is formative for those who take part in it. The first group of norms listed devolve from the communal nature of the liturgy; the second from its pastoral and didactic nature.

26. The Church is a community and a community with a hierarchical structure; the liturgy of the Church should, then, clearly be a community activity in which each member takes part according to the function or place he has in the community.

Firstly the Constitution reminds us that liturgical services are not private acts. Unfortunately they had come to be so regarded by both the clergy and the laity. Priests would frequently refer to "my Mass" and "my Office", and those who attended Mass would look upon it as a privileged moment of private prayer and regard any communal acts of worship as an intrusion upon their privacy with God. The liturgical services, the Constitution says, *are celebrations of the Church*. "To celebrate", writes Dom Hild, "is above all to do something; it is to do something in common and religiously." [7] They are celebrations of the Church and the Church here is not an abstraction like "the State", but in St Cyprian's words, "the sacrament of unity",[8] or as he explains elsewhere, "the holy people united and ordered under their

---

[7] "Le mystère de la celebration" in *La Maison-Dieu,* 20 (1950) p. 103, cited by Père Roguet in his commentary on the Constitution, *La Maison Dieu,* 77, p. 52.

[8] *De Cath. Eccles. Unitate, 7.*

bishops".[9] *They belong to the whole body of the Church; they manifest it and have effects upon it.* Each particular congregation is the microcosm of the diocese, the diocese of the universal Church. The communal liturgy gives outward expression to the invisible worship which is the Church's life of harmonious unity. In the liturgy, the bishop, priests, deacons, and the other servants of the community together with the laity have their different rôles to play, just as in the life of the Church they have their various functions to perform.

27. Therefore, the Constitution stresses, *whenever the rites, according to their specific nature, suppose a communal celebration involving the presence and active participation of the people, this way of celebrating them is to be preferred, so far as possible, to a celebration that is individual and quasi-private.* Some of the Church's liturgical rites no longer suppose a communal celebration, for example, the sacrament of penance; others suppose it to a greater or lesser degree. The sacraments of baptism, confirmation, and first communion, since they mark the initiation of a new member into the community, are essentially communal and suppose the presence of that community. Marriages and funerals belong more to the family than to the parish and it would not be according to the spirit of the Constitution to replace the parish Sunday Mass by a nuptial Mass or a requiem on the pretext of making this a community celebration. The rite of the anointing of the sick supposes the presence of a group of intimate friends and relations around the sick-bed.

The reference to the Mass is of great importance. *Every Mass has of itself a public and social nature* however it should be celebrated, as the Council of Trent has stated,[10] but this

---

[9] Epistle 66. 8. 3.
[10] Session XXII, cf. Denzinger n. 1747 (944); cf. Codex Rubricarum n. 269.

does not always appear. The celebration of Mass with the active participation of the faithful should take precedence over an individual celebration, equally concelebration at a Mass with a congregation should be preferred to a Mass said in the presence of only a server. It is clear that in so far as the piety of new generations of priests is modelled on what is laid down here, the forms of eucharistic piety in the West will be profoundly modified.

28. The following principle introduces a long awaited reform. Already the Instruction *Inter oecumenici* has translated it into practical terms. Those parts which belong to the people or to the choir and are sung or recited by them, should not be said privately by the celebrant; similarly the celebrant should not say privately the lessons which are read or sung by a competent minister or server.[11] Such customs and eventually laws that he should do so grew up from a misunderstanding of the nature of the liturgy. The present article not only forbids the celebrant and the other ministers of the liturgy to appropriate parts which do not belong to them, but insists also that even those who have no special function to perform should do all that pertains to their rôle as members of the congregation. Thus the liturgy is no longer to be "celebrated" only by the priest and his ministers, but by the whole assembly.

29. The servers, readers, commentators, and those who belong to the *schola* or choir perform a true liturgical ministry in their own right even if they are not ordained for it but only appointed for the occasion. The Constitution is here only repeating what was said in the Instruction *De Musica sacra* of September 3rd, 1958.[12] It is especially to be noted

[11] nn. 32 and 33.
[12] English Translation published by the C.T.S. of Ireland (EN 9) nn. 93-103, pp. 32-35.

that the commentator fulfills a true liturgical ministry, though it is to be hoped that what interventions are necessary will eventually be assigned to the competent minister, the priest or the deacon.

30-31. The worshipping community also, for whose sake all the other ministers exist, are to exercise their proper rôle by *acclamations, responses, psalmody, antiphons and hymns, as well as by actions, gestures and bodily attitudes.* Their part in the liturgy is to be indicated by the rubrics of the liturgical books.

These norms will ensure that in the liturgy the Church appears for what it really is: the body of Christ united to its head in the worship of the Father. In the body there are different gifts for the service of all, and so the liturgy is made up from the different contributions of the members of the assembly. The distinctions made by the liturgy according to liturgical functions and clerical rank belong to the whole sacramental structure, but other distinctions which divide society, whether of class, wealth, race or colour should not be allowed to obtrude into the worship of the Church. Civil authorities, however, should be given that honour which is due to their position.

33. Before setting out the norms which devolve from the didactic and pastoral nature of the liturgy the Constitution explains once more that there is no opposition between the worship of God and the sanctification of man through the teaching and grace of the liturgy. The rites of the Church *contain much instruction for the faithful,* because in addition to the readings from Scripture and the sermon, the very prayers, hymns and actions stir us to greater generosity, deepen our understanding of the faith and thus assist us to *offer to God* our *rational service and more abundantly receive his grace.*

34. If the rites of the Church are really to have a formative effect upon those who take part in them, they will need much revision. Times have changed since St Augustine could write: "Our Lord Jesus Christ, as he himself says in the Gospel, has imposed upon us a yoke that is gentle and a burden that is light. He has established the new people by sacraments which are very few in number, of very easy observance and very clear meaning, like baptism celebrated in the name of the Trinity and communion in his blood." [13] Doubtless it will be some little time before the ideal state of the liturgy described in this article of the Constitution is realized, but the goal of our efforts has been indicated.

35. It has long been recognized that owing to the vagaries of a long tradition the choice of Scripture to be read at the various liturgical services is both impoverished and badly selected. This must be changed so that Catholics can become familiar with the whole Bible from hearing it read in Church. But the public reading of the word of God will not have its full effect for the lives of the faithful, unless it be explained and its relevance to the actual situation of those who hear it made apparent. This is the function of the sermon which the Council declares to be part of the liturgy itself.

But apart from biblical preaching and moral exhortation there is also great need to explain to the people the meaning of the liturgical acts in which they take part. The Constitution does not speak here of scholarly expositions on the history of the rites but a living and prayerful initiation which starts from the rites themselves. To this end the Constitution orders that short directives may be spoken by the priest or competent minister at suitable moments within the rites themselves. Examples of such directives are to be indicated in the liturgical books.

[13] Epist. 54. 1.1.

Special services of readings from Scripture and psalms and hymns are encouraged since they are one of the best means to procure that understanding of the history of salvation and the paschal mystery which is so necessary for the life of the Church.

36. Finally the Council gives directions for the language of the liturgy. It is obvious that the liturgical renewal which the Council so earnestly desires will never be a reality so long as the great majority of the faithful do not understand the language in which the liturgy is celebrated. Among all the signs and symbols of the Church's worship language occupies the most important place. So long as the spoken word is intelligible only when it is read in translation from the printed page, true communal participation will never be achieved and the liturgy will be deprived of its didactic and pastoral efficacy to a very large extent.

The Council therefore decrees that *the use of the Latin language is to be maintained in the Latin rites without prejudice to the laws of particular regions in this matter.* This clause should not be regarded as merely a legal fiction inserted to satisfy the more conservative of the Council Fathers. In the first place, if the unity of the Latin rite is to be preserved, there needs to be a norm, and in liturgical matters this should be a living norm of actual practice. Secondly, the Latin liturgy preserves a certain perfection created over the centuries which no vernacular liturgy will be able to equal for a very long time. *But,* the Council continues, *since the use of the mother tongue is frequently of great advantage to the people . . . the limits of its employment may be extended.* This may seem an urbane understatement, but the linguistic situation of the areas where the Latin rites are used varies a great deal. There are some places where Latin remains intelligible to a very large extent; there are others where Latin cannot be replaced by any one vernacular; in the majority of countries the use of Latin has become so rooted in the religious habits of Catholics, that more harm than good may be caused by the abrupt introduction of a change. Finally, it should be remembered that the custom of using several languages in liturgical celebrations is of very long standing in the Church. In many Eastern rites the great eucharistic prayer (corresponding to the Latin Preface and Canon), other prayers of the celebrant, and the lessons are in the language of the people while the dialogues and common chants remain in Greek or another ancient language for the sake of uniformity. The Council approves the introduction of the vernacular from the other end of the scale, which is more in accord with Western habits of thought.

Only the bishops are competent to judge how far the introduction of the people's ordinary language is a necessary and practical means of achieving the Council's aim. The central authority can do no more than indicate those parts of the different ceremonies where the mother tongue may generally be employed with advantage. If local needs exceed the bounds envisaged special concessions will be made. The goal which all must strive to attain has been clearly indicated: *Mother Church earnestly desires that all the faithful should be led to that full, understanding, and active participation in liturgical celebrations which is demanded by the very nature of the liturgy* (14). *The rites . . . should be within the people's power of comprehension and normally should not require much explanation* (34).

The next section represents one of the most momentous decisions of the Council: that the liturgy should be adapted to the culture and traditions of the different nations. All desire for rigid uniformity is renounced and all intention of imposing everywhere Western and Roman customs, though the substantial unity of the Roman rite is to be preserved

(37). In the revised liturgical books the old rubrical conception according to which every movement and gesture of the liturgy was legislated for is to be abandoned: *provision is to be made . . . for the legitimate variations and adaptations to different groups regions and peoples* (38), and within the limits indicated the local ecclesiastical authorities are to specify adaptations of sacramentals, processions, liturgical language, sacred music and the arts, especially in the administration of the sacraments (39).

40. Yet the Council appreciates that *an even more radical adaptation of the liturgy is needed in some places and circumstances.* The local authorities are to consider which elements of the national traditions and cultures might appropriately be admitted into the liturgy. To this end they will be permitted to direct certain experiments and with the help of experts draw up liturgical laws which must be submitted to the Holy See.

This legislation mainly envisages the Churches of Asia and Africa, but it is capable of application much nearer home. In England, for example, the Anglican Church has preserved and developed religious traditions and culture which has inherited a great deal from the practice of the medieval Church and is often in close conformity with the principles laid down by the Constitution. The same is true of the Episcopalians in the United States. If English-speaking Christians are ever again to be united in one Church, whatever is of most value in this tradition should be preserved. For the moment there is no reason why Catholics should not adopt many elements of the Anglican liturgy. The Anglicans themselves are at present engaged in a reform of their liturgy and much might be gained from a close co-operation between the two bodies in working out an English rite which would be in conformity with the tradition and acceptable to both.

IV. THE PROMOTION OF LITURGICAL LIFE
IN THE DIOCESE AND PARISH

41. The Constitution here recalls a truth which has been almost completely forgotten. The centre of the liturgical life of the diocese should be the Eucharist celebrated by the bishop in the midst of his people. This has always been the ideal of the Church since the time of the apostolic Fathers. Only on such occasions does the liturgy fully become the epiphany of the mystery of the Church when *the holy people united and ordered under their bishop* (26) *shows forth the Church to those who are outside as a sign lifted up among the nations* (2). Such gatherings are especially appropriate in the cathedral church, but the bishops would do well to tour the parishes of their dioceses after the example of Pope John XXIII and Pope Paul VI. To make this easier the Instruction, *Inter oecumenici,* gives them permission to celebrate a sung or high Mass without pomp like a simple priest.[14]

42. The parish in its turn *manifests the visible Church established throughout the world* and therefore its liturgical life should really be that of a community. Close relations should be maintained with the bishop by both clergy and laity. Above all, the Sunday celebration of the Eucharist should gather as far as possible into one assembly all the members of the community.

43-46. A final section of the chapter deals with the promotion of pastoral-liturgical action on a national and liturgical scale. It describes the commissions which should be set up to see that the principles of the Constitution are carried into effect and that both clergy and laity receive the necessary instruction. They are essential to the achievement of the Council's aim. It is difficult to believe that those places in

[14] n. 48, c.

which they have not been set up are taking the Constitution seriously.

Once the doctrine and principles set out in the first chapter are understood, the rest of the Constitution will be seen to follow quite naturally without much commentary. The brief remarks that follow will be confined to the second and third chapters.

The sacrament of the Eucharist forms the very centre of the liturgy. It was instituted by our Lord in order to perpetuate on earth the sacrifice of the cross for the salvation of men and the glory of his Father. Christians should be able to take part in it *conscious of what they are doing, with devotion and full collaboration, through an adequate understanding of the rites and prayers*. Therefore the Council decrees that *the rite of the Mass is to be revised in such a way that the intrinsic nature and purpose of its several parts, as also the connection between them, may be more clearly manifested* (50). Since the promulgation of the Constitution much thought and work has gone to the translating of this decree into practical terms, but the difficulties are great. The historical facts, the contributions of catechists and rubricians and tradition are insufficient to provide a true basis for the revision. "The whole Mass must again be re-examined in the light of pastoral liturgy. The rite must be seen both from the nave and from the choir"; so writes Mgr Bugnini, Secretary of the commission for the execution of the Constitution.[15] The work is immense and without precedent. It will be a long time before the project can be finished and presented for the approbation of the Pope.

But without waiting for the new *Ordo Missae*, the Instruction *Inter oecumenici* has already introduced changes to permit the basic structure of the Mass to appear more clearly. The most notable among these is that the celebrant is to stay at his seat all through the liturgy of the word and only

[15] *L'Osservatore Romano*, October 31st, 1964.

return to the altar at the Offertory, and that he does not have to say privately the chants which do not belong to his rôle. The restoration of the prayer over the oblations, formerly called the Secret because it was not heard, and the simplification of the end of the Canon also contribute to this end.[16]

The Constitution orders a much wider selection of lessons at Mass to be spread over a cycle of years (51). The preparation of this new lectionary is advancing and it seems possible that it may provide for three lessons in the Sunday Masses in place of two.

The lessons are to be followed not by a sermon on any theme, but by a homily, which starting from the texts which have been read should expound *the mysteries of the faith and the guiding principles of the Christian life during the course of the liturgical year* (52). Its chief function is to show the relevance of the Scripture and other parts of the celebration to the Christian lives of those taking part, so that the word of God really becomes for them a two-edged sword, revealing the thoughts of hearts and calling to an even deeper conversion.

The "Prayer of the Faithful" in which intercession is made for the Church and the civil authorities, for those oppressed by various needs, for all mankind and for the salvation of the entire world, has been restored in its traditional place, after the homily (53). The liturgy of Good Friday preserves the ancient form of these prayers as they were once made all over the Christian world each Sunday. The Instruction provides a shorter and more usable form.[17]

In order that the eucharistic symbolism instituted by Christ may have its full effect, the Council recommends that the faithful receive in Communion part of what has been offered in the Mass, and not hosts consecrated at some previous

[16] nn. 48-52.
[17] n. 56.

celebration. They are to partake, as it were, of the one loaf which has become Christ's body. Further, on certain occasions to be determined by the Apostolic See, they may communicate not only from the consecrated bread, but also from the chalice.

Finally, the practice of concelebration in which a group of priests offer together the same Eucharist, is to be extended. Formerly it was only used in the West at the Mass of ordination, but it may now become the daily practice of religious houses and communities of priests, for whom the conflicting exigencies of private celebration and communal liturgy have become a serious embarrassment (57-8). The new rite for concelebration is expected to appear shortly.

Among the reforms decreed by the Constitution in the other sacraments and sacramentals some of the most notable are the following.

The present rite for adult and infant baptism group together in an ill-conceived ceremony rites that were originally spread out over a period of many weeks. The result is incomprehensible and disedifying. The Council decrees that for adults the ancient institution of the catechumenate is to be restored. This means that the period of instruction which must necessarily precede baptism is to be organized by the ecclesiastical authorities, and sanctified by the rites originally designed for the purpose. Permission for this had already been granted in 1962, but now it is more strongly recommended in conjunction with the revision of the rites. Disembarrassed of what does not concern them, the rites of baptism for both adults and infants are also to be revised (64-70).

The Constitution clearly teaches that Extreme Unction or, as it is more properly called, the Anointing of the Sick *is not a sacrament reserved for those who are at the point of death* as many have for so long believed. It is to be administered *as soon as any one of the faithful begins to be in danger of death from sickness or old age.* The rite of its administration is also to be revised (73-75).

The marriage rite is normally to take place within the Mass after the reading of the Gospel and the homily—as has also been ordered for religious profession (80) and confirmation (71). But if marriage is contracted outside the Mass, *the Epistle and Gospel of the nuptial Mass should be read as an introduction to the ceremony and the spouses should always be given a blessing* (77-78).

Lastly, the rite of burial is to express more clearly the paschal character of Christian death (81). For by death the Christian who was buried with Christ in baptism and has throughout his Christian life walked through the waters of the world's suffering in the footsteps of his Lord, bearing about the death of Christ in his mortal members, comes finally to share in the victory of Christ's passion to be configured to the glory of his resurrection. As the preface of the requiem Mass declares: "For those who put their trust in you, O Lord, life is transformed, not taken away."

Paulinus Milner, O.P.

PAUL VI: MOTU PROPRIO

SACRAM LITURGIAM

It has always been the great concern of the papacy, of us, and of the bishops of the Church, to preserve, foster, and at need, reform the sacred liturgy. This is evident from numerous acts of public record, but especially from the constitution on this matter which the Second Ecumenical Council of the Vatican approved in solemn session on December 4th, 1963 and we ordered promulgated.

This interest derives immediately from the fact that "in the earthly liturgy we take part in a foretaste of that heavenly liturgy which is celebrated in the Holy City of Jerusalem toward which we journey as pilgrims, where Christ is sitting at the right hand of God, a minister of the holies and of the true tabernacle; we sing a hymn to the Lord's glory with all the warriors of the heavenly army; venerating the memory of the saints, we hope for some part and fellowship with them; we eagerly await the Saviour, our Lord Jesus Christ, until he, our life, shall appear and we too will appear with him in glory" (*Constitution on the Sacred Liturgy,* Article 8).

Thus it is that Christians who worship God, the source and exemplar of all holiness, are drawn and even impelled to achieve that holiness by becoming on this earthly journey "seekers of holy Sion" (Hymn at Lauds, feast of the dedication of a church).

It should be immediately evident that in this area of concern nothing takes precedence for us over the need that all Christians and especially priests have of studying the above-mentioned constitution with care, with a view to observing its requirements with complete fidelity once they have come into force. Since in the nature of the case a knowledge and diffusion of the constitution's liturgical prescriptions should be effected immediately, we earnestly exhort the bishops of the several dioceses with the aid of their priests, "dispensers of the divine mysteries" (cf. 1 Cor. 4. 1), to act swiftly in promoting both the liturgical instruction of the faithful and their active participation[1] in the liturgy internally and externally, taking into account their age and condition, their way of life, and standard of religious culture (Article 19).

It is clear that many prescriptions of the constitution cannot be effected within a short space, since the various rites must be reconsidered thoroughly and the liturgical books carefully worked on. So that this task may go forward with the wisdom and courageous balance required, we initiate a special commission the chief obligation of which will be to bring to completion the matters prescribed in the constitution on liturgy.

There are certain norms of the constitution, however, which surely can be fulfilled now; therefore we wish them to take effect immediately, lest Christians be deprived any longer of the benefits they may expect in the order of grace.

By our apostolic authority and on our own initiative, we decree that from the first Sunday of Lent, February 16th, 1964, at the end of the interim prescribed, the following norms should begin to take effect:

[1] . . . *intersint* in "L'Osservatore Romano" version, January 29th, 1964, becomes *participent*.

1. We would have the requirements indicated in Articles 15, 16, and 17 concerning the teaching of liturgy in seminaries, in houses of religious formation, and in theological faculties studied in the light of curriculum changes now, so that they can be put into effect at the beginning of the next school year.

2. It is likewise our decision that, in accordance with Articles 45 and 46, in every diocese there shall exist[2] a commission, under the direction of the bishop, for exploring and promoting the liturgical apostolate ever more diligently.

At times it may be advisable for several dioceses to have one commission in common.

In every diocese two other commissions should be set up: one on sacred music and the other on sacred art.

It may prove convenient in many cases for these three diocesan commissions to be merged into one.[3]

3. From the date above [February 16th, 1964], we would have a homily preached during Mass[4] on every Sunday and feast day of obligation, in accord with Article 52.

4. We prescribe that that part of Article 71 which says that confirmation during Mass, after the reading of the gospel and homily,[5] may be conferred when convenient,[6] shall take immediate effect.

5. As regards Article 78, the sacrament of marriage must ordinarily take place during Mass,[7] after the gospel and homily. If, however, marriage is celebrated apart from the eucharistic sacrifice, the following order should be observed[8]

---

[2] . . . *condatur* becomes *habeatur* in *A.A.S.*

[3] . . . *si opus erit, in unum concedere poterunt* becomes *non raro congruet, ut in unum coalescant* in *A.A.S.*

[4] . . . *inter Eucharisticum sacrificium* becomes *in Missis* in *A.A.S.*

[5] This phrase added in *A.A.S.*

[6] . . . *ex qua venia datur . . . conferendi* becomes *ex qua . . . conferri potest* in *A.A.S.*

[7] . . . *inter Eucharisticum sacrificium celebrandum esse* becomes *intra Missam celebretur* in *A.A.S.*

[8] . . . *servari jubemus* becomes *serventur* in *A.A.S.*

until the entire rite of this sacrament[9] is devised: at the beginning of the ceremony, after a brief exhortation[10] (cf. Article 35, 3), the epistle and gospel of the nuptial Mass are to be read in the people's language;[11] subsequently the nuptial blessing of the Roman Ritual, title 8, chapter 3, is always[12] to be given.

6. Although the divine Office has not yet been revised in accord with the norms of Article 89, we allow from this date onward those who are not bound to its recitation in choir[13] to omit Prime, and choose from among the other little hours one that best suits the time of day.[14]

We grant this in complete confidence that the sacred ministers will forfeit none of their piety, but will go about their priestly tasks full of love for God and united with him in thought through every hour of the day.

7. Again as regards the Office, in particular cases and for just cause, ordinaries may dispense their subjects wholly or in part from reciting it, or may substitute something else for it (cf. Article 97).[15]

8. Further with respect to the Office, we state[16] that members of any institute dedicated to acquiring perfection who, according to their constitutions, are to recite any parts of the divine Office or any short Office—provided this is drawn up after the pattern of the divine Office and is duly approved

---

[9] . . . *rei* becomes *Sacramenti* in *A.A.S.*

[10] . . . *hortationem* becomes *admonitionem* in *A.A.S.*

[11] . . . *lingua vernacula* added in *A.A.S.*

[12] . . . *semper* added in *A.A.S.*

[13] . . . *qui illius recitandi obligatione astringuntur* becomes *qui chori obligatione non astringuntur* in *A.A.S.*

[14] . . . *in recitatione, quae fiat extra chorum* deleted from this paragraph in *A.A.S.* because of confusion caused with respect to religious bound to the full recitation of the office by their rule.

[15] . . . *ut ea venia iam nunc obtineat praecipimus, cuuis vi . . ac bene considerata* deleted in *A.A.S.*

[16] . . . *constare volumus* becomes *declaramus* in *A.A.S.*

—are to be considered performing the public prayer of the Church (cf. Article 98).

9. Since according to Article 101 of the constitution those who are obliged to recite the divine Office may in various ways be granted the faculty to use translations in their mother tongue instead of Latin, we deem it opportune to indicate that the various versions prepared and voted on[17] by competent territorial ecclesiastical authority be approved, that is, confirmed by the Holy See, in accord with the norm of Article 36, 3 and 4, and the action taken by this authority, in accord with the norm of Article 36, 3. We prescribe the observance of this practice whenever a liturgical[18] Latin text is translated into the vernacular by the aforesaid legitimate authority.

10. Whenever, in the constitution (Article 22, 2) the regulation of the liturgy within the prescribed limits falls under the competence of various legitimately constituted territorial episcopal conferences, we establish that, for now, this term be taken to be understood as national.

In addition to the residential bishops, all who are mentioned in Canon 292 of the Code of Canon Law may participate in these national conferences with the right to vote; coadjutor and auxiliary bishops may also be added.

In these conferences, two-thirds of the votes taken by secret ballot are required for legitimate passage of the decrees.

11. Finally we wish it to be noted that, beyond what we in this apostolic letter on liturgical matters have either changed or ordered to be carried out before the established

[17] . . . *propositas* becomes *conficiendas, et approbandas esse, ad normam art. 36, 3 et 4; acta vero huius auctoritatis, ad normam eiusdem art. 36, 3*, and *recognoscendas atque probandas* becomes *probanda seu confirmanda*, the original wording of the constitution, in *A.A.S.*

[18] . . . *liturgicus* added in *A.A.S.*

time, the regulation of the sacred liturgy comes solely within the competence of the Church: that is, this Apostolic See and, in accord with the law, the bishop; therefore, no other person, even if he be a priest,[19] may add, remove, or change anything in the liturgy on his own authority (Article 22, 1 and 3).

We ordain that all we have established by this *motu proprio* letter shall remain firmly in possession, anything to the contrary notwithstanding.

Given at Rome, at St Peter's, January 25th, 1964, the feast of the Conversion of St Paul the Apostle, in the first year of our pontificate.

Pope Paul VI

---

[19] . . . *etiamsi sacerdoti* becomes *ne sacerdoti quidem* in *A.A.S.*

Reprinted through the courtesy of the National Catholic Welfare Conference.

CONGREGATION OF RITES: INSTRUCTION ON IMPLEMENTING THE LITURGICAL CONSTITUTION

FOREWORD

1. The nature of this instruction

1. The Constitution on the Sacred Liturgy justly ranks among the first fruits of the Second Ecumenical Vatican Council. Its legislation governs what is noblest in the Church's activity. The amount of good that will come from it will depend on how deeply the clergy and the faithful learn to appreciate its genuine spirit and on their wholeheartedness in putting the Constitution into effect.

2. The Commission for implementing the Constitution on the Sacred Liturgy, set up by the reigning Sovereign Pontiff, Paul VI, through his Apostolic Letter *Sacram Liturgiam* has already begun its work, which is to put into effect the direc-

tives of the Constitution and of the said Apostolic Letter and to make full provision for the correct understanding and fulfilment of these documents.

3. It is supremely important, however, that from the outset what these documents lay down shall be applied everywhere correctly, and that any doubts about their interpretation shall be resolved. Hence, by order of the Sovereign Pontiff, this Commission has prepared the present Instruction, defining more clearly the duties of bishops' conferences regarding the liturgy, explaining more precisely some of the principles stated in general terms in the above-mentioned documents, and allowing, or in some cases decreeing, that certain matters may be brought into effect even now before the liturgical books are revised.

II. Some principles to be noted

4. In deciding what is to be brought into effect even at this stage the intention has been to make the liturgy reflect ever more perfectly the mind of the Council concerning the active participation of the faithful.

Moreover, the general renewal of the sacred liturgy is much more likely to be welcomed by the faithful if it proceeds gradually, step by step, and if it is presented to them and explained to them by their pastors by means of planned instructions.

5. But first it must be clearly understood that the aim of the Second Vatican Council's Constitution on the Sacred Liturgy is not simply to bring about changes in the liturgical forms and texts but rather to give inspiration and encouragement to that instruction of the faithful and that pastoral activity which has the liturgy for its source and finds in the liturgy the height of its expression (cf. Const. art. 10). Changes which have so far been introduced as well as those which are to be introduced later into the sacred liturgy have this as their end and object.

6. The value of organizing pastoral activity around the liturgy lies in this, that it expresses the paschal mystery by actually living it. The paschal mystery is the mystery in which the Son of God became man, accepted an obedience which brought him even to death on the cross, and now, when he is risen from the dead and ascended into heaven, makes it possible for the world to share in his divine life. So it is that men now die to a life of sin, fashion themselves anew according to the model which is Christ, and now no longer live with their own life but with the life of him who died for them and who rose again (2 Cor. 5. 15).

This comes about through faith and through the sacraments of faith, principally baptism (cf. Const. art. 6) and the most sacred mystery of the holy Eucharist (cf. Const. art. 47), and around these are gathered the other sacraments and sacramentals (cf. Const. art. 61), and that cycle of feasts which in the course of the year unfold Christ's paschal mystery in the Church (cf. Const. art. 102-107).

7. And so, although the liturgy does not exhaust the entire activity of the Church (cf. Const. art. 9), it is only right to give some attention to the problem of linking up pastoral work with the sacred liturgy, and of making pastoral liturgical activity not a thing separate and distinct from other pastoral works, but something intimately united with them.

It is particularly necessary that there should be an intimate connection between the liturgy and such things as catechizing, religious instruction, and preaching.

III. The awaited harvest

8. Bishops, therefore, and all who labour with them in the priesthood, should organize the whole of their pastoral mission more and more around the liturgy. In this way the faithful, sharing fully in the sacred rites, drinking deeply from the source of divine life, will become Christ's leaven and the

salt of the earth. They will bear witness to that divine life and be instrumental in transmitting it to others.

CHAPTER I: SOME GENERAL RULES

I. The application of these rules

9. The practical rules found in the Constitution or in this Instruction, and everything which this Instruction permits or decrees to take effect even before the revision of the liturgical books, apply only to the Roman rite, but, with the proper reservations, they may be applied to other Latin rites also.

10. Everything which this Instruction commits to the competent regional ecclesiastical authority can and must be put into effect only by the lawful decrees of that authority.

In each and every case a clear indication should be given of the date and under what circumstances these decrees are to take effect. A reasonable interval of time should always be allowed for the instruction of the faithful and their training in carrying out the decrees.

II. The liturgical education of clerics
(Const. art. 15-16, and 18)

11. As regards the liturgical education of clerics:

(a) Wherever theological degrees are given there should be a chair of liturgy so that all students may acquire a proper liturgical training. In seminaries and in religious houses of studies local Ordinaries and major superiors must see to it that a special, well-trained teacher of liturgy is provided soon.

(b) In accordance with art. 15 of the Constitution, the training of teachers to take charge of liturgical studies ought to be begun with as little delay as possible.

(c) Institutes of pastoral liturgy for the further liturgical education of the clergy, those especially already working in the Lord's vineyard, are to be set up as soon as arrangements can be made.

12. In accordance with art. 16 of the Constitution, liturgy must be taught for a suitable regular period to be indicated by the competent authority in the time-table of studies and according to a teaching-method likely to be effective.

13. Liturgical ceremonies must be performed as perfectly as possible, that is:

(a) Rubrics must be carefully observed and the ceremonies performed with decorum under the careful eye of those in charge and after the necessary practice.

(b) Those clerics who are deacons, subdeacons, acolytes, or lectors should frequently perform the liturgical duties of their respective orders. Clerics should also learn how to be commentators and cantors.

(c) Churches and oratories, sacred furnishings generally, and sacred vestments must conform to a decent standard of Christian art—and this applies also to modern art forms.

III. The liturgical formation of the spiritual life of the clergy
(Const. art. 17)

14. In order that clerical students may be trained to take a full part in liturgical ceremonies, to draw their spiritual life from them and thereafter impart it to others, the Constitution on the Sacred Liturgy is to be fully implemented in seminaries and religious houses of studies in accordance with the ruling given in the documents of the Holy See. This must be given the full support and co-operation of superiors and teachers. The early stages of a cleric's training in the sacred liturgy should be through books on the liturgy, those particularly which deal with its theological and spiritual aspect (and such books should be in plentiful supply in the library), through sermons and meditations which draw their main inspiration from the sacred Scripture and the liturgy (cf. Const. art. 35, 2), and through the carrying out of those cere-

monies which are customary and are part of Christian formation according to the various seasons of the liturgical year.

15. The holy Eucharist, the centre of the whole spiritual life, is to be celebrated daily, adopting different forms of celebration according to the clerical status of those who take part (cf. Const. art. 19).

On Sundays, however, and on the major feasts, Mass should be sung, and everyone in the house should be present. There should be a homily and, as far as possible, all those who are not priests should receive holy Communion. When the need of the faithful does not require priests to say a separate Mass, these will be able to concelebrate, especially on the more solemn feasts, once the new rite has been promulgated.

It is greatly to be desired that, at least on major feastdays, church students should take part in the Eucharist with the bishop in the cathedral church (cf. Const. art. 41).

16. It is especially fitting that clerics, even those not yet bound by obligation to say the divine Office, should recite or sing Lauds in common each morning as a morning prayer, and in the evening, Vespers as an evening prayer, or Compline at the end of the day. The staff too, as far as possible, should take part in this common recitation. Furthermore, the daily time-table must allow clerics in sacred orders sufficient time for the fulfilment of their obligation to say the divine Office.

It is fitting that, at least on major feastdays, church students sing Vespers in the cathedral church, wherever this can be arranged.

17. Devotional practices organized in accordance with the laws or customs of the locality or of the particular institute are to be held in due regard. Care must be taken, however, to ensure that they are in harmony with the sacred liturgy (see Const. art. 13) and that they take account of the seasons of the liturgical year.

IV. *The liturgical formation of religious*

18. What is stated in the preceding paragraphs about the liturgical formation of the spiritual life of clerics is also to be applied, with the necessary reservations, to religious, both men and women.

V. *The liturgical instruction of the faithful*

19. Pastors of souls should strive to carry out, sedulously and patiently, the Constitution's ruling concerning the instruction of the faithful in the liturgy and their internal and external active participation in it, 'having regard to their age and social standing, their way of life and their standard of religious culture' (Const. art. 19). They must take particular care to secure the liturgical instruction and active participation of those who belong to religious sodalities for the laity. Such people have a duty to share more intimately in the Church's life and to co-operate with their priests in promoting the liturgical life of the parish (cf. Const. art. 42).

VI. *The competent liturgical authority* (Const. art. 22)

20. The regulation of the sacred liturgy is a matter for the authority of the Church. No one may proceed on his own initiative. (This reacts only too often to the detriment of the liturgy and of its development by competent authority.)

21. It is for the Holy See to revise and approve the general liturgical books, to regulate the sacred liturgy in matters affecting the universal Church, to give its approval or confirmation to the decrees and decisions of the regional authority, and to receive from the regional authority their proposals and requests.

22. It is for the bishop to make regulations concerning the liturgy in his own diocese, in accordance with the letter and the spirit of the Constitution on the Sacred Liturgy, and of

the decrees of the Holy See and of the competent regional authority.

23. The various kinds of regional bishops' conferences which, in virtue of art. 22, 2 of the Constitution, have power to make regulations concerning the liturgy, are to be understood, *for the time being,* to be as follows:

Either (*a*) conference of all the bishops of a particular nation, in accordance with the Apostolic Letter, *Sacram Liturgiam,* n. 10;

or (*b*) a lawfully constituted group of bishops—or of bishops and other local ordinaries—of several nations;

or (*c*) a conference to be set up with leave from the Holy See of bishops and other local ordinaries of several countries, especially in the case of those countries where the bishops are so few that it is better for them to form a conference of several different countries having the same language and cultural outlook.

Where special local conditions call for still other arrangements, the matter should be referred to the Holy See.

24. The following are to be summoned to the above-mentioned conferences:

(*a*) residential bishops;

(*b*) abbots and prelates *nullius*;

(*c*) vicars and prefects apostolic;

(*d*) those who have a permanent appointment as administrators apostolic of dioceses;

(*e*) all other local ordinaries, excepting vicars general.

Coadjutor and auxiliary bishops may be invited by the president on the simple majority vote of those who have a deliberative voice in the conference.

25. The summoning of the conference, unless other provision is lawfully made in certain localities and in view of special circumstances, is the responsibility of:

(*a*) the respective president, in the case of conferences already lawfully established;

(*b*) in other cases, the archbishop or bishop who lawfully has the right of precedence.

26. The president, with the consensus of the Fathers, decides on the order to be observed in the matters for discussion, and he it is who opens, adjourns, defers, and closes the actual conference.

27. All the persons mentioned in paragraph 24 are entitled to a deliberative vote, not excepting coadjutor and auxiliary bishops, unless expressly stated otherwise in the deed of convocation.

28. For the lawful passing of decrees, a two-thirds majority is required on a secret ballot.

29. An account of the proceedings of a competent regional authority is to be forwarded to the Holy See for approval or confirmation, and should include the following items:

(*a*) the names of those present at the conference;

(*b*) a report on the matters dealt with;

(*c*) the result of the ballot on each of the decrees.

These Acta, prepared in duplicate, should bear the signature of the president and secretary of the conference, together with the appropriate seals, and should be sent to the Commission for implementing the Constitution on the Sacred Liturgy.

30. Acta which include decrees concerning the use and the degree of the vernacular to be admitted in the Liturgy should, in accordance with art. 36, 3 of the Constitution and the Apostolic Letter, *Sacram Liturgiam,* n. 9, contain the following items in addition to those set out in the preceding paragraph:

(*a*) an indication of the individual parts of the liturgy which it is decided to have said in the vernacular;

(*b*) two copies of the vernacular liturgical texts, one of which will be returned to the bishops of the conference;

(*c*) a short account of the criteria on which the work of translation has been based.

31. The decrees of a regional authority which need the

Holy See's approval or confirmation, may not be promulgated and put into effect until the Holy See has given its approval or confirmation.

VII. *The office of individuals in the liturgy* (Const. art. 28)

32. Those parts which concern the choir and the people, if they are in fact said or sung by them, are not said privately by the celebrant.

33. Neither are the lessons which are read or sung by the competent minister or by a server, recited privately by the celebrant.

VIII. *Special honours not to be paid to private persons*
       (Const. art. 32)

34. Individual bishops or, if considered desirable, regional and national conferences of bishops must see to it that the ruling of the Council which forbids the giving of special honours to private persons or social classes, whether in the ceremonies or by external display, shall be put into practice in their respective territories.

35. For the rest, let priests in charge of souls in all prudence and charity spare no pains to demonstrate even externally the equality of the faithful particularly in the celebration of Mass and the administration of the sacraments and sacramentals. Moreover, they should avoid anything that would give the impression that their thought is of monetary reward.

IX. *The simplification of certain rites* (Const. art. 34)

36. In order that liturgical actions may evince that noble simplicity which accords better with the present-day mentality:

(*a*) bowing to the choir by the celebrant and ministers is to be restricted to the beginning and the end of the sacred function;

(*b*) the incensation of the clergy (other than those who are bishops) is to be one triple swing of the censer towards each side of the choir;

(*c*) the incensation of the altar is to take place only at the altar at which the liturgical function is being celebrated;

(*d*) kissing of the hands and of things given or received is to be omitted.

X. *Services of the Word of God* (Const. art. 35, 4)

37. In places where there is no priest and no possibility of celebrating Mass on Sundays or Holydays of Obligation an effort should be made, if the bishop thinks fit, to hold a service of the Word of God, led by a deacon, or even by a layman deputed to do so.

The service should take much the same shape as the liturgy of the Word celebrated at Mass. As a rule, the epistle and gospel from the day's Mass should be read in the vernacular, preceded by and interspersed with some singing, especially of the psalms. If the one who presides is a deacon, he should give a homily. If he is not a deacon, he should read a homily indicated by the bishop or parish priest. The rite as a whole should conclude with community prayer—that is, the prayer of the faithful—and the Sunday collect.

38. It is fitting that services also of the sacred Word of God, which are to be encouraged on the vigils of more solemn feasts, on some of the weekdays of Advent and Lent and on Sundays and Holydays, should be planned on the model of the liturgy of the Word in Mass, although there need only be one reading from sacred Scripture.

But if there are several lessons a reading from the Old Testament should generally precede one from the New Testament, and the reading of the holy gospel should be the climax. In this way the history of salvation will be put into clear perspective.

39. To ensure that these services are dignified and devo-

tional, the liturgical commissions in the various dioceses should make it part of their business to offer help and advice.

XI. *Translations of liturgical texts into the language of the people* (Const. art. 36, 3)

40. In translating liturgical texts into the language of the people, it is fitting that the following rules be observed:

(*a*) Translations of liturgical texts are to be made from the liturgical Latin. Translations of passages from Scripture must also conform to the liturgical Latin text, although it is always allowed, in order to make the meaning clearer, to have regard to the original or to another translation.

(*b*) The work of preparing a translation of liturgical texts is to be entrusted especially to the liturgical commission referred to in art. 44 of the Constitution and paragraph 44 of this Instruction, aided where possible by the Institute of Pastoral Liturgy. If there is no such commission, responsibility for the work of translation should be given to two or three bishops who should select a team, laymen not excluded, of those well versed in Scripture, in liturgy, in the biblical and Latin languages, in the vernacular language and also in music. If liturgical texts are to be properly translated into the language of the people attention must be paid at one and the same time to a number of factors.

(*c*) Where the occasion demands it, a joint plan concerning translations should be formed with the bishops of neighbouring territories.

(*d*) In the case of multi-lingual nations, translations should be made into each of the various languages and submitted to the special examination of the bishops concerned.

(*e*) Attention must be paid to the dignified appearance of the book from which the vernacular liturgical text is read. The very appearance of the book should arouse in the faithful a greater reverence for the word of God and for sacred things generally.

41. In those liturgical functions which happen in some

places, with a congregation that speaks a different language from that spoken locally—a gathering of people for example who have come from abroad or of people who are cared for not by a local parish priest but by a priest appointed to care for a language group—the local Ordinary may allow the use of a version in their own language if this translation has been properly approved by the competent authority of a country where their language is spoken.

42. New melodies for the singing of the vernacular parts by the celebrant and ministers are to be approved by the competent regional ecclesiastical authority.

43. Particular liturgical books duly authorized before the promulgation of the Constitution on the Sacred Liturgy and indults granted up to that time shall retain their validity unless they are contrary to the Constitution, until the partial or total revision of the liturgy determines otherwise.

XII. *The liturgical commission within the bishops' conference* (Const. art. 44)

44. The liturgical commission to be set up by the regional authority should be chosen as far as possible from among the bishops themselves; it should at least consist of one or two bishops with the addition of a number of priests, well versed in liturgical and pastoral matters and especially nominated for this work.

It is desirable for the members of the commission together with the consultors to meet several times a year and discuss things.

45. To this commission the regional authority may very well entrust the following business:

(*a*) the promoting of studies and experiments in accordance with art. 40, 1 and 40, 2 of the Constitution;

(*b*) the furthering throughout the entire region of projects designed to foster the liturgy and the application of the Constitution;

(*c*) the preparation of study-schemes and practical aids

made necessary by the decrees of the full conference of bishops;

(d) the task of regulating liturgical-pastoral action in the entire nation, of supervising the fulfilment of decrees of the plenary conference, and of reporting on all these matters to the conference;

(e) the organization of frequent meetings and the promotion of joint projects among the societies or groups in the same region whose interest is in Scripture, catechetics, pastoral problems, music, and sacred art, and indeed with every type of religious association for the laity.

46. Members of the Institute of Pastoral Liturgy, and any who by reason of their knowledge and experience may have been invited to assist the liturgical commission, should be ready and willing to offer their services also to individual bishops for the more effective promotion of pastoral-liturgical action in their diocese.

XIII. *The diocesan liturgical commission* (Const. art. 45)

47. The following are the duties of the diocesan liturgical commission, under the direction of the bishop:

(a) to be conversant with the state of pastoral-liturgical activity in the diocese;

(b) to put into effect the proposals of the competent authority in liturgical matters, and also to keep themselves informed of all that is being said and done in this matter in other countries;

(c) to suggest and to promote practical schemes likely to further the liturgical movement especially such as will help priests already working among the people;

(d) to help individuals, or even the whole diocese, to draw up a pastoral-liturgical programme, to be completed in stages and with due regard to all the circumstances; where need arises to be able to give the names, and even secure the services of those qualified to help the priests concerned, and also to give advice about the best means of putting the programme into effect;

(*e*) to ensure in a way similar to that indicated for the commission set up within the bishops' conference [para. 45 (*e*)] that the diocesan schemes for the promotion of the liturgy have the goodwill and co-operation of other associations.

CHAPTER II: THE MOST HOLY MYSTERY OF THE EUCHARIST

I. *The rite of the Mass* (Const. art. 50)

48. Until the entire rite of the Mass has been revised, the following rules are to be observed:

(*a*) Those parts of the proper of the Mass which are sung or recited by the choir or by the people are not said privately by the celebrant.

(*b*) The celebrant may sing or recite the parts of the ordinary of the Mass together with the people or the choir.

(*c*) Psalm 42 is omitted from the prayers to be said at the foot of the altar at the beginning of Mass. All the prayers at the foot of the altar are omitted whenever another liturgical service immediately precedes the Mass.

(*d*) In solemn Mass the paten is not held by the subdeacon, but is left on the altar.

(*e*) The secret prayer, or prayer over the offerings, is to be chanted in sung Masses, and recited aloud in other Masses.

(*f*) The doxology at the end of the Canon, from the words *Per ipsum* to the words *Per omnia saecula saeculorum. Amen,* inclusive, is to be chanted or recited aloud. Throughout the whole doxology the celebrant, omitting the signs of the cross, holds the chalice with the host slightly elevated. At the end he genuflects only after the response *Amen* given by the people.

(*g*) In low Masses the *Pater Noster* may be recited in the vernacular by the people together with the celebrant; in sung Masses it may be sung in Latin by the people together with the celebrant, and if the regional ecclesiastical authority so decrees, even in the vernacular to melodies approved by the same authority.

(*h*) The embolism (*Libera nos quaesumus,* etc.) after the Lord's Prayer is to be chanted or recited aloud.

(*i*) In distributing holy Communion the formula *Corpus Christi* is to be used. As the celebrant says these words he holds the host raised a little above the ciborium for the communicant to see; the communicant replies *Amen,* and then receives Communion from the priest, who does not make a sign of the cross with the host.

(*j*) The Last Gospel is omitted; the Leonine prayers after Mass are no longer to be said.

(*k*) It is allowed to celebrate a sung Mass with only a deacon to assist.

(*l*) Bishops, when need arises, may celebrate a sung Mass in the form used by ordinary priests.

II. *Lessons and chants between the lessons* (Const. art. 51)

49. In Masses celebrated with the people present, the lessons, epistle, and gospel are to be read or sung facing the people:

(*a*) in solemn Mass, at the ambo or at the altar-rails;

(*b*) in sung Mass or low Mass, if read or sung by the celebrant, then either at the altar or at the ambo or at the altar-rails, as may be convenient; if by someone other than the celebrant, then at the ambo or at the altar-rails.

50. In Masses which are celebrated with the people present but are not solemn Masses, the lessons and epistle, together with what is sung or recited, may be read by a qualified lector, or by one of the servers, while the celebrant

sits and listens. The gospel may be read, however, only by a deacon or another priest, who says the *Munda cor meum,* asks the blessing, and at the end presents the book of gospels to the celebrant for him to kiss.

51. In sung Masses, if the vernacular is used for the lessons, epistle, and gospel, these may be read and not sung.

52. The procedure for reading or singing the lessons, epistle, the chants which follow them, and the gospel is as follows:

(*a*) In solemn Mass, the celebrant sits and listens to the lessons and epistle as they are read as well as whatever is to be sung in between. The subdeacon, after singing or reading the epistle, goes to the celebrant, and is there blessed by him. Then the celebrant, still seated, puts incense into the thurible and blesses it. While the *Alleluia* and its verse are being sung, or towards the end of other singing following the epistle, the celebrant rises and blesses the deason. Standing there he listens to the reading of the gospel, kisses the book of gospels and, after the homily, intones the creed, if there is to be one. At the end of the creed he returns with the ministers to the altar, unless he is to lead the prayer of the faithful.

(*b*) In sung or low Masses in which the lessons, epistle, intervening chants and the gospel are sung or read by the minister referred to in paragraph 50, the celebrant acts in the manner described above.

(*c*) In sung or low Masses in which the gospel is sung or read by the celebrant, while the *Alleluia* and its verse are being sung or recited, or towards the end of whatever other singing follows the epistle, the celebrant goes to the lowest step of the altar and there bows low while he says the *Munda cor meum.* Then he goes to the ambo or to the altar-rails and sings or reads the gospel.

(*d*) If in a sung or low Mass all the lessons are being sung or read at an ambo or at the altar-rails by the celebrant himself, then he, standing in the same place, reads, if need be, the chants also which come after the lessons and epistle. He turns to the altar to say the *Munda cor meum.*

III. *The homily* (Const. art. 52)

53. A homily is to be delivered on Sundays and Holydays of Obligation at all Masses attended by the people. No exception is to be made for conventual, sung or even pontifical Masses.

On other days a homily is recommended, especially on some of the weekdays of Advent and Lent, and on any other occasions when people attend church in considerable numbers.

54. By a homily on the sacred text is meant an explanation of some point either from the text of the readings from the sacred Scripture or from the text of the ordinary or proper of the Mass of the day, having in mind either the feast or mystery which is being celebrated or the particular needs of the audience.

55. If courses of sermons at Mass are planned for any particular periods, care must be taken to ensure that the subject matter is in harmony with the greater seasons and festivals of the liturgical year, or with the unfolding story of our redemption (cf. Const. art. 102-104). The homily after all is a part of the liturgy of each particular day.

IV. *The community prayer, or prayer of the faithful*
(Const. art. 53)

56. In places where the community prayer, or prayer of the faithful, is already an established custom, it is to take place before the Offertory, after the *Oremus,* and for the time being according to the formula already in use in the particular area. The celebrant may lead the prayer either from the place where his seat is, from the altar, from an ambo, or from the altar-rails.

The things to be prayed for, the invocations, may be chanted by a deacon or a cantor or some server able to do it, reserving to the celebrant the introductory words and the concluding prayer, which will ordinarily be: *Deus, refugium nostrum et virtus* (cf. *Missale romanum,* Orationes diversae, n. 20) or, on occasion, some other prayer which happens to be better suited to a particular need.

In places where the community prayer, or prayer of the faithful, is not yet customary, the competent regional authority may decree its introduction in the manner described above, using for the time being formulas approved by that authority itself.

V. *The parts of the Mass which may be said in the vernacular* (Const. art. 54)

57. In sung or low Masses celebrated with the people present, the competent regional ecclesiastical authority may allow the use of the vernacular in the following parts of the Mass, provided its decrees are approved, that is to say, confirmed, by the Holy See:

(*a*) especially in the reading of the lessons, and of the epistle and gospel, and in the community prayer or prayer of the faithful;

(*b*) also, as local conditions may demand, in those parts of the ordinary of the Mass, which may be sung or recited by the people, i.e. *Kyrie, Gloria, Credo, Sanctus-Benedictus,* and *Agnus Dei,* and in the antiphons at the Introit, Offertory, and Communion, as well as in what is sung between the lessons;

(*c*) furthermore, in all acclamations, greetings, and dialogue formulas: in the formulas *Ecce Agnus Dei, Domine, non sum dignus,* and *Corpus Christi* at the communion of the faithful, and in the Lord's Prayer together with its introduction and the prayer *Libera nos* which follows it.

Missals for liturgical use, however, must contain the Latin text as well as the vernacular translation.

58. It is for the Holy See alone to grant permission to use the vernacular in other parts of the Mass said or sung by the celebrant alone.

59. Priests shall take great care that the faithful, and particularly the members of religious organizations for the laity, also know how to sing or say together in Latin those parts of the ordinary of the Mass which are rightfully theirs. They should be taught especially the use of the simpler melodies.

VI. *The faculty of repeating communion on the same day*
    (Const. art. 55)

60. The faithful who receive Communion in the Mass of the Easter Vigil or in the midnight Mass of Christmas may also receive Communion again in the second Mass of Easter and in one of the Masses celebrated on Christmas day.

CHAPTER III: THE OTHER SACRAMENTS AND THE SACRAMENTALS

I. *The rôle which may be conceded to the vernacular*
   (Const. art. 63)

61. The competent regional authority may allow the following use of the vernacular, provided its decrees are approved, that is to say confirmed, by the Holy See:

(*a*) in the rites of Baptism, Confirmation, Penance, Anointing of the Sick, and Matrimony, not excluding the essential forms, and in the distribution of Holy Communion;

(*b*) in the conferring of Orders: in the allocutions at the beginning of each ordination or consecration as well as in the examination of the candidate for episcopal consecration, and in all the admonitions;

(*c*) in the sacramentals;

(*d*) in the funeral rites.

If a more extensive use of the vernacular seems desirable, the ruling of art. 40 of the Constitution should be observed.

II. *What should be omitted in the rite for supplying the baptismal ceremonies* (Const. art. 69)

62. In the rite for supplying the ceremonies omitted at infant baptism (see the Roman Ritual, tit. II, ch. 5) the exorcisms found under n. 6 (*Exi ab eo*), 10 (*Exorcizo te, immunde spiritus—Ergo, maledicte diabole*), and 15 (*Exorcizo te, omnis spiritus*) are to be omitted.

63. In the rite for supplying the ceremonies omitted at adult baptism (see the Roman Ritual, tit. II, ch. 6) the exorcisms found under n. 5 (*Exi ab eo*), 15 (*Ergo, maledicte diabole*), 17 (*Audi, maledicte satana*), 19 (*Exorcizo te— Ergo, maledicte diabole*), 21 (*Ergo, maledicte diabole*), 23 (*Ergo, maledicte diabole*), 25 (*Exorcizo te—Ergo, maledicte diabole*), 31 (*Nec te latet*) and 35 (*Exi, immunde spiritus*) are to be omitted.

III. *Confirmation* (Const. art. 71)

64. If confirmation is administered during Mass, it is fitting that the Mass should be celebrated by the bishop himself, who will then administer confirmation wearing the Mass vestments.

The Mass within which confirmation is given may be celebrated as a second class votive Mass of the Holy Spirit.

65. After the gospel and homily, and before the reception of confirmation, it is recommended that the candidates renew their baptismal promises, according to the rite lawfully in use in the particular region, unless this has already taken place before the Mass began.

66. If the Mass is celebrated by someone other than the bishop, the bishop himself ought, if he can, to assist at the Mass wearing the vestments prescribed for the conferring of

confirmation. These may be either the colour of the Mass or white. The bishop himself gives the homily, and the celebrant resumes the Mass only after the actual confirmation ceremony is over.

67. Confirmation is conferred according to the rite prescribed in the Roman Pontifical, but at the words *In nomine Patris, et Filii, et Spiritus Sancti* which follow the formula *Signo te,* only a single sign of the cross is to be made.

IV. *The continuous rite for the anointing of the sick and viaticum* (Const. art. 74)

68. When the anointing of the sick and viaticum are administered at the same time, if there is not already a continuous rite in the local Ritual, the following order is to be observed: after the sprinkling and entrance prayers found in the rite of anointing, the priest shall, if necessary, hear the confession of the sick person, then administer the anointing, and finally give viaticum, omitting the sprinkling and the prayers that go with it and also the *Confiteor* and the absolution.

If, however, the apostolic blessing with a plenary indulgence at the hour of death is to be conferred on the same occasion, this must be given immediately before the anointing, omitting here also the sprinkling and the prayers that go with it and the *Confiteor* and the absolution.

V. *The imposition of hands in episcopal consecration* (Const. art. 76)

69. All bishops present at an episcopal consecration may impose hands; they vest in choir dress. But the words *Accipe Spiritum Sanctum* are to be said only by the consecrating bishop and the two co-consecrators.

VI. *The rite of matrimony* (Const. art. 78)

70. Unless there is a good reason for omitting the celebration of Mass, matrimony is to be celebrated within the rite

of the Mass, after the gospel and the homily. The homily is never to be omitted.

71. Whenever matrimony is celebrated within the Mass it is always the votive Mass *pro Sponsis* that is to be said, unless the rubrics dictate that only a commemoration is to be made of it. This obtains even during what are known as the closed seasons.

72. As far as possible, the parish priest himself, or his delegate for the wedding, should celebrate the Mass; but if it should be another priest who assists, the celebrant must take care not to proceed with the Mass until the rite of matrimony has been completed.

The priest who assists at the wedding only, and does not himself celebrate the Mass, is to be vested in surplice and white stole and, if it is customary, in a cope; and he is to preach the homily. But the blessing after the *Pater noster* and the other before the *Placeat* is always to be given by the priest celebrating the Mass.

73. The nuptial blessing is always to be given within the Mass, even in the closed seasons, and even though either or each of the spouses has been married previously.

74. In the celebration of matrimony outside Mass:

(*a*) At the beginning of the ceremony, in accordance with the Apostolic Letter, *Sacram Liturgiam,* n. 5, a brief instruction is to be given. This is not a homily, but a simple introduction to the marriage ceremony (cf. Const. art. 35, 3). A sermon or homily, however, is given on the sacred text (cf. Const. art. 52) after the reading of the epistle and gospel from the nuptial Mass. Thus the order of the whole rite is as follows: a brief introductory instruction, the reading of the epistle and gospel in the vernacular, a homily, the celebration of the marriage, and the nuptial blessing.

(*b*) For the reading of the epistle and gospel of the nuptial Mass, if there is no vernacular text approved by the competent regional ecclesiastical authority, a translation approved by the local ordinary may be used for the time being.

(*c*) Between the epistle and gospel singing is allowed. And after the completion of the marriage rite, before the nuptial blessing, it is strongly recommended that there should be an *oratio fidelium,* of petitions spoken by the priest and answered by the people, in a formula approved by the local ordinary. It should include prayers for the married couple.

(*d*) At the end of the rite, the blessing is always to be given to the married couple even in the closed seasons, and even though either or each of them has been married previously. It is to be given according to the formula in the Roman Ritual, tit. VIII, ch. III, unless another blessing is contained in any Ritual approved for use locally.

75. If marriage is celebrated during the closed seasons the parish priest must warn the couple to make their plans with due regard to the special character of the liturgical season.

VI. *Sacramentals* (Const. art. 79)

76. In the blessings of candles on February 2nd and the blessing of ashes at the beginning of Lent, no more than one of the prayers found in the Roman Missal for these blessings need be said.

77. The blessings contained in the Roman Ritual, tit. IX, ch. 9, 10 and 11, and hitherto "reserved", may now be given by any priest, excepting the blessing of a bell for the use of a blessed church or oratory (ch. 9, n. 11), the blessing of a foundation stone for a church (ch. 9, n. 16), the blessing of a new church or public oratory (ch. 9, n. 17), the blessing of an antimension (ch. 9, n. 21), the blessing of a new cemetery (ch. 9, n. 22), papal blessings (ch. 10, n. 1-3), and the blessing and erection of the Stations of the Cross (ch. 11, n. 1) since this is reserved to a bishop.

CHAPTER IV: THE DIVINE OFFICE

I. *The divine Office for those bound to the obligation of choir* (Const. art. 95)

78. Until the completion of the revision of the divine Office:

(*a*) Communities of canons, monks, nuns, and other regulars or religious bound by law or their constitutions to choir, are to celebrate daily, besides their conventual Mass, the full divine Office in choir.

Individual members who are in major orders or who are solemnly professed in these communities, not however lay brothers or lay sisters, though they may be lawfully dispensed from choir, must recite privately each day any canonical hours for which they are not present in choir.

(*b*) Cathedral and collegiate chapters must, in addition to the conventual Mass, fulfil the obligation of those parts of the Office in choir which are imposed on them by universal or particular law.

In their private recitation of the Office individual members of these chapters must include, besides the canonical hours to which all clerics in major orders are bound (cf. Const. art. 96 and 89), those hours also which are recited in choir by their chapter.

(*c*) In mission territories, however, while the practice of religious or capitular choir Office is to be maintained wherever it has been lawfully established, individual members of religious Orders or chapters who must be absent from choir by reason of their pastoral ministry, may, with the permission of the local ordinary—not however of the vicar general or delegate—avail themselves of the concession granted in the Apostolic Letter, *Sacram Liturgiam,* n. VI.

II. *The faculty to dispense from the divine Office or to commute it* (Const. art. 97)

79. The faculty granted to all ordinaries to dispense their subjects in individual cases and for a good reason from the obligation of reciting the whole or any part of the divine Office, or to commute it, is extended also to major superiors of non-exempt clerical religious Institutes and of Societies of clerics who live in community life without vows.

III. *Little Office* (Const. art. 98)

80. No Little Office can be considered to be modelled on the divine Office if it does not consist of psalms, lessons, hymns, and prayers, and does not bear some relation to the hours of the day and to the liturgical seasons as they occur.

81. For the time being, to fulfil the purpose of taking part in the public prayer of the Church, any of those Little Offices may be used which have hitherto been lawfully approved, provided that they conform with the requirements enumerated in the above paragraph.

But before any new Little Offices are used for taking part in the public prayer of the Church they must be approved by the Holy See.

82. The translation of the text of the Little Office into the vernacular for use as the public prayer of the Church must be approved by the competent local ecclesiastical authority and its decrees approved, that is to say confirmed, by the Holy See.

83. The competent authority for granting the use of the vernacular in the recitation of the Little Office to those who are bound to this Office by their constitutions, or for dispensing from or commuting the obligation of recitation, is the ordinary or major superior in every case.

IV. *The divine Office or Little Office recited in common by members of religious Orders and Societies* (Const. art. 99)

84. The obligation of reciting in common either the divine Office or a Little Office or parts of either imposed by their constitutions on members of Societies living under vows,[1] does not affect the permission to omit the hour of Prime, and to select from among the other little hours the one that best suits the time of the day (cf. Apostolic Letter, *Sacram Liturgiam,* n. VI).

V. *The language to be used in the recitation of the divine Office* (Const. art. 101)

85. In reciting the divine Office in choir, clerics are bound to the Latin tongue.

86. The faculty granted to the ordinary of allowing the use of the vernacular, in individual cases, to clerics for whom the use of Latin is a serious obstacle to their praying the Office properly, is also extended to major superiors of non-exempt clerical religious Institutes and of Societies of clerics living in community but without vows.

87. The serious obstacle required for granting the above concession is to be measured taking into account the physical, moral, intellectual and spiritual circumstances of the applicant. This faculty, granted for the sole purpose of rendering the recitation of the divine Office easier and more devout, is in no way intended to detract from the obligation incumbent on priests of the Latin rite of learning the Latin language.

88. The translation into the local language of a divine Office according to any other than the Roman rite is to be prepared and approved by the ordinaries who are concerned with that particular language group. Wherever there are

[1] *Sodalibus statuum perfectionis.*

elements of the Office common to both rites, the translation approved by the regional authority is to be used. The text must then be submitted for confirmation to the Holy See.

89. Breviaries for the use of clerics who, in accordance with art. 101, 1 of the Constitution, have obtained permission to recite the divine Office in the vernacular, should contain the Latin text as well as the vernacular translation.

CHAPTER V: THE PROPER CONSTRUCTION OF CHURCHES AND ALTARS IN ORDER TO FACILITATE THE ACTIVE PARTICIPATION OF THE FAITHFUL

I. The lay-out of churches

90. In building new churches and in repairing or adapting old ones great care must be taken to ensure that they lend themselves to the celebration of divine services as these are meant to be celebrated, and to achieve the active participation of the faithful (cf. Const. art. 124).

II. The high altar

91. It is better for the high altar to be constructed away from the wall so that one can move round it without difficulty, and so that it can be used for a celebration facing the people. It ought to occupy a central position in the sacred edifice, thus becoming naturally the focal point of attention for the whole congregation.

In choosing the material for the construction and decoration of the altar, existing laws are to be observed.

The sanctuary must be large enough to allow plenty of room for the ceremonies.

III. Seating for the celebrant and ministers

92. Taking into account the general shape of each individual church the seats for the celebrant and for the minis-

ters are to be so placed as to be easily seen by the congregation.

The celebrant when seated should appear as truly presiding over the whole gathering.

At the same time, if the seat for the celebrant is behind the altar all appearance of a throne must be avoided, since that belongs only to the bishop.

IV. *Side altars*

93. Side altars are to be few in number. As far as the general shape of the building allows, they should be placed in chapels in some way cut off from the main body of the church.

V. *The ornamentation of altars*

94. The cross and candlesticks normally required to be placed on the altar for the various liturgical services, may, at the discretion of the local ordinary, be placed instead in close proximity to it.

VI. *The reservation of the Blessed Sacrament*

95. The Blessed Sacrament is to be reserved in a solid, burglar-proof tabernacle in the centre of the high altar or of another altar if this is really outstanding and distinguished. Where there is a lawful custom, and in particular cases to be approved by the local ordinary, the Blessed Sacrament may be reserved in some other place in the church; but it must be a very special place, having nobility about it, and it must be suitably decorated.

It is lawful to celebrate Mass facing the people even if on the altar there is a small but adequate tabernacle.

VII. *The ambo*

96. There should be, if possible, a pulpit (ambo) or pulpits for the public reading of the sacred texts. They should

be so arranged that the minister can be clearly seen and heard by the congregation.

VIII. *The position of the choir and organ*

97. The choir and organ shall be so arranged that it is clear to all that the singers and the organist form part of the congregation and can indeed fulfil their liturgical function.

IX. *The places of the faithful*

98. The congregation must be accommodated in such a way as to ensure that they can pay full attention both outwardly and inwardly to all that is happening in the sanctuary. It is a good thing, as usually is the case, for benches or seats to be provided for their use; but the custom of reserving seats for private individuals is to be discontinued forthwith in accordance with art. 32 of the Constitution.

Care too must be taken that the faithful can not only see the celebrant and ministers, but also hear them. Modern technical aids should be used.

X. *The baptistry*

99. In the construction and furnishing of the baptistry, careful attention must be paid to making the dignity of the sacrament of baptism clearly evident. It must be a place which lends itself on occasion to the more public administration of the sacrament (cf. Const. art. 27).

The present Instruction, prepared by order of His Holiness Pope Paul VI by the Commission for implementing the Constitution on the Sacred Liturgy, was presented to His Holiness by James Cardinal Lercaro, President of the Commission.

The Holy Father, after he had given due consideration to this Instruction with the assistance of the above-mentioned Commission and of this Sacred Congregation of Rites, in an Audience granted to Arcadio Maria Cardinal Larraona,

Prefect of the Sacred Congregation of Rites, gave it both in its entirety and in detail his special approval, confirmed it by his authority and ordered it to be published and carefully observed by all concerned, as from March 7th, 1965, the First Sunday of Lent.

All things to the contrary notwithstanding.

Rome, September 26th, 1964.

JAMES Cardinal LERCARO
Archbishop of Bologna

*President of the Commission for
implementing the Constitution
on the Sacred Liturgy*

ARCADIO M. Cardinal
LARRAONA
Prefect of S.C.R.

✠ HENRY DANTE
*Titular Archbishop of Carpasia
Secretary of S.C.R.*

Reprinted through the courtesy of the Catholic Truth Society, London, England.

SELECTED BIBLIOGRAPHY

Amiot, François. *History of the Mass, The Twentieth Century Encyclopedia of Catholicism,* Vol. 110. New York: Hawthorn Books, 1959.

Barry, Colman J. *Worship and Work. Collegeville,* Minn.: Liturgical Press, 1956.

Baumstark, Anton. *Comparative Liturgy.* Westminster, Md. Newman Press, and London: Mowbray, 1958.

Bohen, Marian, O.S.U. *The Mystery of Confirmation.* New York: Herder and Herder, 1963.

Bouyer, Louis. *Liturgical Piety.* Notre Dame, Ind.: University of Notre Dame Press, 1955. English edition, *Liturgy and Life.* London: Sheed and Ward, 1958.

————. *The Liturgy Revived.* Notre Dame, Ind.: University of Notre Dame Press, 1965.

————. *The Paschal Mystery.* London: George Allen & Unwin, 1951.

————. *Rite and Man.* Notre Dame, Ind.: University of Notre Dame Press, 1963.

Casel, Odo, O.S.B. *The Mystery of Christian Worship.* Westminster, Md.: Newman Press; London: Darton, Longman & Todd, 1962.

Challenge of the Council: Person, Parish, World, The. Washington, D.C.: Twenty-fifth North American Liturgical Week, 1964.

Church and the Liturgy, The Concilium, Vol. II. Glen Rock, N.J.: Paulist Press, 1965.

Crichton, James D. *Changes in the Liturgy:* Considerations on the degree *Inter oecumenici.* New York: Alba House, and London: Geoffrey Chapman, 1965.

————. *The Church's Worship:* Considerations on the Liturgical Constitution of the Second Vatican Council. New York: Sheed and Ward, and London: Geoffrey Chapman, 1964.

Dalmais, Irenée-Henri, O.P. *Eastern Liturgies, The Twentieth Century Encyclopedia of Catholicism,* Vol. 112. New York: Hawthorn Books, Inc., 1960.

Davis, Charles. *Liturgy and Doctrine.* New York and London: Sheed and Ward, 1960.

————. *Sacraments of Initiation, Baptism and Confirmation.* New York: Sheed and Ward, 1964. English edition, *The Making of a Christian.* London: Sheed and Ward, 1964.

Dawson, Christopher. *The Dividing of Christendom.* New York: Sheed and Ward, 1965.

Denis-Boulet, Noële M. *The Christian Calendar, The Twentieth Century Encyclopedia of Catholicism,* Vol. 113. New York: Hawthorn Books, Inc., 1960.

Eisenhofer, Ludwig, and Joseph Lechner. *The Liturgy of the Roman Rite.* New York: Herder & Herder; Edinburgh: Nelson, 1961.

Gelineau, Joseph, S.J. *Voices and Instruments in Christian Worship,* translated by Howell Clifford, S.J.. Collegeville, Minn.: Liturgical Press, 1964.

Hockett, W. (ed.). *The Modern Architectural Setting for the Liturgy.* London: S.P.C.K., 1963.

Hofinger, Johannes, S.J. (ed.). *Liturgy and the Missions: The Nijmegen Papers.* New York: Kenedy; London: Burns & Oates, 1960.

Jungmann, Joseph Andreas, S.J. *The Mass of the Roman Rite, Its Origins and Development* (Missarum Solemnia), translated by F.A. Brunner, C.SS.R. Two volumes. New York: Benziger Brothers, 1951 and 1955.

Kilmartin, Edward J., S.J. *The Eucharist in the Primitive Church.* Englewood Cliffs, N.J.: Prentice-Hall, 1965.

Klauser, Theodor. *The Western Liturgy.* London: Mowbray, 1952.

Koenker, E.B. *The Liturgical Renaissance in the Roman Catholic Church.* Chicago: University of Chicago Press, 1954.

Korolevsky, C. *Living Languages in Catholic Worship,* translated by Donald Attwater. New York and London: Longmans, 1957.

Link, Mark J., S.J. *Christ Teaches Us Today.* Chicago: Loyola University Press.

Marco, Angelus A. de, O.F.M. *Rome and the Vernacular.* Westminster, Md.; Newman Press, 1961.

————. *A Key to the New Liturgical Constitution.* New York: Desclee, 1964. Marshall, Romey P., O.S.L., and Michael J. Taylor, S.J. *Liturgy and Christian Unity.* Englewood Cliffs, N.J.: Prentice-Hall, 1965.

McManus, Frederick R. *The Council and the Liturgy.* Washington, D.C.: National Catholic Welfare Conference, 1965.

————. (ed.). *The Revival of the Liturgy.* New York: Herder and Herder, 1963.

McNaspy, C.J., S.J. *Our Changing Liturgy.* New York: Hawthorn Books, Inc., 1966.

Miller, J.H., C.S.C. *Signs of Transformation in Christ.* Englewood Cliffs, N.J.: Prentice-Hall, 1963.

––––––. (ed.) *Yearbook of Liturgical Studies,* Vol. 5, 1964. Collegeville, Minn.: Liturgical Press, 1965.

Milner, Paulinus, O.P. *The Worship of the Church, The New Library of Catholic Knowledge,* Vol. 9. New York: Hawthorn Books, Inc., and London: Burns and Oates, 1964.

Murphy, John L. *The Mass and Liturgical Reform.* Milwaukee: Bruce Publishing Co., 1957.

Murray, Placid, O.S.B. (ed.) *Studies in Pastoral Liturgy,* Vol. 1. Maynooth: The Furrow Trust, 1961.

Nocent, Adrian. *The Future of the Liturgy.* New York: Herder and Herder, 1963.

O'Connell, J. B. *Sacred Music and Liturgy* (the Instruction of the Sacred Congregation of Rites, translated with a commentary). London: Burns & Oates, 1959.

Pocknee, C. E. *The Christian Altar in History and Today.* London: Mowbray, 1963.

Rousseau, Dom Olivier, O.S.B. *Progress of the Liturgy.* Westminster, Md.: Newman Press, 1951.

Ryan, V. O.S.B. (ed.) *Studies in Pastoral Liturgy,* Vol. 2. Maynooth: The Furrow Trust, 1963.

Schmemann, Alexander. *Sacraments and Orthodoxy.* New York: Herder and Herder, 1965.

Semmelbroth, Otto, S.J. *The Preaching Word.* New York: Herder and Herder, 1965.

Sheerin, John B., C.S.P. *Christian Reunion: The Ecumenical Movement and American Catholics.* New York: Hawthorn Books, Inc., 1966.

Sheppard, Lancelot. *Blueprint for Worship.* Westminster, Md.: Newman Press, and London: Darton, Longman and Todd, 1964.

––––––. *The Liturgical Books, The Twentieth Century Encyclopedia of Catholicism,* Vol. 109. New York: Hawthorn Books, Inc., 1962.

––––––. (ed.) *True Worship.* Baltimore: Helicon Press, Inc., 1963.

Vagaggini, Cyprian. *Theological Dimensions of the Liturgy.* Collegeville, Minn.: Liturgical Press, 1959.

Liturgy. Collegeville, Minn.: Liturgical Press, 1959.

Wolf, Donald, S.J., and James V. Schall, S.J. *Current Trends in Theology.* New York: Doubleday & Co., Inc., 1965.

Van Zeller, Hubert, O.S.B. *The Mass in Other Words.* Springfield, Ill.: Templegate Publishers, 1965.

INDEX

Belgium, 22–23, 38, 44, 50, 54, 125
Benedictine Congregation of Beuron, 21. *See also* Beuron
Benedictine Liturgical Conference, 37
Benedictines, 35, 36, 38, 39, 43, 51, 145; and liturgy, 87
Bet-undsangmesse, 47
Beuron, Abbey of, 21, 22, 43
Bibel und Liturgie, 45
Bible, 50, 107, 148, 169 (*see also* Scriptures; Word of God; specific Books); and catechesis, 71–73, 148; Constitution on, 169, 174, 219; and liturgy, 59–68
Bible Missal, 140–41
Bilingual rituals, 119–20. *See also* specific countries
Bishop, Edmund, 10
Bishops, 54–56, 109, 110, 121, 131–41 *passim,* 229, 232–33; Congregation of Rites on, 235, 236, 239–42, 243, 244, 245–49, 254–55; Constitution on, 165, 166, 169, 171, 172, 181, 213–16, 221, 223, 257; Constitution on art and, 194, 195, 196; Constitution on consecration of, 180, 253, 255; Constitution on music and, 191; and language, 245–46; seating for, 262
Bishops' Commission on the Liturgical Apostolate, 130, 131
Blessed Sacrament, 49, 50, 87 (*see also* Host, the); reservation of, 262
Blessings, 256, 257; reserved, 181
Bologna, archbishop of, 39, 55
Books, liturgical, 170, 240; revision of, Constitution on, 166, 167, 214–15, 218, 219, 222, 238; translations of, 245–46
Books, music, 191–92. *See also* Music
Botte, Dom, 43
Bouyer, Fr L., 19, 27*n,* 49, 105, 107*n;* on canonical study of

liturgy, 146; on Dom Casel, 82*n,* 83, 86; on evolution of devotions, 86–90; on Jubé as liturgical pioneer, 108–9
Bread and wine, 100, 101, 114, 226. *See also* Communion; Host, the
Breviary, 11, 13*n,* 96–98, 135, 137, 138, 261 (*see also* Divine Office); Constitution on, 173
British Isles, 141. *See also* England; Great Britain; Ireland; Scotland; Wales
Bugnini, Mgr, 224
Bulletin liturgique et paroissial, 23
Burgos, Spain, 38
Burial (funeral) rites, 181, 216, 227, 254
Byzantine rites, 45, 102, 144–47 (*see also* Eastern Churches), and concelebration, 109–10

Cabrol, Dom, 24
Calendar reform, 11, 97, 169–97. *See also* Seasons; Year
Caloen, Dom Gérard van, 22, 23, 67
Canada, 137
Canon(s), 108, 109, 136, 185, 221, 225, 248, 258; canonical study of the liturgy, 146; Code of Canon Law, 232
Capelle, Dom, 43
Caribbean Islands, 137–38
Casel, Dom Odo, 24, 27, 28, 62; and Christian mystery, 82–86
Casper, Joseph, 45
Catalonia, Spain, 38
Catechesis, catechumenate, 48, 69–80, 117, 149, 189; Constitution on, 178–79; sacraments and, 118, 120, 125, 178
Cathedral churches, 239; music (choirs) in, 185, 191, 258
Catholic Action, 49, 89
Catholic Directory, 32
Celebrant, the, 104–5, 106, 217, 221, 224–25, 243, 246, 248*ff;*

THE CONTRIBUTORS

LANCELOT SHEPPARD, editor of *The People Worship*, is the editor of the English-language edition of *The Twentieth Century Encyclopedia of Catholicism*, and was Editor-in-Chief of the periodical *Twentieth Century Catholicism*. He is the author of *The Liturgical Books* and *The Mass in the West*, and translated into English the selections in this volume written by the French sacerdotal communities.

THE SACERDOTAL COMMUNITIES OF ST. SÉVERIN OF PARIS AND ST. JOSEPH OF NICE have long been active in liturgical work, and have contributed much in thought and writing to the contemporary liturgical revolution.

THE REV J. RICHARD QUINN teaches Sacramental Theology at Saint John's Seminary in Brighton, Massachusetts. He has taken part in national and regional liturgical programs, and writes regularly on the liturgy.

FR CLIFFORD HOWELL, S.J., is well known as a lecturer on liturgical matters in the United States and throughout the English-speaking world. He teaches liturgy at Heythrop College, Chipping Norton, England.

FR PAULINUS MILNER, O.P., is a lecturer in the history of philosophy at Hawkesyard Priory, the Dominican House of Studies in Staffordshire, England. He studied for his doctorate at the Institut Supérieur de Liturgie in Paris.

A HAWTHORN BOOK